I0901063

IMAGES
of America

THE CONRAD WEISER AREA

ON THE COVER: This homestead was built after 1729 and operated as a working farm until the 1920s. At that time, a movement was proposed to make the homestead a park. That movement became a reality in 1928 when the property became the Conrad Weiser Memorial Park. The cover photograph was taken at that time. In 1935, the State of Pennsylvania purchased the property. Today, the homestead is run by a group called Friends of the Conrad Weiser Homestead. (Courtesy of Carl Ganster.)

IMAGES
of America

THE CONRAD WEISER AREA

Carl Ganster and Carl Reidler
Introduction by Lynn Otto

ARCADIA
PUBLISHING

ISBN 978-1-4671-2347-1

Published by Arcadia Publishing
Charleston, South Carolina

Printed in the United States of America

Library of Congress Control Number: 2014954872

For all general information, please contact Arcadia Publishing:
Telephone 843-853-2070
Fax 843-853-0044
E-mail sales@arcadiapublishing.com
For customer service and orders:
Toll-Free 1-888-313-2665

Visit us on the Internet at www.arcadiapublishing.com

Dedicated to Lester Breininger Jr., our beloved biology teacher, who taught us the importance of preserving our local history

Contents

Acknowledgments

Thanks are due to Curtis Ganster, John Grimes, Earl W. Ibach, Ryan A. Zerbe, C. Donald Moyer, Carl H. Bloss, Greg Boyer, Robert Bausher, Randy Gardner, May Blatt, Donald Brown, Barnett's Garage, Tulpehocken Settlement Historical Society, David Sonon, Pete Lengle, James Feeg, Leonard Rohrbach, and Lynn Otto. We also want to thank Carl H. Bloss for proofreading all captions. Unless otherwise noted, all photographs come from the authors' collections.

INTRODUCTION

Photographs and postcards are truly snapshots in time. Taken to remember people, places, and objects, they tell us about our past. Unfortunately, when talking about the 18th century and the early history of the Tulpehocken Valley, we can only draw our images from the written word. But these words can stimulate snapshots in our mind. Such is the case when remembering Conrad Weiser, the Tulpehocken Valley's most famous early occupant. Let us start to form our postcard.

Conrad Weiser was born in the German Palatinate town of Affstätt on November 2, 1696. After the death of Conrad's mother, Anna Magdalena, in 1709, Conrad's father, Johan, decided to move his eight children to America. Their destination was the royal colony of New York. Their occupation was to raise hemp and produce pine tar and pitch in the Hudson Valley. When this endeavor did not work out, the Weiser family and others moved to the Schoharie Valley, near Albany, New York.

During this period, young Conrad spent a winter with the Mohawk Indians. Although not pleasurable, this experience would prove invaluable to Conrad in his future. In 1720, he took a bride, marrying Anna Eve Feeg. This union was the source of strength for things to come and produced 14 children, seven of whom lived to adulthood. However, conditions did not improve greatly for the German immigrants, and in 1729, Conrad, Anna Eve, and four of their children moved from New York to a fertile land in Pennsylvania called the Tulpehocken Valley. There, Conrad built his farm in the shadow of Eagles Peak. This would be his home for the next 31 adventurous years.

Early on in his life in the Tulpehocken Valley, Conrad recognized the apparent need for a skilled interpreter who could help in Indian negotiations. Drawing on his experience of living with the natives, he became a skilled negotiator, and over the next 30 years, his service to the colony of Pennsylvania was invaluable. Through this experience, he formed a lifelong bond with Sachem Shikellamy. Their friendship would continue until Shikellamy's death in 1748. Conrad's plantation grew to 900 acres, and he maintained a tannery, orchard, and vineyard while splitting his time between Indian policy and his home life.

In 1750, Berks County was formed through Conrad's help, and he served as justice of the peace and, later, the first judgeship in Berks County. In addition to purchasing several lots and establishing a home, he helped lay out the town of Reading. During the French and Indian War, he served as lieutenant colonel of the 1st Battalion of the newly formed Pennsylvania Regiment. Finally, Conrad Weiser was laid to rest after his death on July 13, 1760. His plantation passed to his son and was later sold to a Mr. Sheetz. Little evidence of the Weiser plantation remained into the 19th century except the little stone building and Conrad's grave maker. It appeared as if the Tulpehocken Valley had forgotten all about the efforts of this man. Or had it?

By the 1920s, a movement was afoot to somehow commemorate Conrad Weiser and his achievements. Starting with a donation of 20 acres for $1 from Le Roy R. Valentine, owner of the Weiser property at that time, the Conrad Weiser Memorial Park Association began to realize its plan to memorialize Conrad Weiser. After raising $30,000, the park association sought the help of the Olmstead Brothers of Brookline, Massachusetts, to design the park. Slowly, the park and restorations were under way. The dedication of the Conrad Weiser Memorial Park finally took place on September 1, 1928. More than 25,000 people attended this event. Rev. Dr. P.C. Croll delivered the dedicatory address. Many snapshots and postcards from this time period exist, showing us the way the park and house looked in those early days. Since that time, this lovely park has seen many owners, lastly the Pennsylvania Historical and Museum Commission (PHMC). In 2009, the historical area of the park was closed because of cuts within the state budget. However, a recent management agreement between the PHMC and the Friends of the Conrad Weiser Homestead allowed the historical area to reopen for public viewing.

Many things have changed in the years between 1729 and today. People, places, and objects continuously evolve. Surely, the surrounding Tulpehocken Valley area has grown, with the addition of new roads, new buildings, and new towns. Yet if we look beneath the shadow of Eagles Peak, the same stone house and gravesite remain unchanged.

—Lynn Otto
Vice President, Friends of the Conrad Weiser Homestead

One

Marion Township

In 1723, the first settlers made Marion Township their home. At the time, it was called Tulpehocken, named after the creek that runs through it. Marion had the first church, Reed's in 1727, and the first mill, that of Leonhardt Reed in about 1730. As time went by, the settlement grew, and a second church, Christ Lutheran, was built in 1743. In 1749, the first forge, Tulpehocken Eisenhammer (later, Charming Forge), was started in the western part of Marion. Charming Forge ceased production in the 1890s.

Starting in Reading and running west into Dauphin County, the first turnpike, the Berks-Dauphin Turnpike, was opened in 1805. The road improved commerce for local residents, as it ran through Marion. The turnpike lasted into the 1920s, when the state appropriated the road.

In 1808, Andrew Stouch purchased land along this road and built a tavern, after which houses sprang up on the north side of the turnpike. By the 1820s, Jacob Shitz had laid out lots on the south side of the turnpike; thus, Stouch Town was born. In 1832, a post office was established, and the name was changed to Stouchsburg. The post office closed in 1972.

In the late 1820s, Marion saw another boost to the area. The Union Canal was opened, which ran from Reading in the east to Harrisburg in the west.

Until the 1840s, Marion was made up of Tulpehocken and Heidelberg Townships. In 1843, its citizens petitioned the county court to set aside a separate township called Marion. The petition was granted the following year, and Marion established its own government.

Meanwhile, settlers cleared the land for farming and built limestone houses and barns. Today, residents are blessed with many of those remaining homes and barns, as well as some of the best farmland found in Berks County.

With the exception of Stouchsburg, modern-day Marion is a farming community. In 2010, its population was 1,688, and it ranks near the top in farmland and preservation acres in Berks County. Charming Forge looks much like it did 100 years ago.

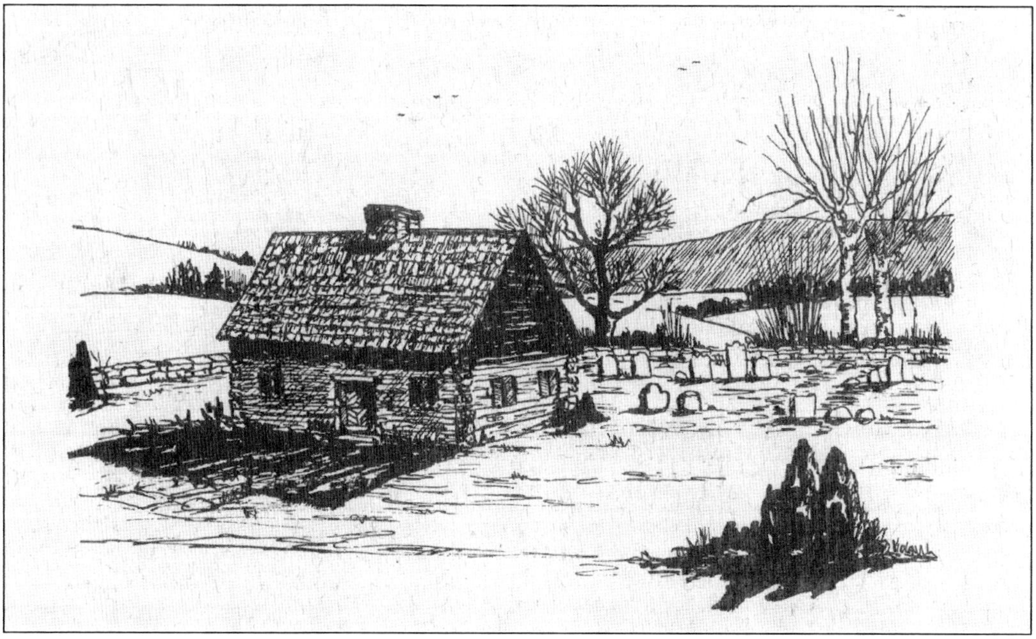

Pictured here in an artist's rendering from around 1970 is the first church in western Berks County. This church was built in 1727 on Reed's Cemetery, along Sheridan Road. Used by Lutheran, Reformed, and Moravian congregations, the church remained in service until 1744, when a second church was built at the same location. At that time, each congregation established their own church, and the original structure became Reed's Lutheran Church. (Courtesy of Carl Ganster.)

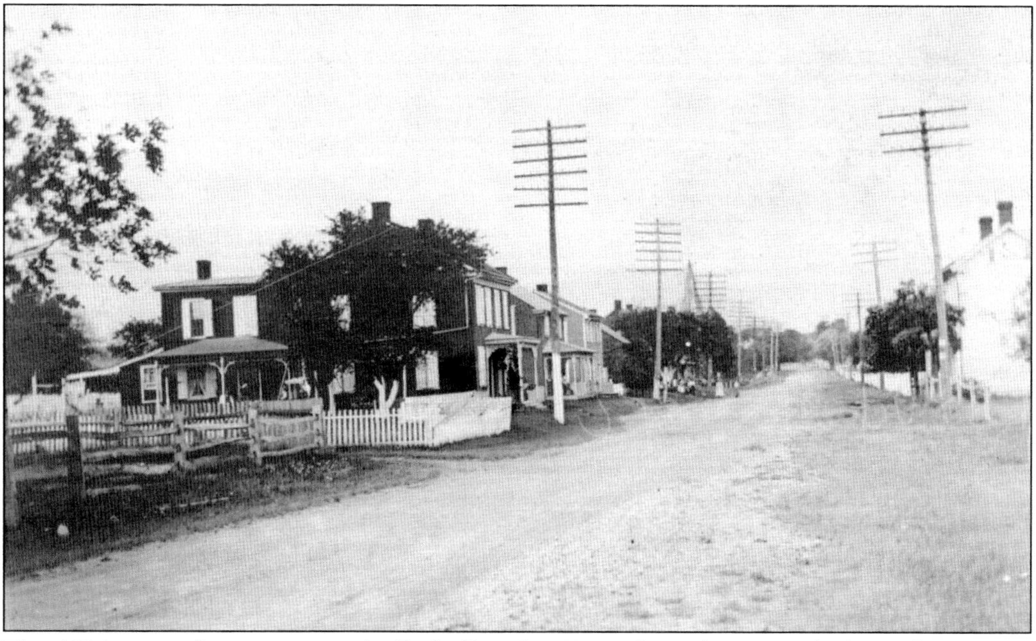

This 1906 postcard view captures the Berks-Dauphin Turnpike at the east end of Stouchsburg. On the 1876 map of Stouchsburg, a school was located on the right. This area was called Snitzville because of a large apple orchard; the word *snitz* is Pennsylvania Dutch for "apple." (Courtesy of Carl Ganster.)

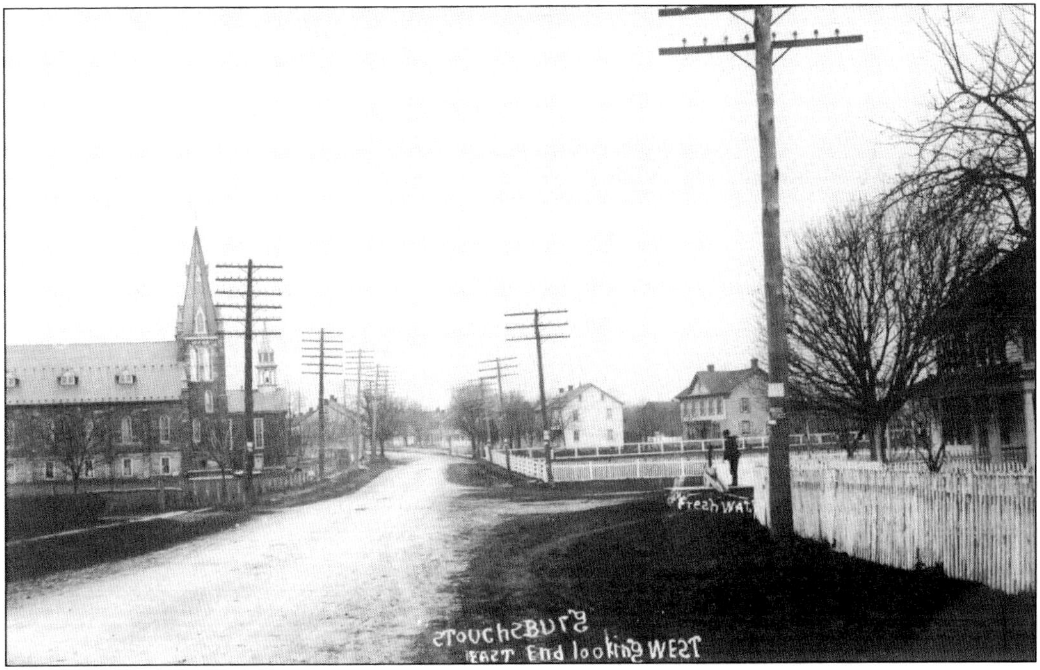

On the right, 37 Main Street is the address of the former Eagle Hotel, built by Henry Bennethum around 1830. During the Union Canal's days, this was a popular place for the canal workers. The next house on the right is the former Stouchsburg Academy, built in 1838 and operational until 1878. The last building on the right is the former Cooper tobacco factory. On the left is the 1895 Reed's Church, followed by St. Peter's Church, built in 1849. (Courtesy of Carl Ganster.)

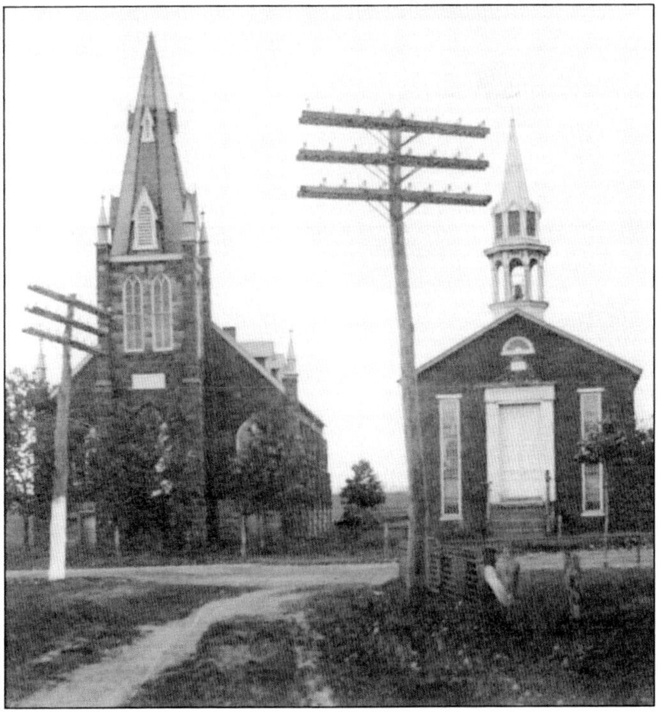

This 1907 postcard depicts Reed's Church (left) and St. Peter's Church. The former is the fourth church for Reed's and the first in Stouchsburg. Construction was started in 1895, but not completed until 1911. St. Peter's was built in 1849 and served as a chapel for Reed's, Christ Lutheran, and Trinity Reformed, which was just over the Marion line in Jackson Township, Lebanon County. Because Stouchsburg had no church in town, this location was used as a community Sunday school and church in inclement weather. In later years, it was called the Stouchsburg Union Sunday School. St. Peter's was torn down in the 1930s. (Courtesy of Carl Ganster.)

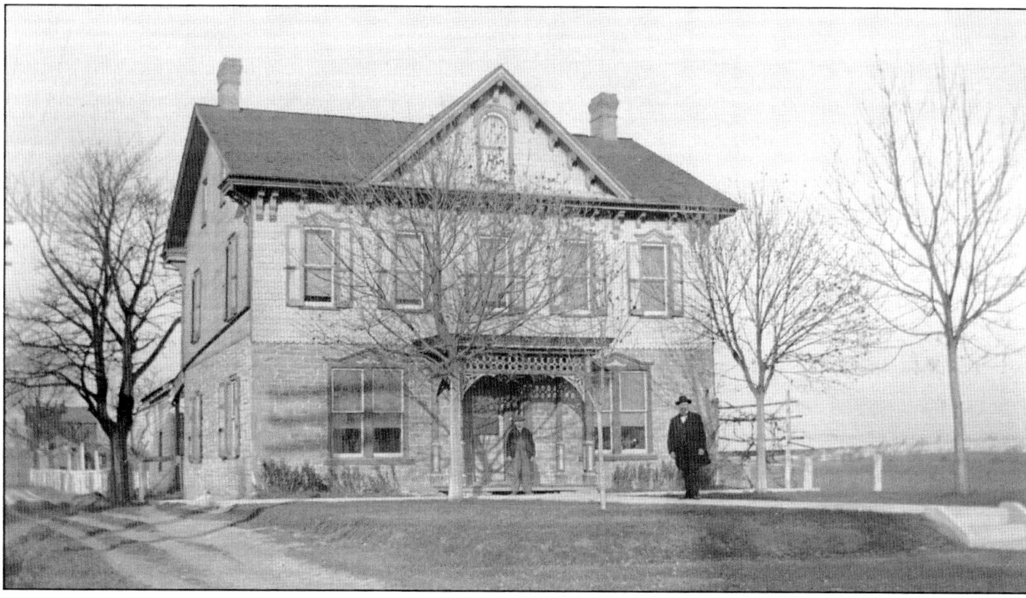

Stouchsburg Academy, also known as the White Hall Academy, was built in 1838 and incorporated in 1842. At that time, George Lechner was the president, and Jonathan Klopp served as the treasurer. One share of stock was sold for $40 in May 1842. The academy closed in 1878 and was sold to Samuel Reed for $510. A second story was added after the closure and subsequent sale. Today, 43 Main Street is owned by Christopher Heffelfinger. Frank Reed is the man standing on the walkway. (Courtesy of Carl Ganster.)

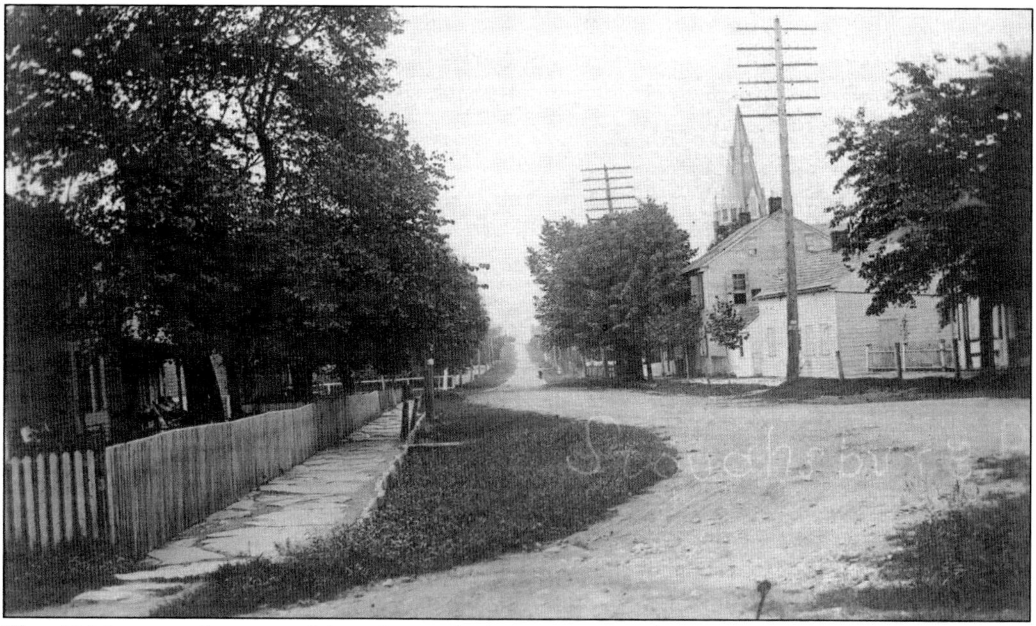

This 1906 postcard captures Main Street, looking west. On the 1876 map of Stouchsburg, Main Street was called Cumberland Street, and the little log house on the right was lot No. 1 on Jacob Shitz's town layout in the 1820s. It burned down in February 2015. Also visible are the two steeples of the churches. Note the dirt road; on the left is Marion Drive, which at present crosses over Route 422, one block away. (Courtesy of Carl Ganster.)

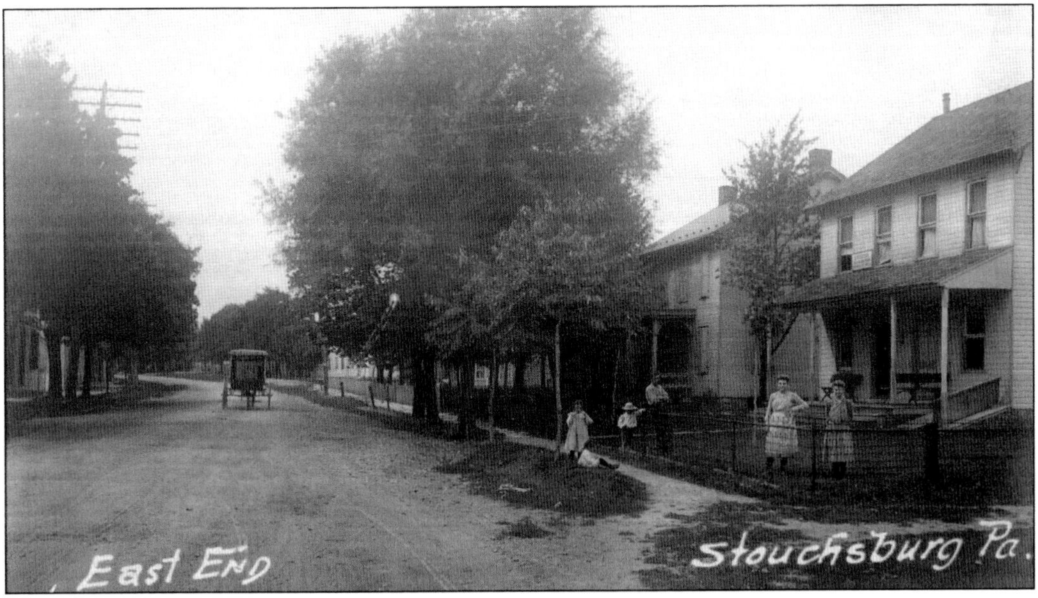

Pictured here is the east end of Stouchsburg around 1910. On the right are 45 and 47 Main Street, owned by the Cooper family for three generations. Henry W. Cooper started out as a photographer about 1870; he later turned to cigars and tobacco to make a living. His son John C. Cooper continued the business, followed by Luke Schoener, who stopped processing tobacco in the early 1960s. Henry Cooper also ran a tollgate for the Berks-Dauphin Turnpike from this location. The two young girls seen standing behind the fence are John C. Cooper's daughters Maude (left) and Ella (right). Both girls never married and lived on the property until they passed away in the 1960s and 1970s. (Courtesy of Carl Ganster.)

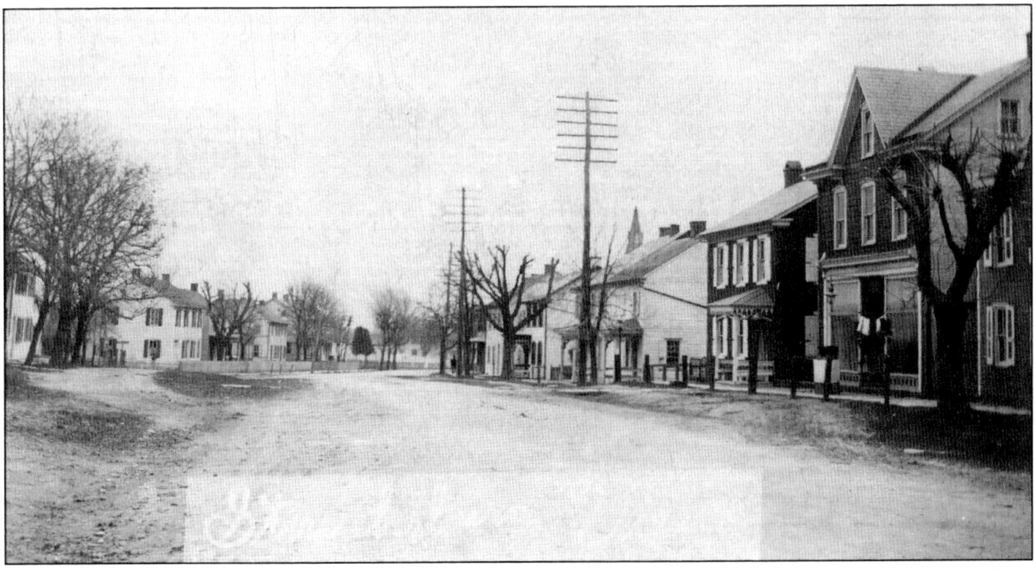

Looking east on Main Street in this 1909 postcard, the first building on the right is the Calvin Unger Store, which was said to have everything. Notice the extra-wide street in the center of town and the hitching posts in front of the business. The house to the left of center was the home of Dr. J.A. Fisher in 1876. In 1950, Marion Grange No. 1853 purchased the store building, and it has been the grange hall ever since. (Courtesy of Carl Ganster.)

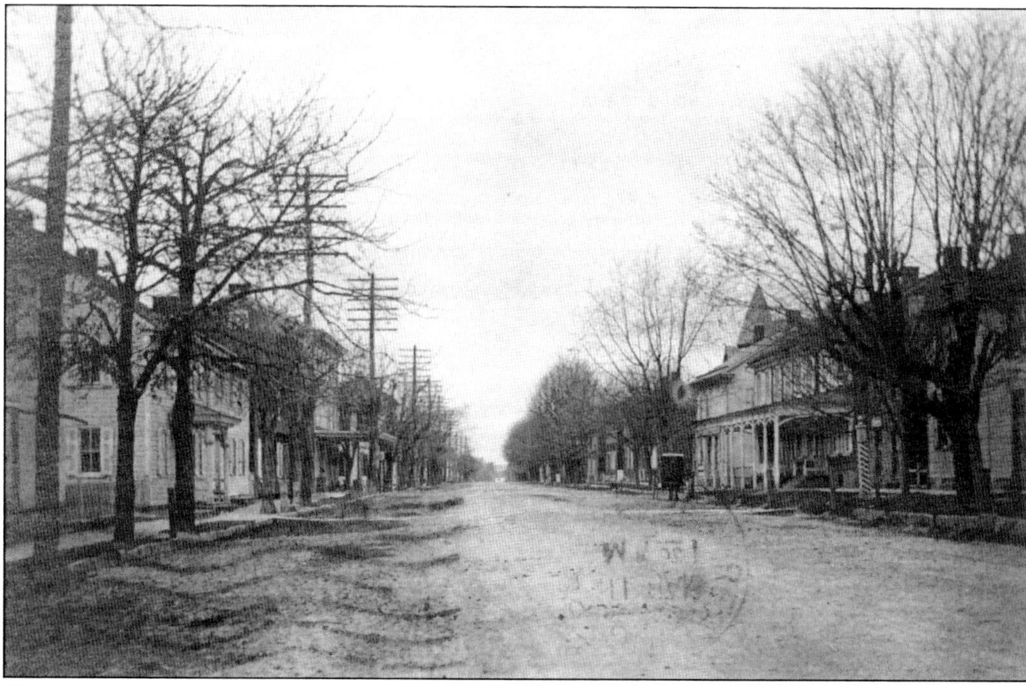

This 1907 postcard of the central part of Stouchsburg looks west. On the left is the American House, the larger building with a porch. Across the street, the other building with a porch is the Samuel Keiser Store, which served as the post office in 1876. Note the striped post on the right that appears to be a barber's pole. (Courtesy of Carl Ganster.)

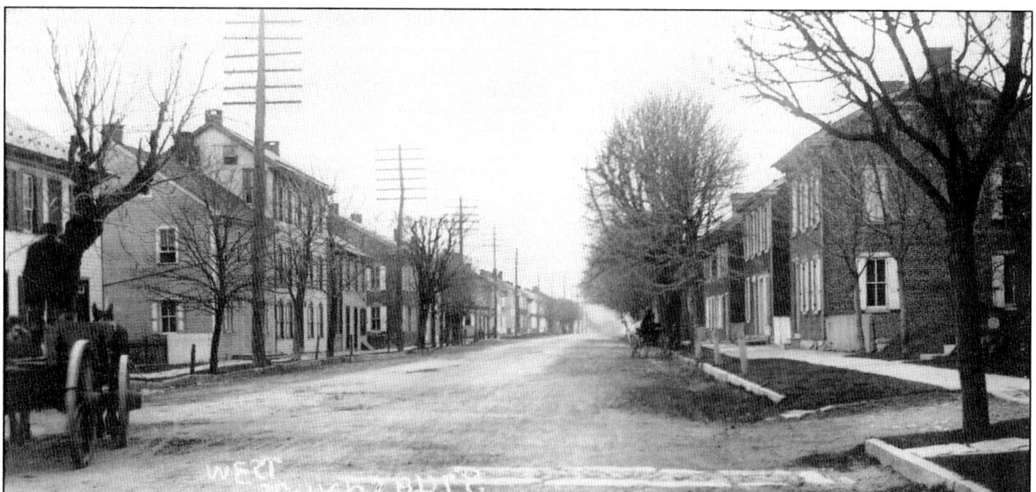

This 1910 postcard captures another view of Main Street, looking west. The building on the left behind the horse-drawn wagon was the Ruth Motor Company around 1920. Later, Roy Miller ran a small grocery store here, from the 1950s to 1969. The three-story building on the left was a cigar factory started by Reily Zerbe in 1883. It produced 4.3 million cigars in that year alone. The structure was originally a two-story building, but a third story was added around 1890. Zerbe sold his business to Charlie Peiffer, who made cigars into the 1920s. The second building on the right was George Kapp's tailor business in the 1870s and 1880s. From the 1940s to the early 1960s, it served as the town's post office. (Courtesy of Carl Ganster.)

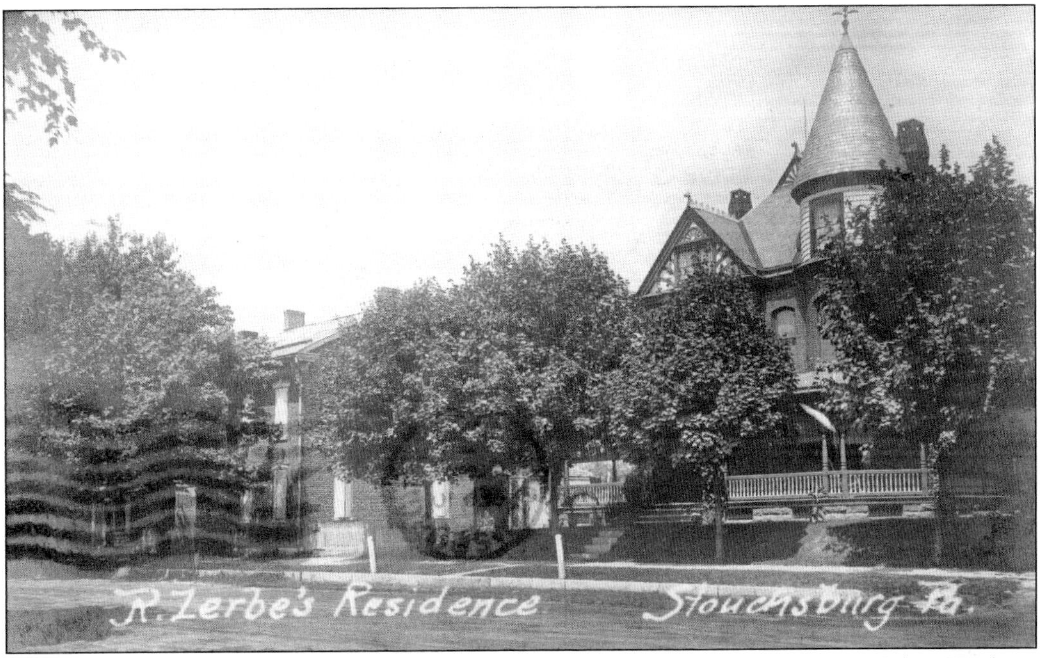

Pictured here is Reily Zerbe's house on Main Street. With the help of contractor John Weidner, Zerbe built the 14-room house, complete with its own gas plant, in 1895. His father, James Zerbe, was one of the first cigar makers in Stouchsburg. This building later served as a maternity hospital operated by Dr. Ed Ruth in the 1940s. It then became the site of Dr. A.A. Nagle and Dr. John Marshall's medical practice from the 1950s until about 1970, followed by the law firm of Jonathan Batdorf from the 1980s until about 2002. The beautiful structure burned down in 2006 and was replaced with a modern home. (Courtesy of Carl Ganster.)

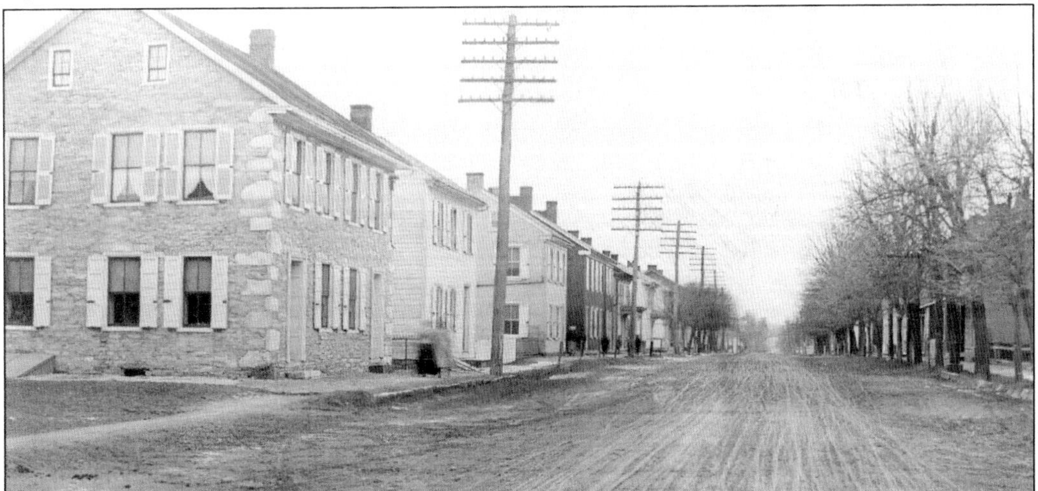

This c. 1915 postcard captures the west end of Stouchsburg. The early limestone house on the left is one of only two limestone homes in town. Most residences are either log or brick. Stouchsburg had its own brick factory just north of town on Marion Drive, where the Stouchsburg Nursery once stood. In the 1960s, Ben Dow owned this house, and he would play Christmas music on a loudspeaker that could be heard throughout most of the town. Barbara Brown is the present owner of this fine home. (Courtesy of Carl Ganster.)

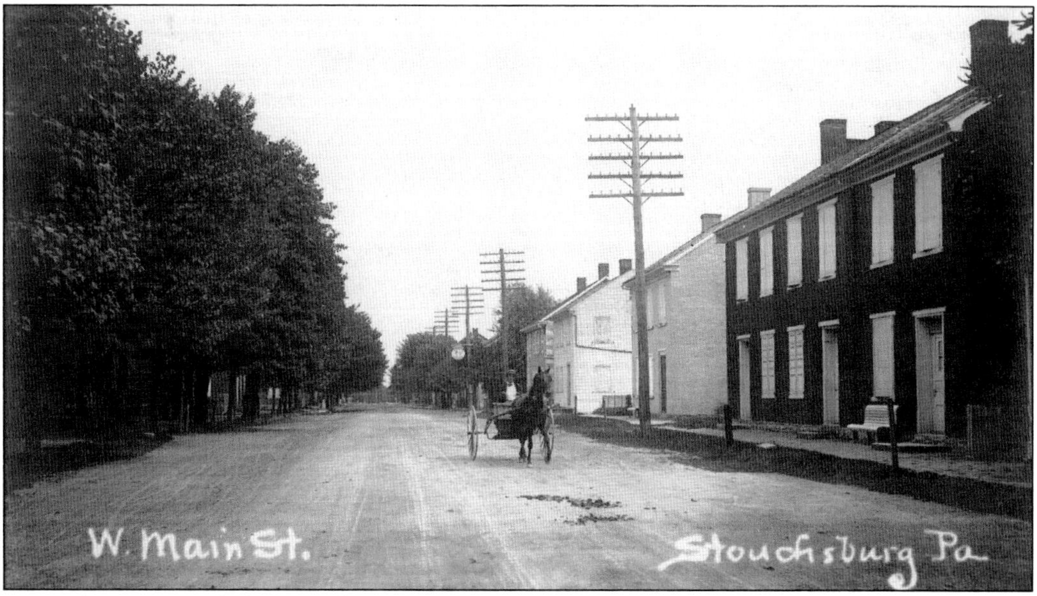

Around 1910, a single horse pulls a small cart along Main Street in Stouchsburg. The house on the right was probably the first brick home built in town, around 1840. Notice the Marion House sign in the distance and the hitching posts along the street. (Courtesy of Carl Ganster.)

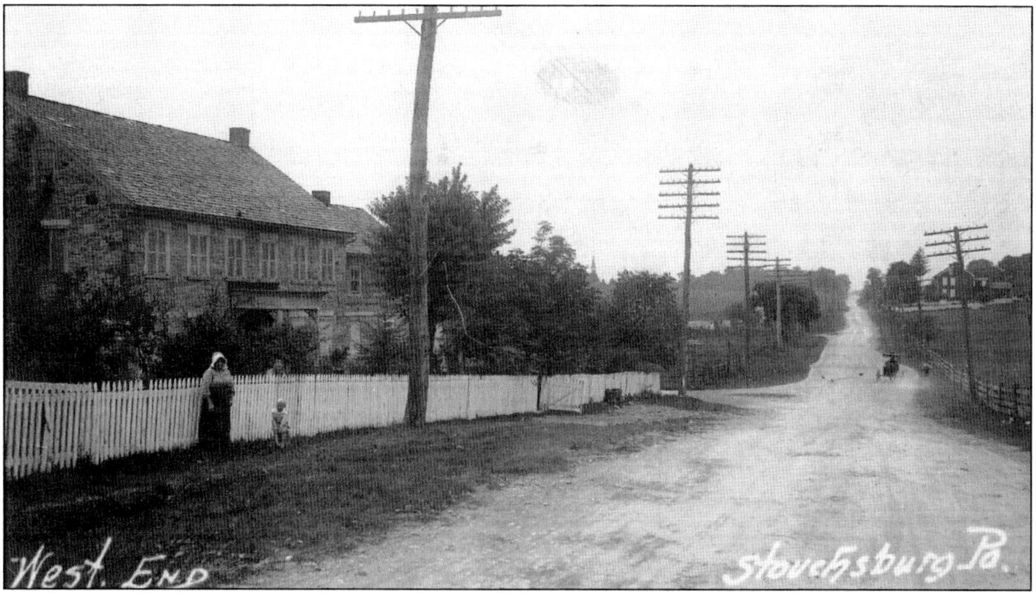

Pictured here around 1910, the house on the left is the oldest home in Stouchsburg and one of the oldest in Marion Township. Peter Spycker built the lower part around 1740 and the middle part around 1750. His son Henry built the main upper part around 1790. Peter served as judge for Berks County from 1763 to 1790. Henry served in the state legislature from 1784 to 1790. It was also the site where 300 men met to march against the hostile Indians in 1755. Jacob Shitz, who owned this property in the 1820s, laid out lots on the south side of Main Street. He died in debt, and some lots were sold on December 17, 1827. Dr. Newcomet, the town physician, owned the property around 1900, and the present owner is Robert Nelson. Over the last 25 years, individual lots have been deeded from this property. (Courtesy of Carl Ganster.)

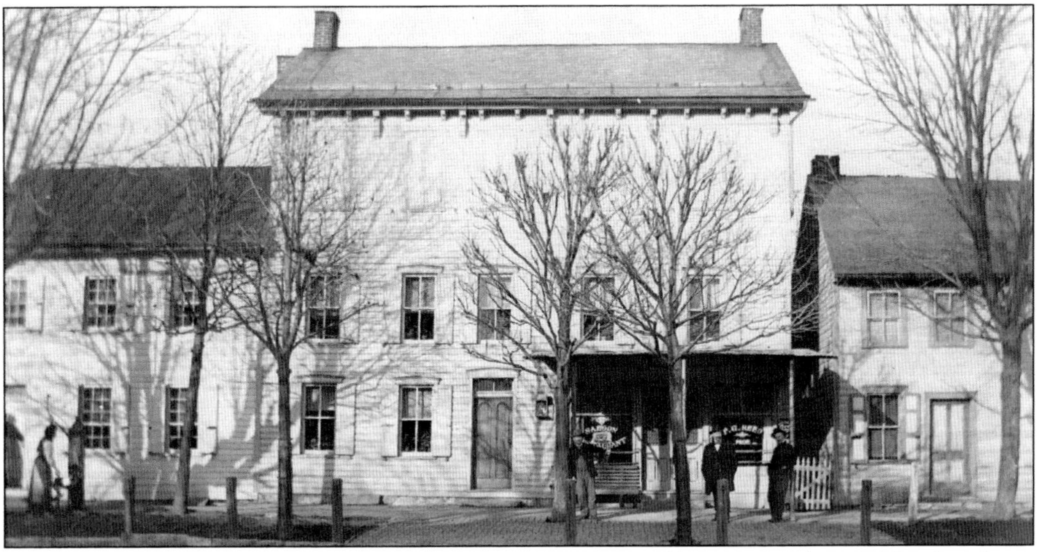

The F.G. Reed Hotel at 85, 87, and 89 Main Street is pictured here around 1910. This hotel was called Wolf's Café from 1938 to 1950. It is said that Wolf's was a very popular eatery before Route 422 was built north of town. Mike Andruzack ran the hotel from 1950 to 1974, and Serrafino was the last hotelkeeper, closing the hotel in the late 1970s. The building to the right was owned by James Manbeck, and in 1915, he sold the property to the Marion Fire Company for $1,105. Note the wooden pump on the left side, as well as the hitching posts. (Courtesy of Carl Ganster.)

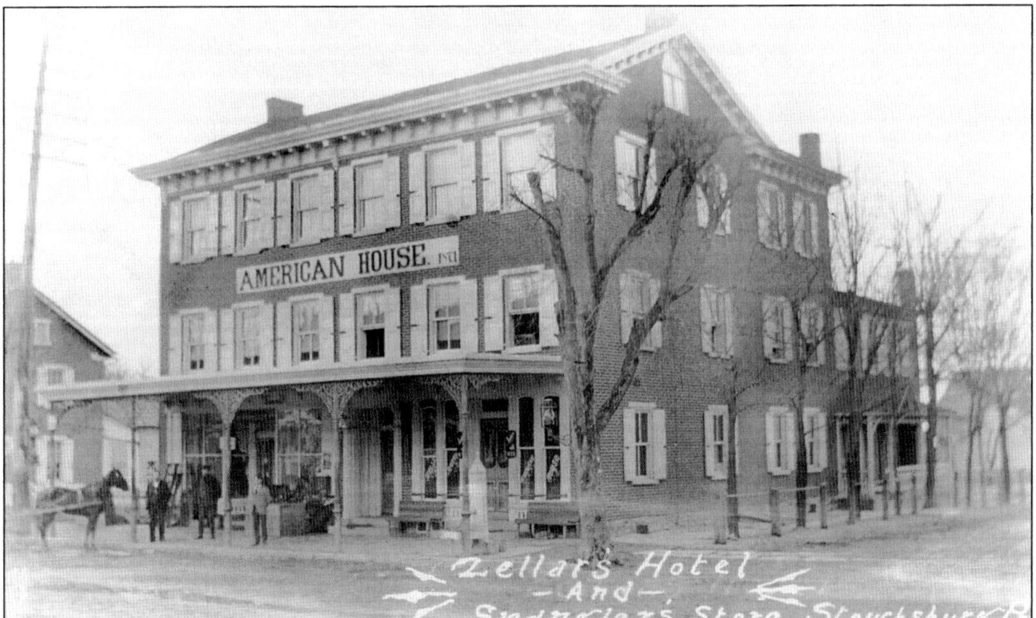

Pictured here in 1909 is the American House hotel and store, located at 89 Main Street. This hotel was built in 1877 by Isaac Moyer, a Civil War veteran who named it after a hotel in Washington, DC. This structure served as a hotel, general store, lodge hall, community meeting place, and personal residence, and it is now a home for senior citizens. In the 1960s and 1970s, it was called Klein's Hotel. Note the old wooden town pump and streetlamp on the corner of the lot. (Courtesy of Carl Ganster.)

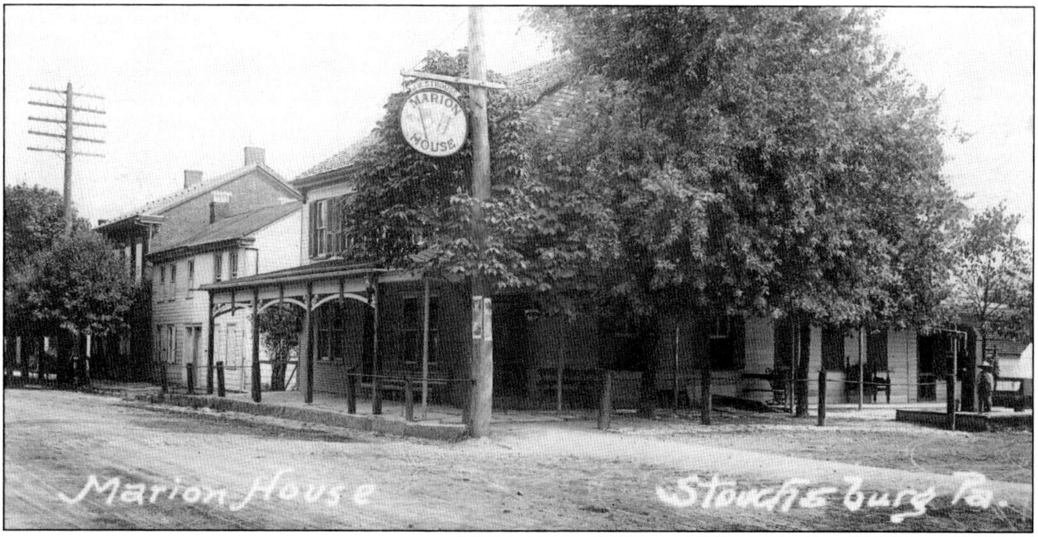

Located at 116 Main Street, the Marion House Hotel is pictured here around 1910. This hotel was built by Lida Jimy or William Dieffenbach around 1830. In 1860, it became known as the Marion House, which it remained until about 2000, when it became the Black Dog Café. It was the longest-running business in Marion Township until the café closed in August 2014. The building in the middle is a log house built in the 1820s. The next house on the left was owned by the Smaltz family, who ran a small cigar factory in the rear of the structure. The Black Dog Hotel reopened in 2014, continuing the presence of a hotel on Main Street for almost 200 years. (Courtesy of Carl Ganster.)

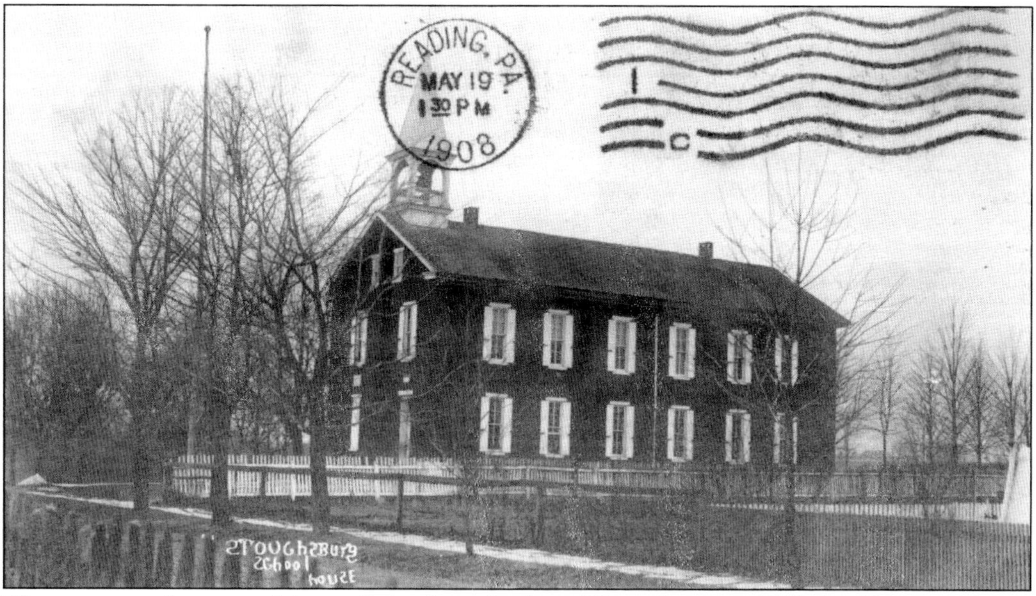

The two-story, four-room Marion School was built on Water Street in 1877. In 1932, an addition was made to the front of the school, which divided the building into six classrooms and a library. The school was known as the Marion Township High School until 1954, when the Conrad Weiser School District was formed. From 1954 to March 1970, it was called the Marion Elementary Center and served grades one through six. At that time, all Marion Township schoolchildren were bused to the Conrad Weiser West Elementary in Womelsdorf. (Courtesy of Carl Ganster.)

The Marion Fire Company was organized in 1908 and housed its hand pumper in a shed at the ball field on Scharff Road. In 1915, a home on Main Street was purchased for $1,105 to serve as the fire station. The building was dedicated on October 7, 1916, with a parade and carnival. This image of the celebration hangs in the meeting room on the second floor. Fire trucks ran from this building until 1986, and the company built a modern four-bay engine house along Route 422 just east of Church Road in 2006. Between 1986 and 2006, the trucks were housed in a building on Scharff Road. (Courtesy of the Marion Fire Company.)

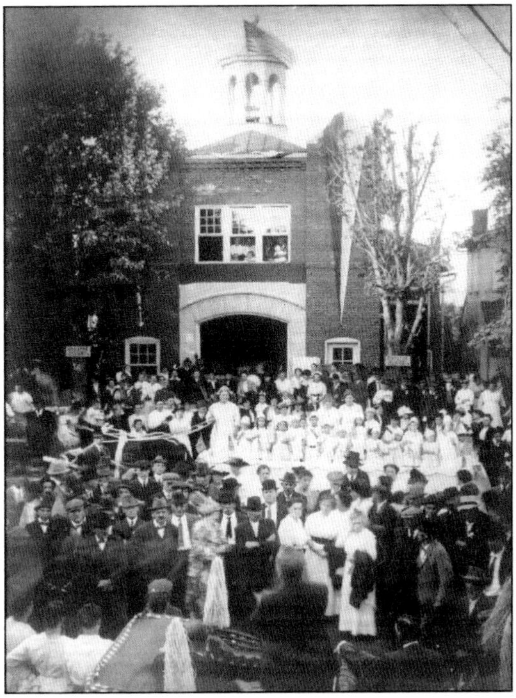

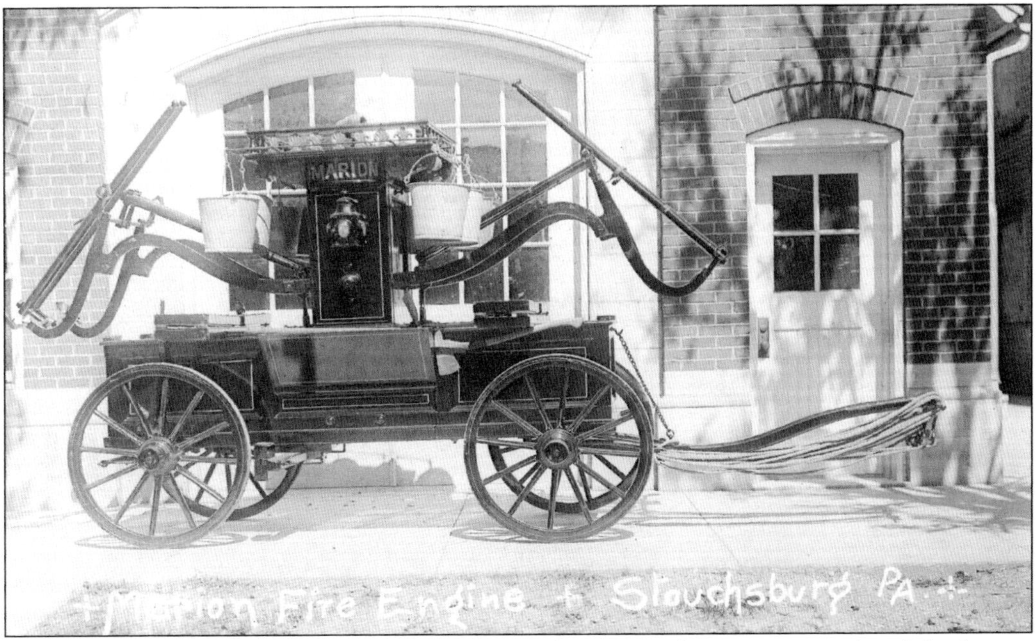

Pictured here in 1916, this hand pumper was the first piece of equipment used to fight fires in Marion Township. It was made by John Agnew of Philadelphia around 1830. The community purchased it about 1870, but no organized firefighting unit was founded until 1908. The unit was used until 1923, when a new Hahn pumper was purchased at a cost of $3,990. This hand pumper was also hand pulled, and it took a bucket brigade and 16 men to operate the pump. It is said that this apparatus could pump a stream of water over the school on Water Street. The Marion Fire Company still owns this antique. (Courtesy of Carl Ganster.)

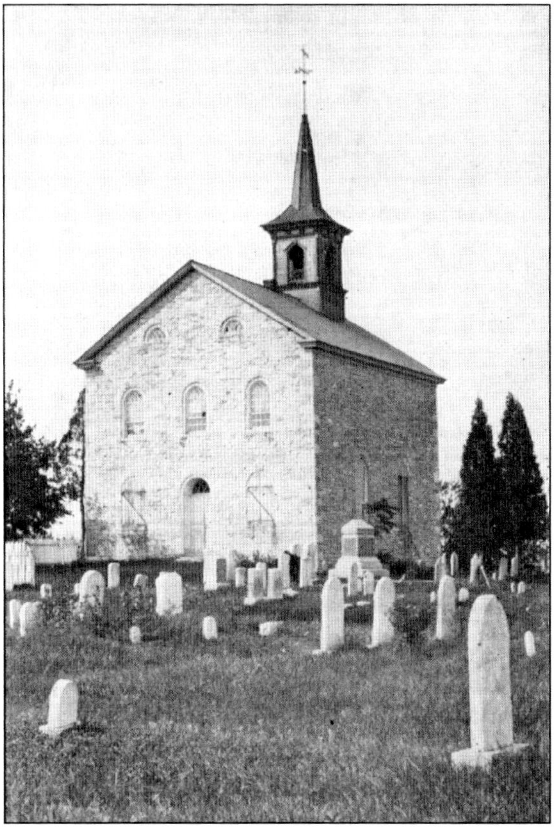

Pictured here is the third and last Reed's Church built on the grounds of Reed's Cemetery on Sheridan Road. Christopher Ried, Jacob Ried, Peter Kaiser, and Geo Kaiser served as the building committee, and the cornerstone was laid on April 23, 1837. This church was torn down around 1902. At that time, a new church was built in Stouchsburg. Reed's Cemetery has tombstones dating back to the 1740s, making it one of the oldest burial grounds in Berks County. (Courtesy of Carl Ganster.)

This is a c. 1900 view of the interior of the third Reed's Church. Some of the original items from the church are still used in the Sunday school at the current Reed's Church in Stouchsburg. (Courtesy of Carl Ganster.)

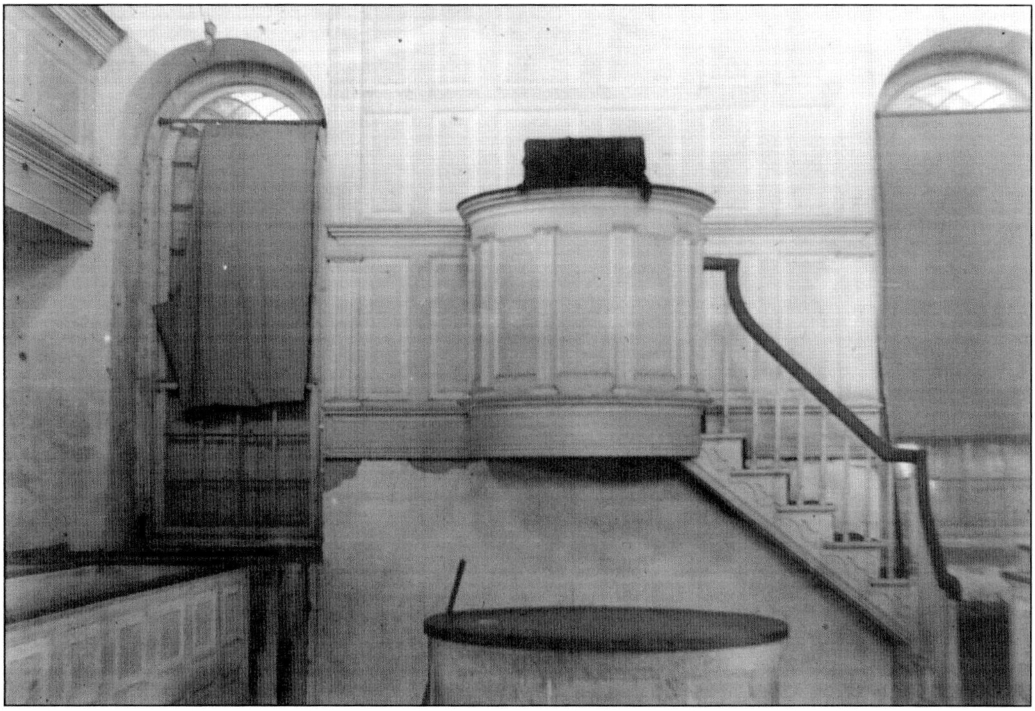

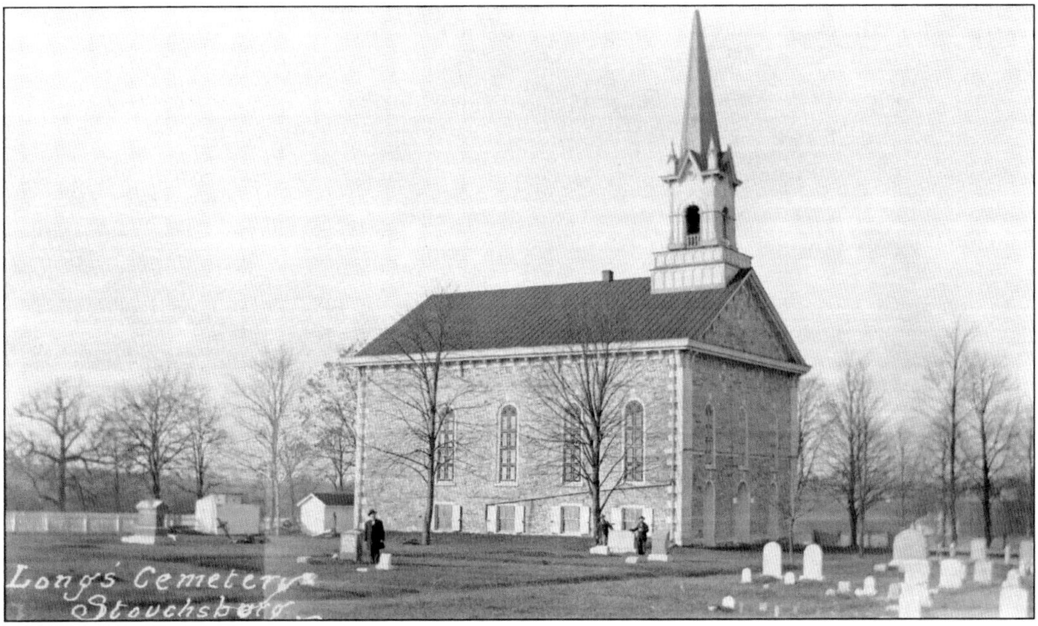

Conrad Weiser helped organize the original Christ Lutheran Church, first built in 1743. The second church, pictured here around 1910, was constructed in 1786. This church was severely damaged on November 7, 1884, from a dynamite factory explosion nearby, and it was struck by lightning and burned on August 1, 1887. The church was rebuilt using the original 30-inch-thick walls, the only thing left standing after the fire. A pastor by the name of A. Johnson Long served the church for over 30 years, from 1874 to 1908, so it is often referred to as Long's Church. In the early 1960s, an educational center was added to the rear of this building. The cemetery has tombstones dating back to the mid-1700s. (Courtesy of Carl Ganster.)

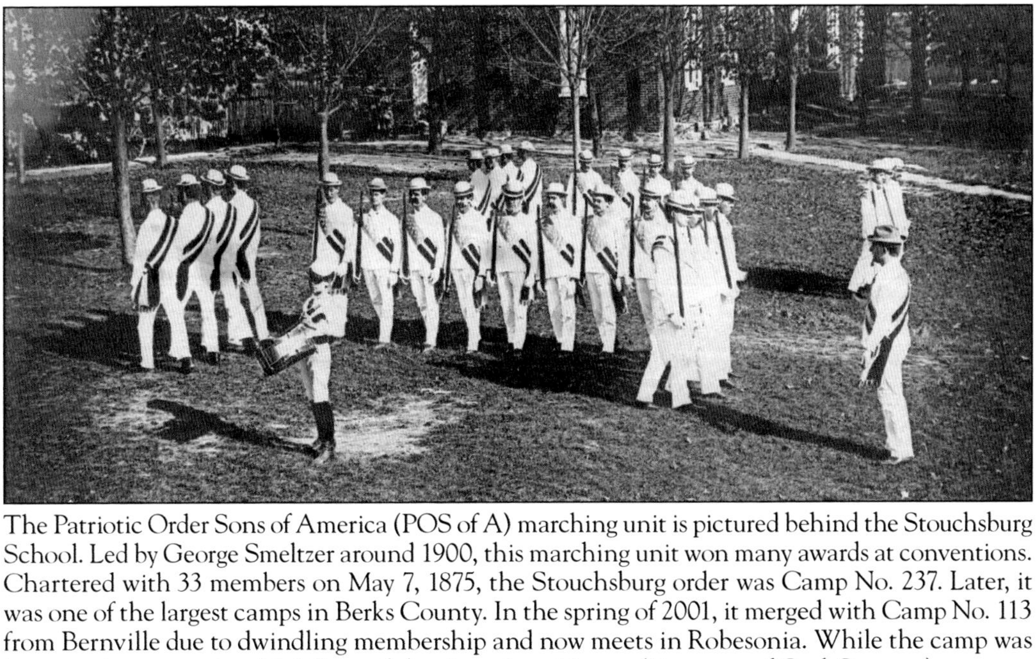

The Patriotic Order Sons of America (POS of A) marching unit is pictured behind the Stouchsburg School. Led by George Smeltzer around 1900, this marching unit won many awards at conventions. Chartered with 33 members on May 7, 1875, the Stouchsburg order was Camp No. 237. Later, it was one of the largest camps in Berks County. In the spring of 2001, it merged with Camp No. 113 from Bernville due to dwindling membership and now meets in Robesonia. While the camp was in town, it met on the third floor of the American House. (Courtesy of Carl Ganster.)

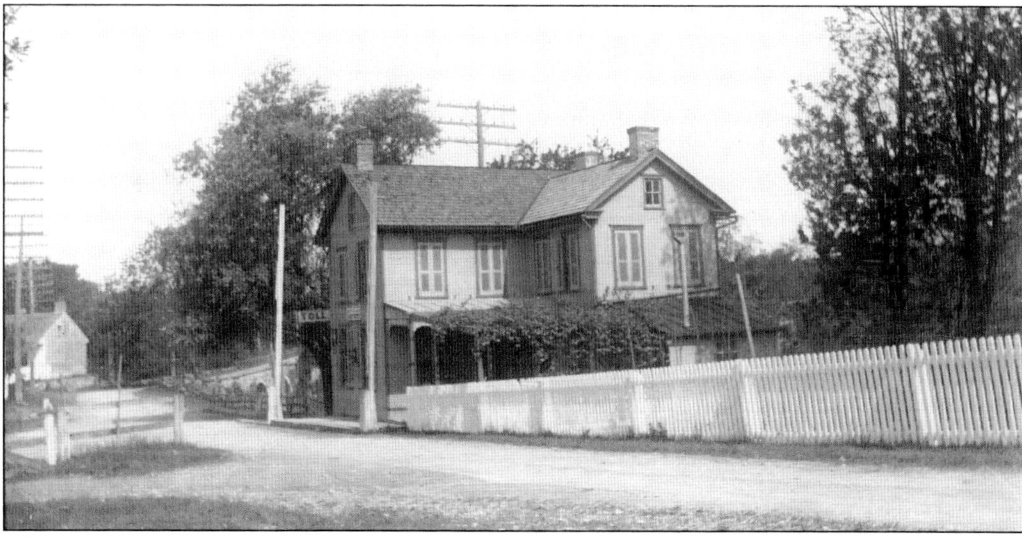

The Waterloo tollgate of the Berks-Dauphin Turnpike stood at the bottom of the hill on William Penn Boulevard when coming from Womelsdorf, before the new bridge that was built in 2013. It cost 24¢ for a buggy and one horse to travel to Wernersville and 39¢ for two horses. The last toll was collected here on August 30, 1917. The turnpike closed in 1917 when the state took over the road, and the tollhouse was subsequently torn down. (Courtesy of Carl Ganster.)

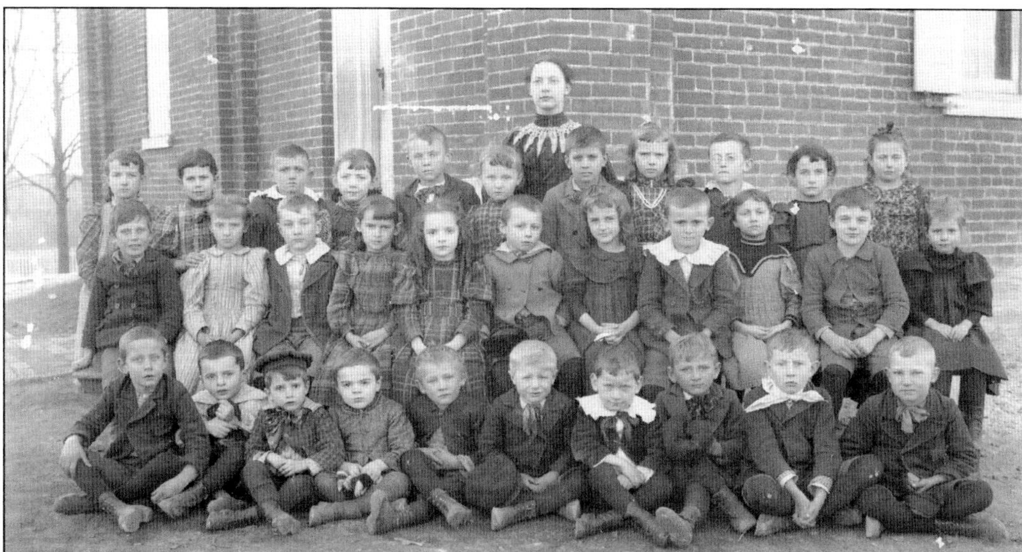

The Marion School's primary class, taught by Florence Mertz, is pictured here at the school on Water Street around 1900. From left to right are (first row) Harry Killmer, Douglas Gesger, Harry Weidman, Frank Kurr, George Kline, Milton Royer, John Bickel, Roy Troutman, Claude Schadler, and Paul Rhine; (second row) Fred Bubb, Amy Troutman, Charlie Reed, Nettie Kline, Mary Walborn, Levi Troutman, Sadie Kline, Harry Strause, Celia Hooster, Howard Kurr, and Rhoda Weidman; (third row) Lillie Kline, Winnie Snyder, Earl Spohn, Ray Searle, Harry Potteiger, Edith Seibert, Fred Royer, Mannie Zimmerman, Clarence Houncker, Edna Kline, and Mary Whitman. Later, Milton Royer owned Royer's Mill, Mary Walborn was postmistress, Howard Kurr was an undertaker and furniture salesmen, and Ray Searle had a toy store in town. (Courtesy of Carl Ganster.)

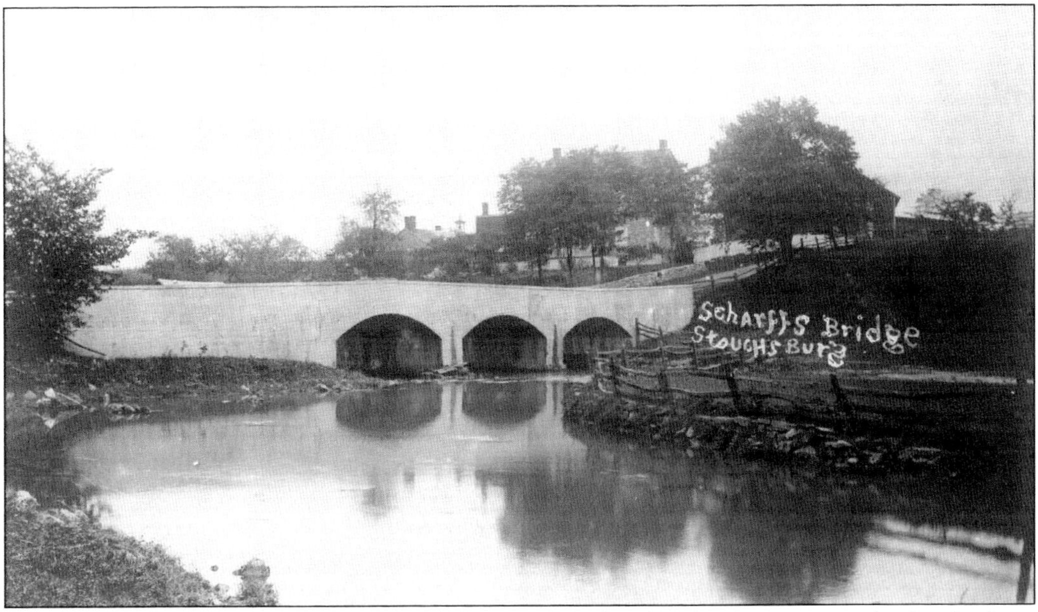

In 1904, the three-arch Scharff Bridge was supposed to be the first cement bridge built in Pennsylvania. The original two-arch bridge was built of limestone. On the hill behind the bridge is the Scharff homestead, built in 1837. This farm, which stayed in the Scharff family until the 1960s, had its own electric plant and sawmill. Today, Susan Stum owns the limestone farmhouse. (Courtesy of Carl Ganster.)

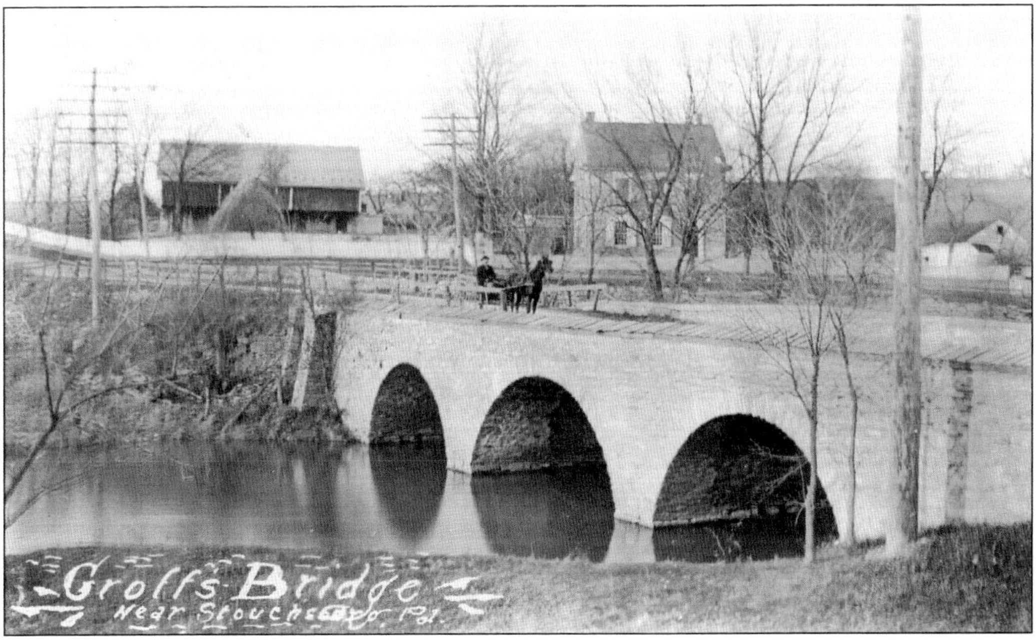

Pictured here in 1909, Groff's Bridge was built in 1816 to service the Berks-Dauphin Turnpike. Locally, it is was known as the S-Bridge due to the number of curves. Many locals would be surprised to know that the bridge had an official name. After 185 years of use, it was closed on May 21, 2001, then torn down. The new bridge was built and opened in the spring of 2013. (Courtesy of Carl Ganster.)

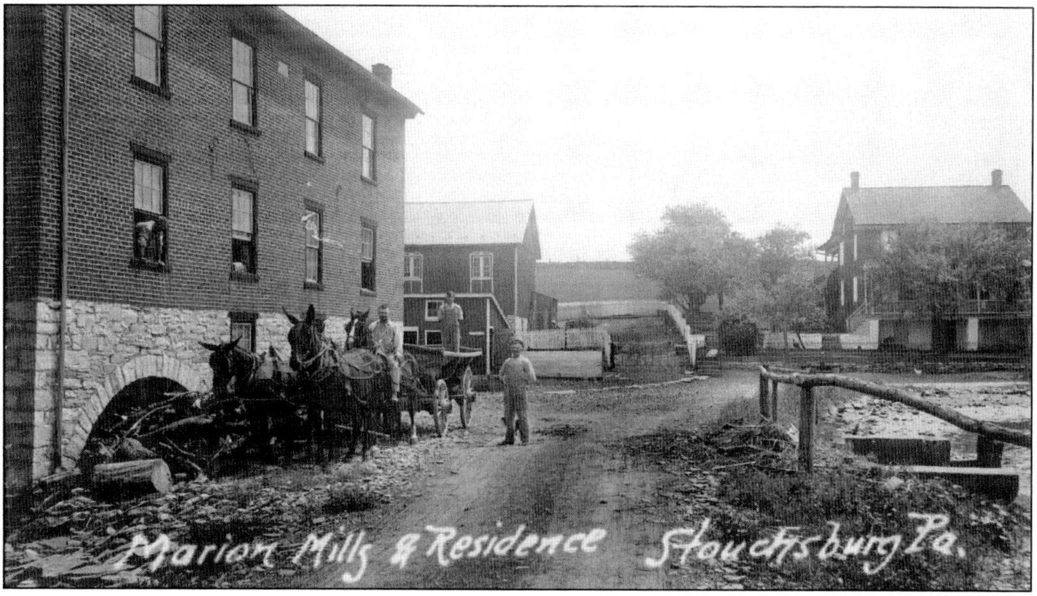

In 1860, the Royer family built the Marion Mill on Richland Road. An earlier mill, built around 1800 and owned by Jacob Shitz in the 1820s, stood behind this one. Around 1960, Milton Royer sold his family's mill to Aaron Burkholder, and a fire destroyed it in November 1962. The older mill survived the fire but was torn down in the 1990s. In the spring of 1963, the Marion Rod and Gun Club purchased the property and continues ownership today. The barn in the middle serves as the clubhouse. (Courtesy of Carl Ganster.)

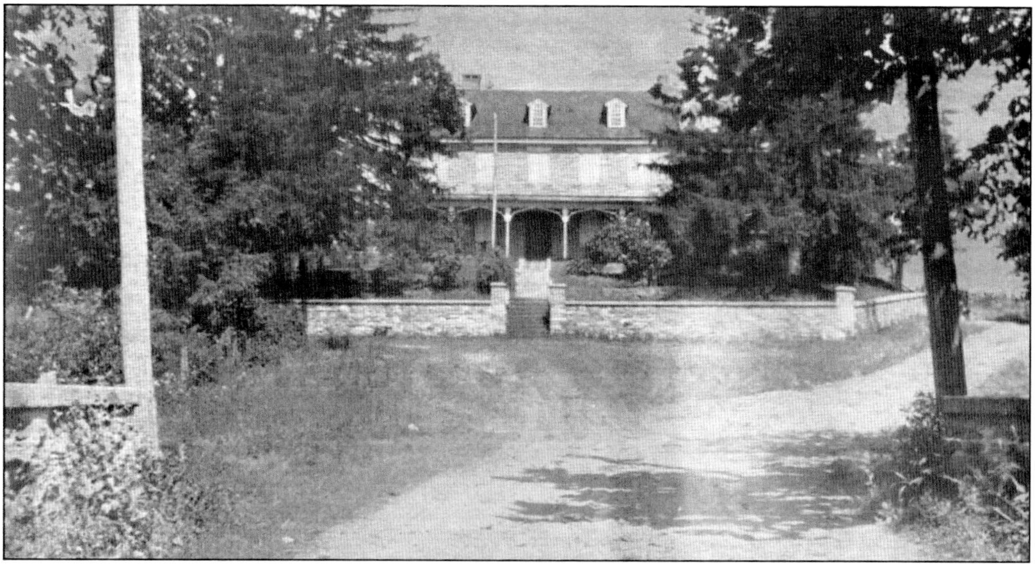

On the western edge of Marion Township is a small village called Charming Forge. The village was founded in 1749 by J. George Nickoll and Michael Miller, who built a dam to create enough waterpower for a forge hammer. Part of the Charming Forge Mansion, pictured here around 1930, was constructed in 1749, with the main portion built between 1780 and 1784. In the 1990s, the mansion was restored to its 1780s style. During the Revolutionary War, Hessian prisoners of war were hired to cut a 250-foot channel through limestone in the front yard of the mansion. Chip Henderson is the current owner of this historic home and village. (Courtesy of Carl Ganster.)

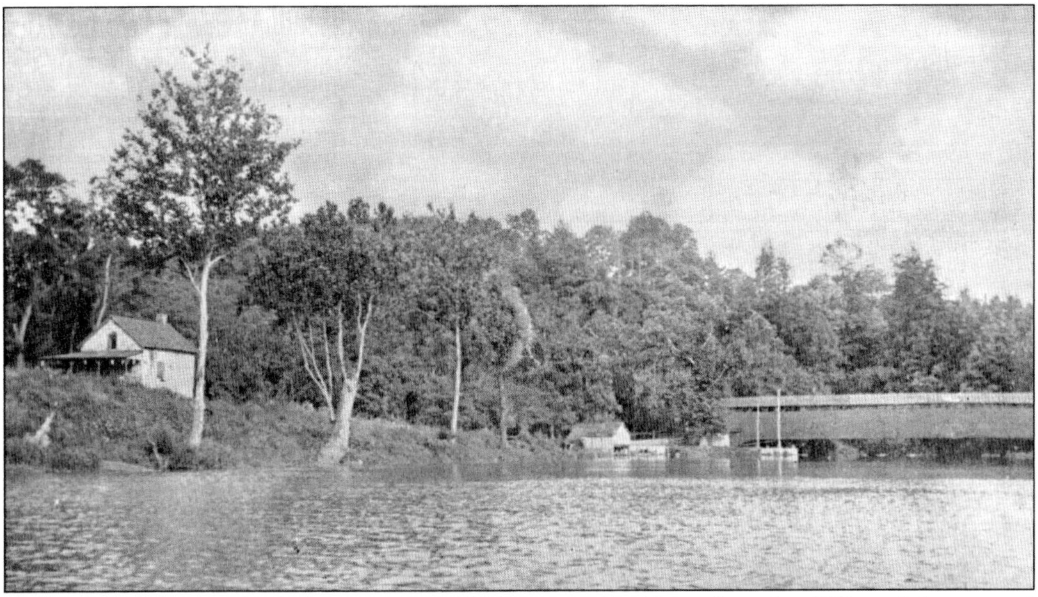

Pictured here along Tulpehocken Creek are old limestone buildings from the 1700s and the covered bridge at Charming Forge. This bridge was built in 1873 and torn down in 1938. It was the only covered bridge in Marion Township, connecting Marion to Heidelberg Township. The dimensions of the bridge were 186 feet long, 16 feet wide, and 13 feet high. (Courtesy of Carl Ganster.)

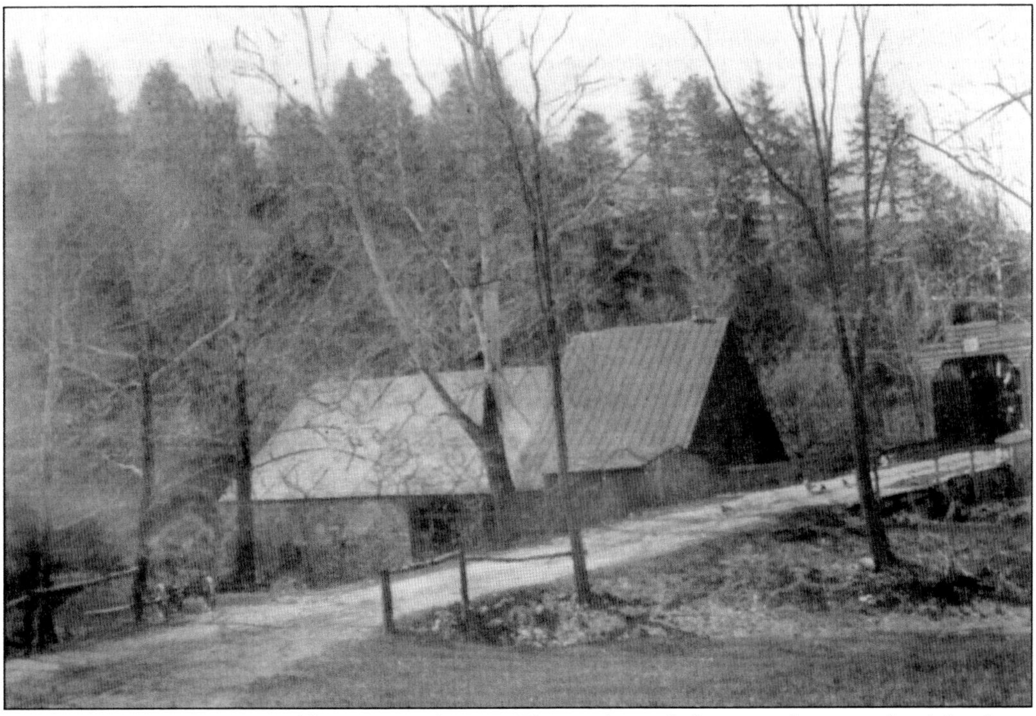

Charming Forge is pictured here around 1888. This is the only known photograph of the forge building. The forge was built in 1749 and torn down around 1890. It stood on the left side of the road, right before the covered bridge, and some of the iron produced here is said to have been used in the Revolutionary War. (Courtesy of Carl Ganster.)

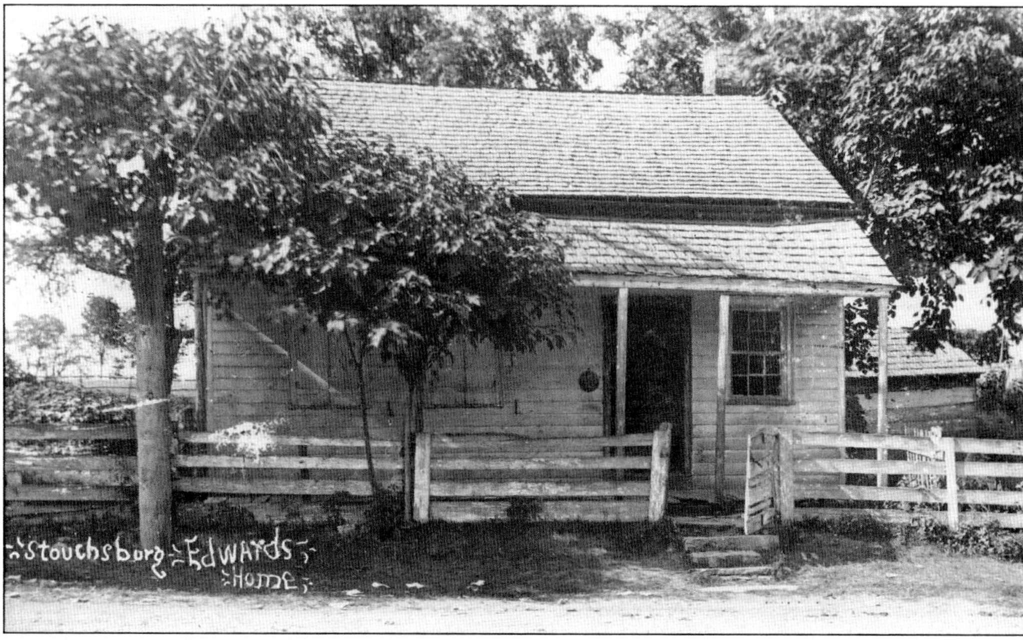

Seen here around 1905 is the Edwards home, where a murder took place in 1901. Kate Edwards, along with the help of her daughter Mary, murdered her husband (Mary's father), John, and hid his body. Kate was pregnant with the child of her lover, a black man by the name of Samuel Greason. Kate and Samuel were both sentenced to be hanged in the courtyard of the Berks County Prison. The baby, Alma, was born while Kate was in jail and remained there until her mother's execution. (Courtesy of Carl Ganster.)

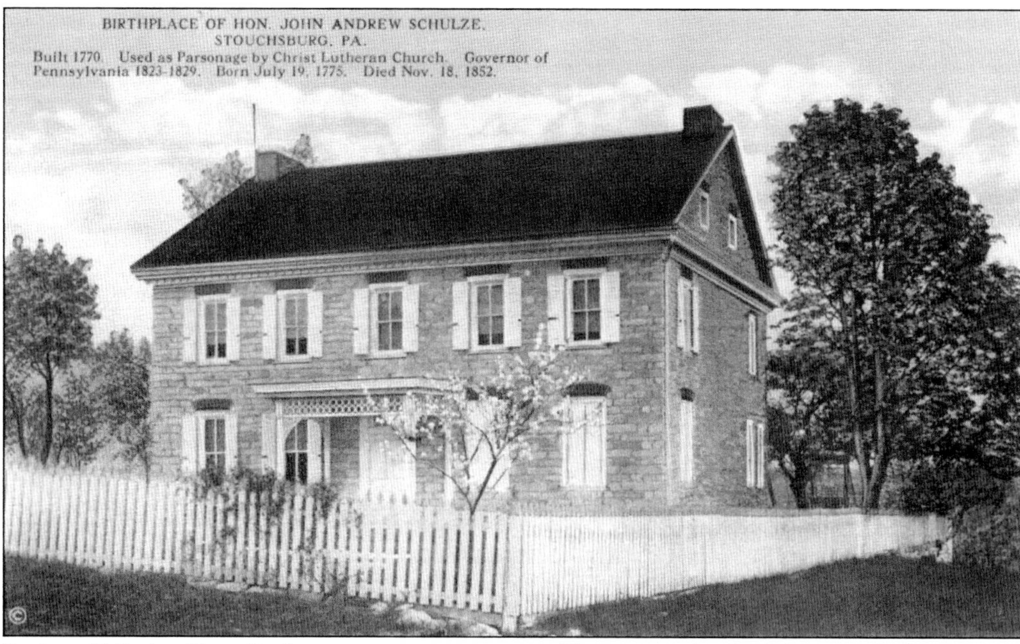

Built in 1770, the Christ Lutheran parsonage is pictured here around 1930. John A. Schultz, governor of Pennsylvania from 1823 to 1829, was born here on July 19, 1775. (Courtesy of Carl Ganster.)

Two

Womelsdorf Borough

Womelsdorf is the oldest borough in the Conrad Weiser area. On May 1, 1762, John Womelsdorf laid out 75 lots on his 250-acre farm on the Tulpehocken Path, which started at Conrad Weiser's home and continued to Shamokin. Womelsdorf's father purchased the farm in 1750, and the new town was called Middletown, as it was located midway between Reading and Lebanon. In September 1762, the first lots were sold, and the deeds stipulated that each residence would be a 24-foot-by-20-foot log house with a chimney of double brick. Jacob Seltzer Sr. is said to have constructed the first building, a hotel, of stone.

By 1774, Womelsdorf had faced some financial troubles and was forced to sell the remaining lots to Jacob Seltzer for £208 and one shilling ($503.56). Some militia companies were formed in Womelsdorf for the Revolutionary War, and the first church was started in 1792 for both Lutheran and Reformed congregations. This church stood on the hill on the north side of town at the present-day cemetery. Pres. George Washington visited in November 1793 and stayed at the Stouch Tavern, built between 1785 and 1788. The tavern still stands today, bearing the same name. President Washington also paid a visit in October 1794 when en route to western Pennsylvania.

The first post office west of the Schuylkill River was established in 1807, and Womelsdorf was designated as a borough in 1833. At that time, the population was listed as 750. In 1834, the borough purchased its first firefighting equipment, and a local newspaper was being printed by 1840. In 1855, Womelsdorf had a town jail, followed by a police department two years later. The present fire company was organized in 1895, and the Womelsdorf Union Bank was established in 1903.

The town continued to grow, and by the 2010 census, its population had reached 2,810. Womelsdorf boasts many stores, two banks, four churches, and a funeral home. It is also home to Conrad Weiser West Elementary School, which serves children in the western part of the school district.

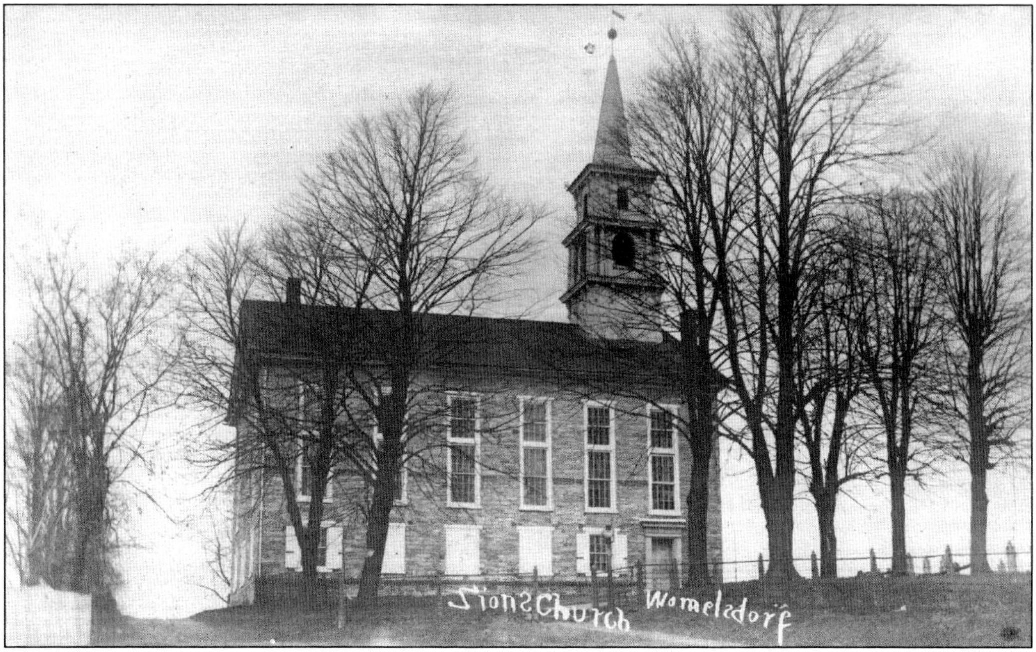

Zion Lutheran and Reformed Church was built at the cemetery at the end of North Front Street to serve both Lutheran and Reformed congregations. The cornerstone for the sanctuary was laid on June 30, 1792. In 1915, both congregations agreed to build separate churches on High Street. This church was torn down in May 1958. (Courtesy of Carl Ganster.)

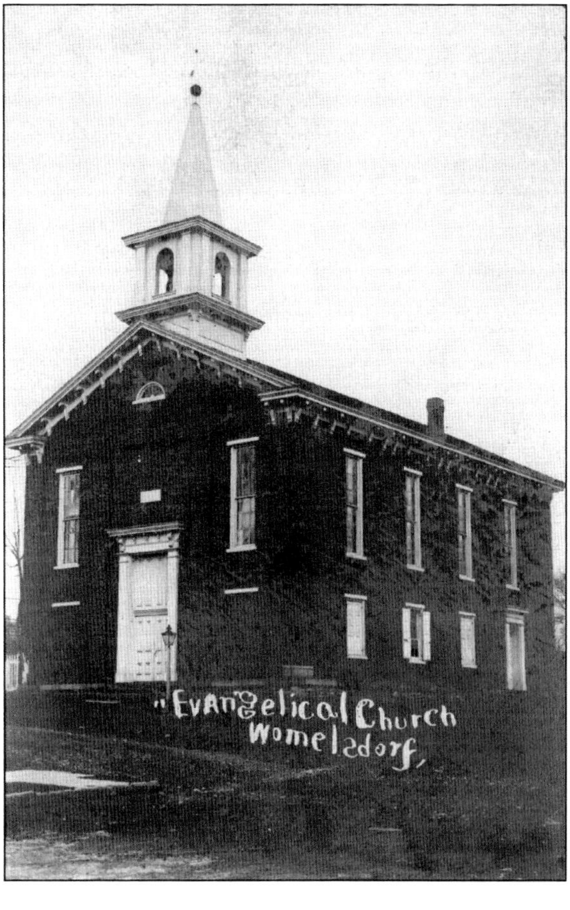

The Evangelical Church, built on the corner of Front and Franklin Streets around 1830, is pictured here in 1909. In 2010, this church was closed, and the congregation moved to the former Fulton Bank building on Lyman Street. (Courtesy of Carl Ganster.)

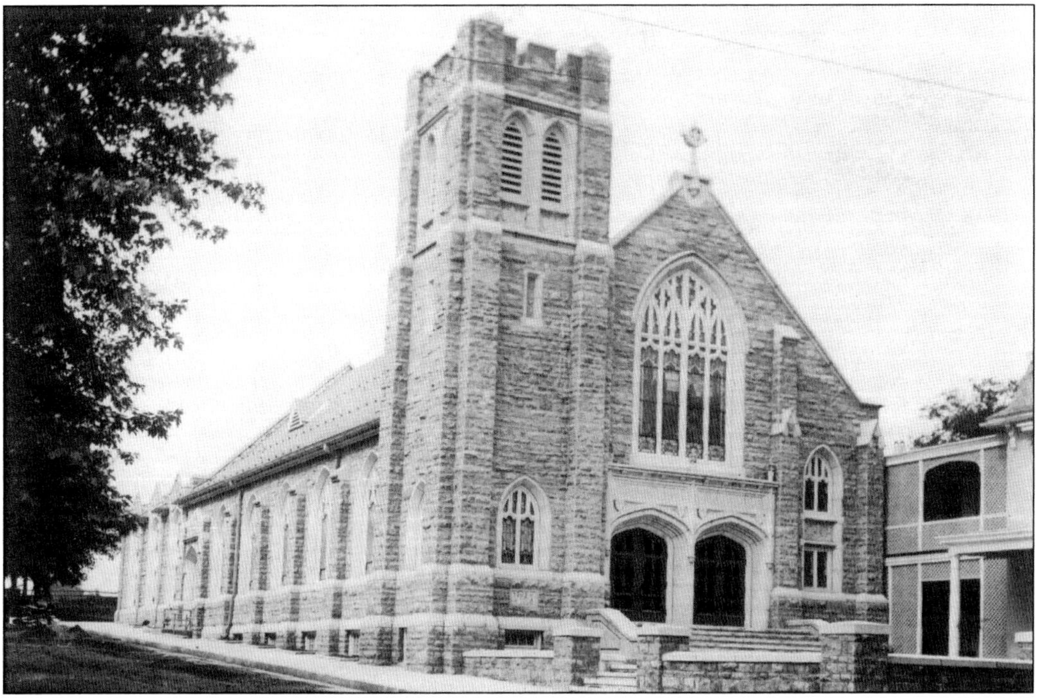

The Zion Evangelical Lutheran Church at Second and High Streets is seen here around 1920. On April 5, 1915, the Lutheran congregation voted in favor of soliciting funds to erect a new church. Its cornerstone was laid on October 16, 1916, and the first service was held on January 20, 1918. The total cost of construction was $35,000. (Courtesy of Carl Ganster.)

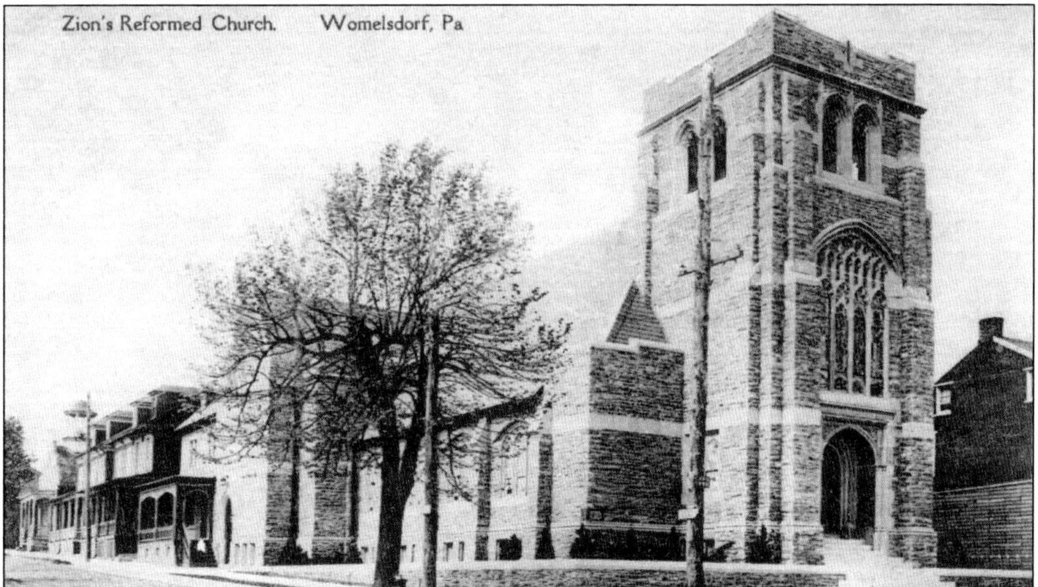

Zion's Reformed Church at Third and High Streets is pictured here about 1930. On April 13, 1915, the Reformed congregation voted to establish their own church. The cornerstone was laid on July 24, 1916, and the church was dedicated on November 25, 1917. The total cost, including the parsonage, was $50,000. (Courtesy of Carl Ganster.)

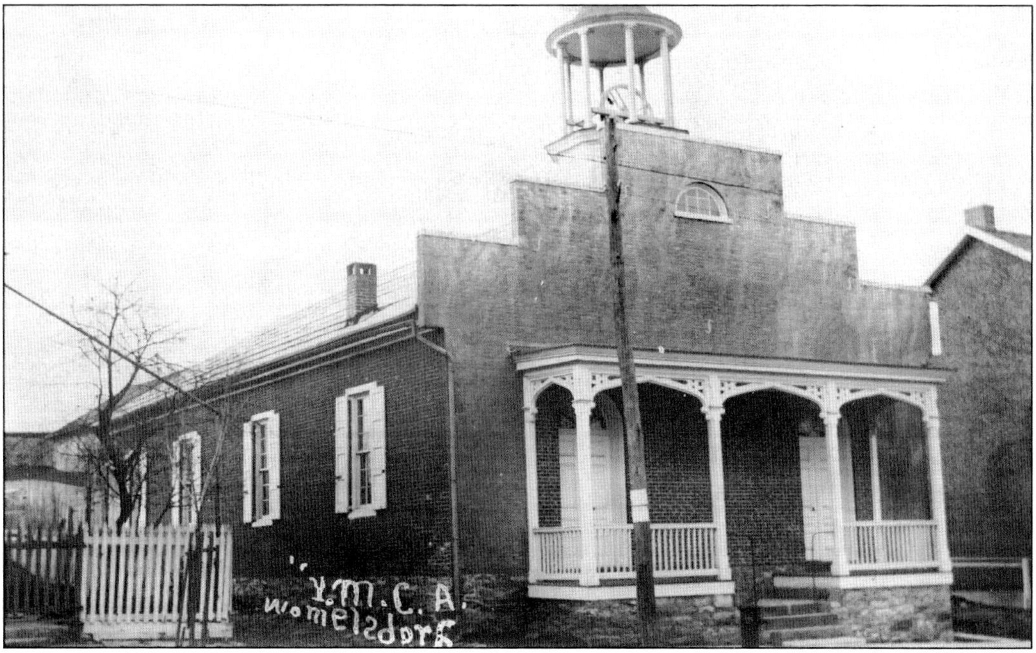

The Womelsdorf YMCA on South Second Street was originally a Presbyterian church built in 1834. The church lasted until 1854, and years later, it became the YMCA, pictured here in 1908. For a time, it also housed a school while a new one was being built. According to Earl W. Ibach, the building was torn down about 1940. (Courtesy of Ryan A. Zerbe.)

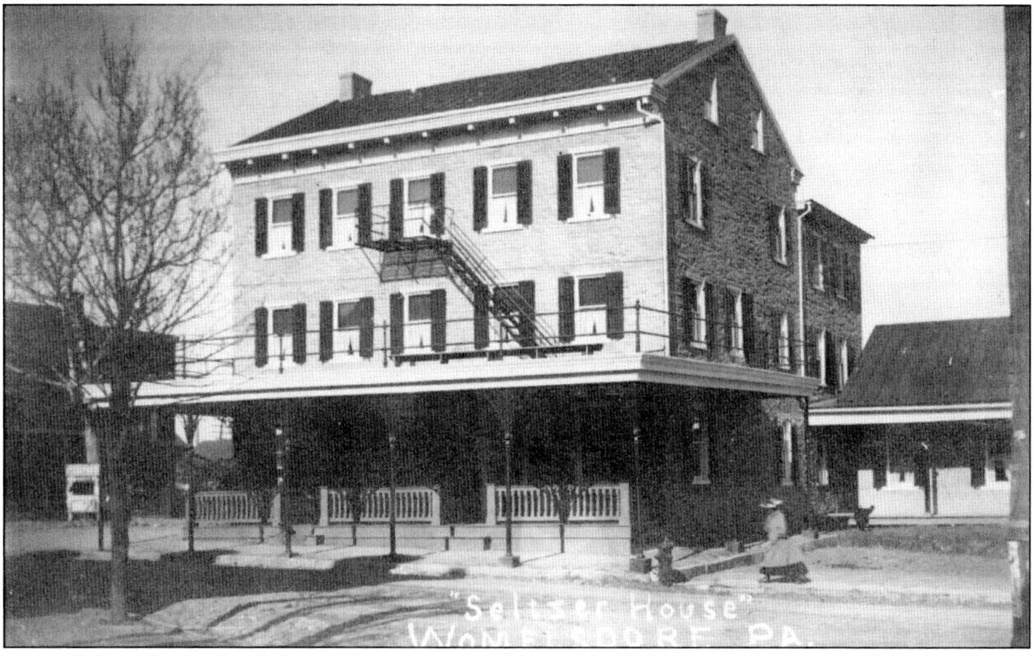

Jacob Seltzer built the Seltzer House, pictured here about 1910, as a two-story hotel in 1800. Jacob's son Michael added a third story around 1825, and it remained a hotel until 1937, when Jack Hafer retired and sold the property. Since 1937, the building has been an apartment house. (Courtesy of Ryan A. Zerbe.)

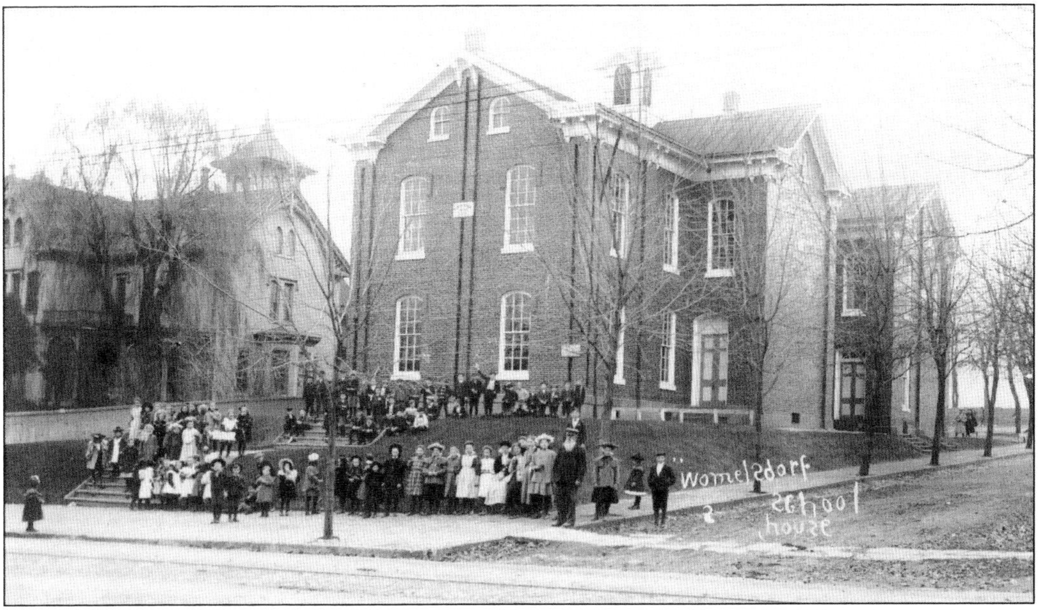

The Womelsdorf Public School, shown here before 1909, was built in 1880 and torn down in 1960. It stood at Third and High Streets, across from the Lutheran church. Before public schools, Womelsdorf had private academies. Henry W. Stiegel, the famous glassmaker and part owner of Charming Forge, taught school in Womelsdorf in the 1700s. The Womelsdorf Union Academy operated from 1825 to 1855, at which time the public school opened in Womelsdorf. There was also a Womelsdorf Academy that ran from 1866 to 1876. (Courtesy of Ryan A. Zerbe.)

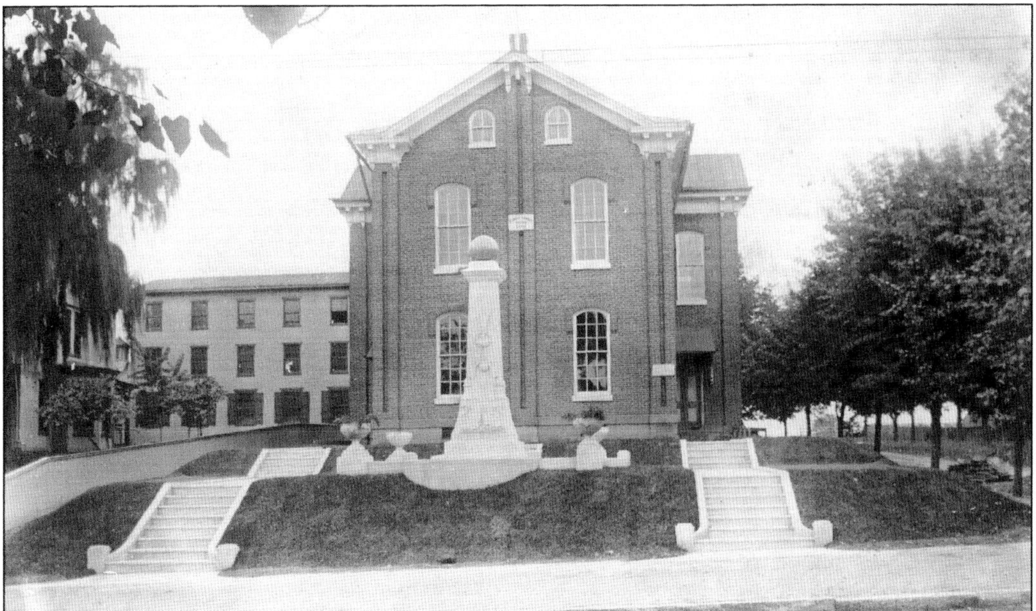

Pictured here in 1909 are the old school and the Conrad Weiser monument, which was dedicated on September 25, 1909, with a parade. The POS of A Washington Camp No. 67 from Womelsdorf was given permission to erect the monument in front of the school. The monument was later moved to the Conrad Weiser Park, east of Womelsdorf. (Courtesy of Ryan A. Zerbe.)

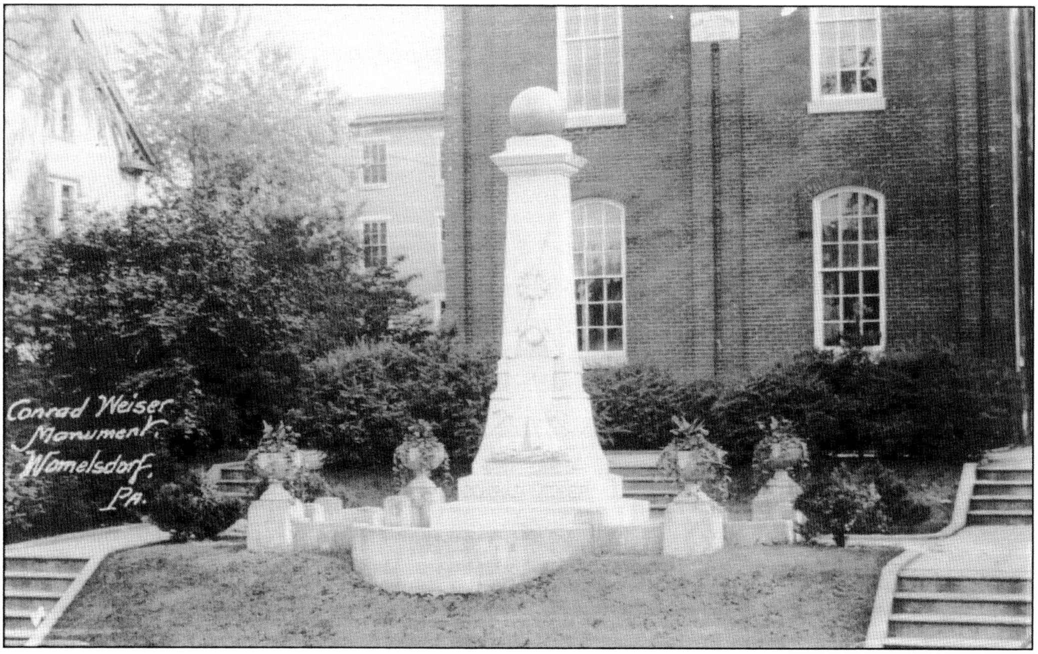

This is a close-up view of the Conrad Weiser monument in 1909. (Courtesy of Carl Ganster.)

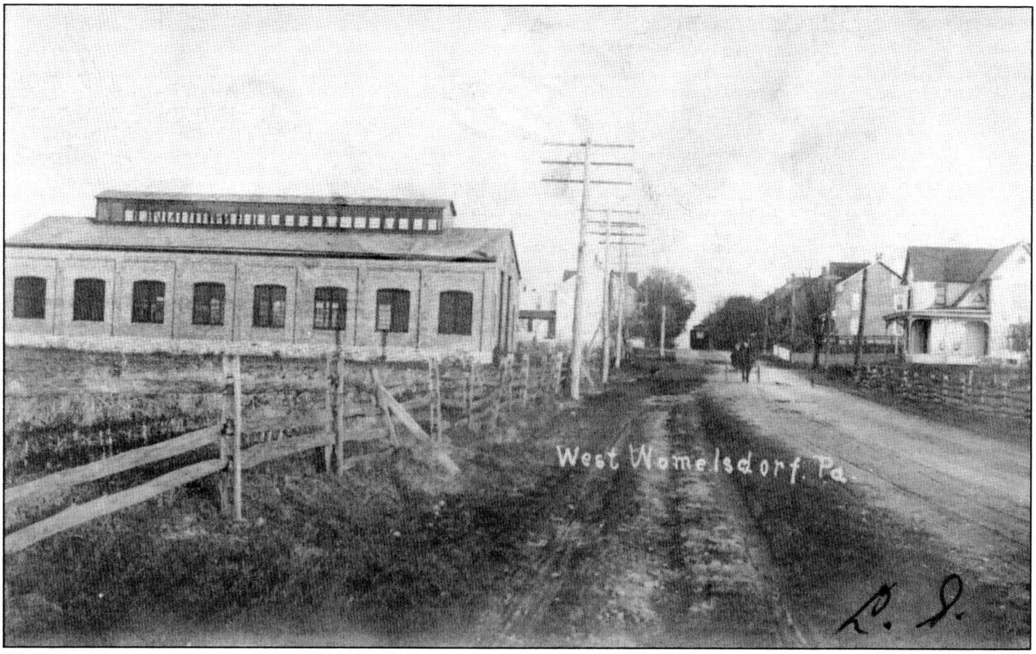

This is the west end of town as it appeared in the early 1900s. The building on the left was the Womelsdorf Car Barn, located at what is now Fourth and High Streets. It housed trolley cars for the line that ran from Reading to Womelsdorf. The car barn was built in 1896 and torn down in the late 1930s. (Courtesy of Ryan A. Zerbe.)

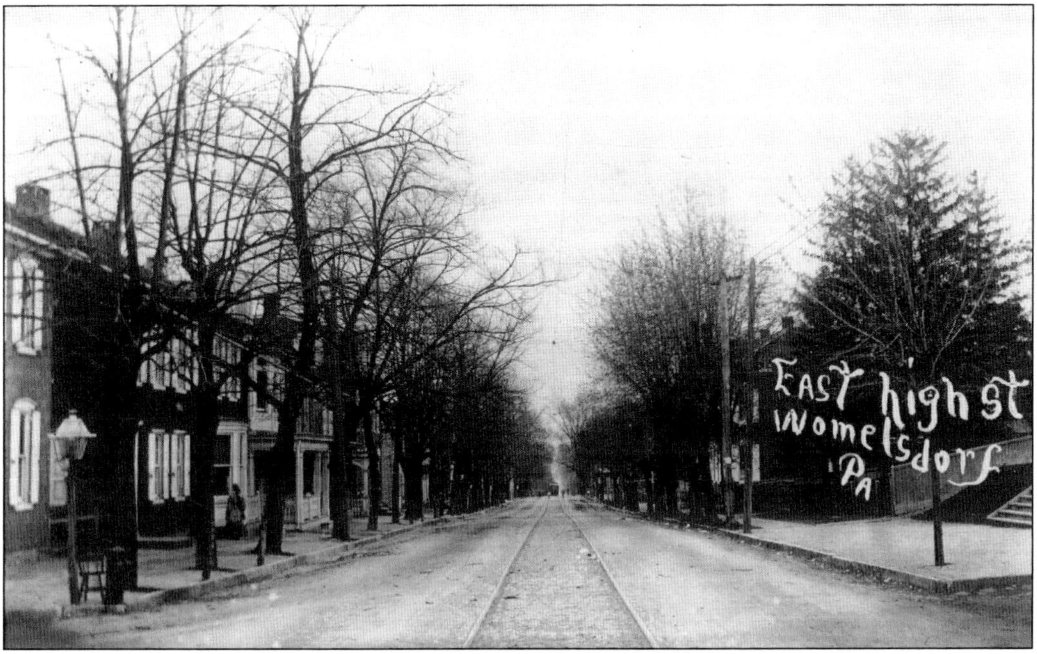

This 1908 photograph of East High Street was taken at the corner of Third Street, looking east. Note the streetlight on the left and the trolley tracks running down the middle of High Street, a lovely tree-lined avenue. (Courtesy of Ryan A. Zerbe.)

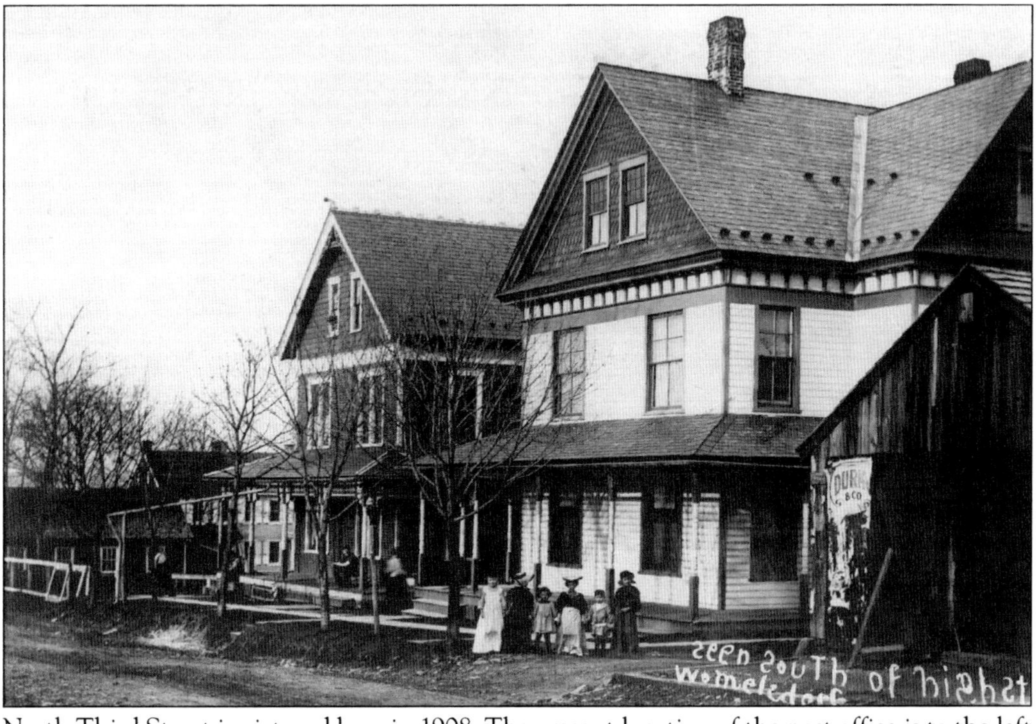

North Third Street is pictured here in 1908. The present location of the post office is to the left of these two houses, and the thoroughfare is now Route 419, leading to Route 422. (Courtesy of Ryan A. Zerbe.)

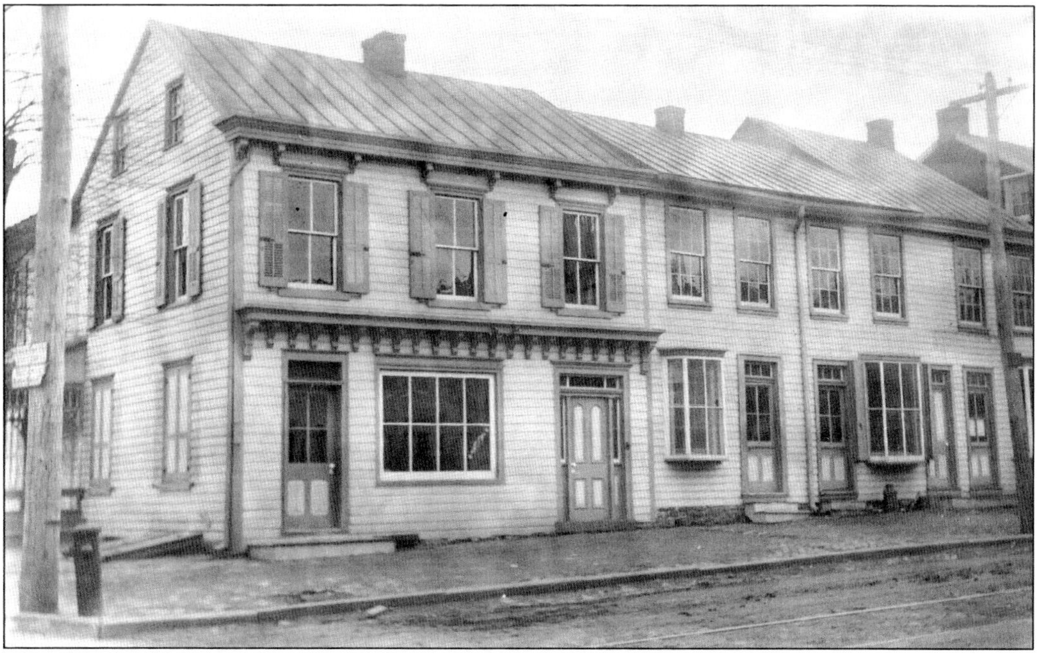

The present-day Zion Reformed Church now occupies this corner of Second and High Streets, pictured here before 1915. In that year, this property, lot No. 25 on Womelsdorf's town plan, was purchased for $4,500 for the new church. Note the fire hydrant on the corner. (Courtesy of Ryan A. Zerbe.)

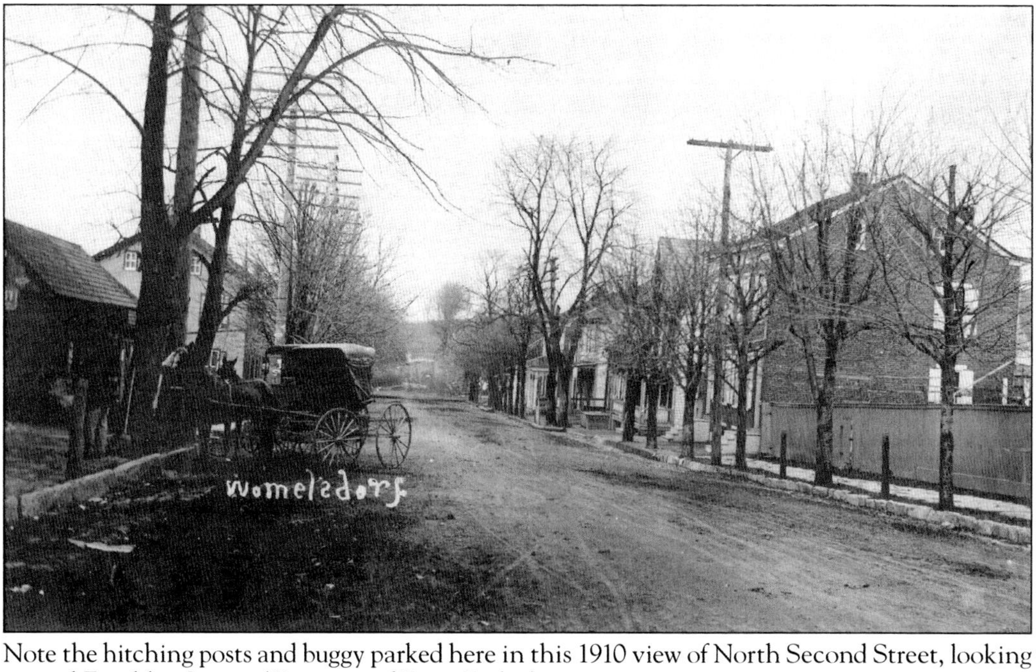

Note the hitching posts and buggy parked here in this 1910 view of North Second Street, looking toward Franklin Street. (Courtesy of Ryan Zerbe.)

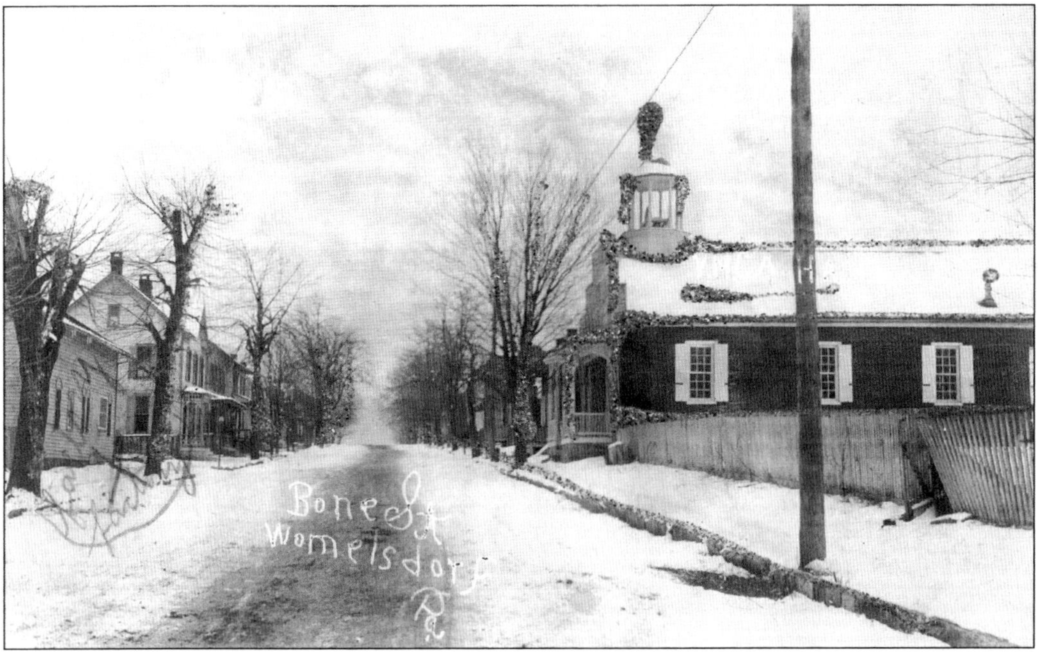

Pictured here around 1910 is Bone Street, now South Second Street. The 1834 Presbyterian church turned YMCA is on the right. The Hiester & Hirst hosiery factory is on the left, where John Smaltz later built a large cigar factory. Valley Forge Flag later made flags there, and now apartments occupy the site. This is Route 419 leading to Newmanstown in Lebanon County. (Courtesy of Ryan Zerbe.)

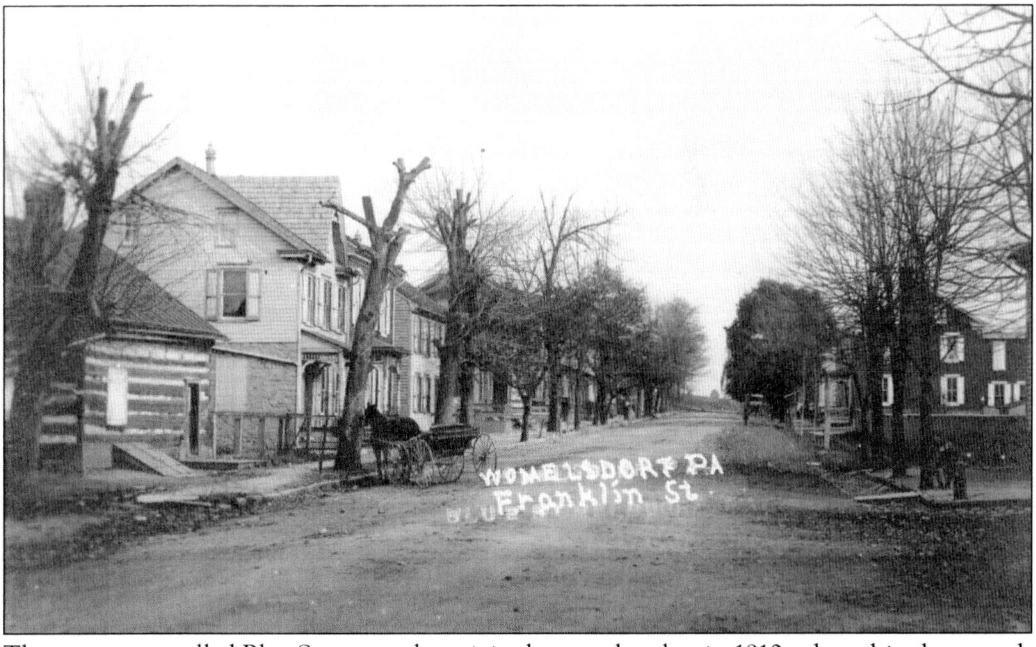

This street was called Blue Street on the original town plan, but in 1910, when this photograph was taken, it was known as Franklin Street. (Courtesy of Carl Ganster.)

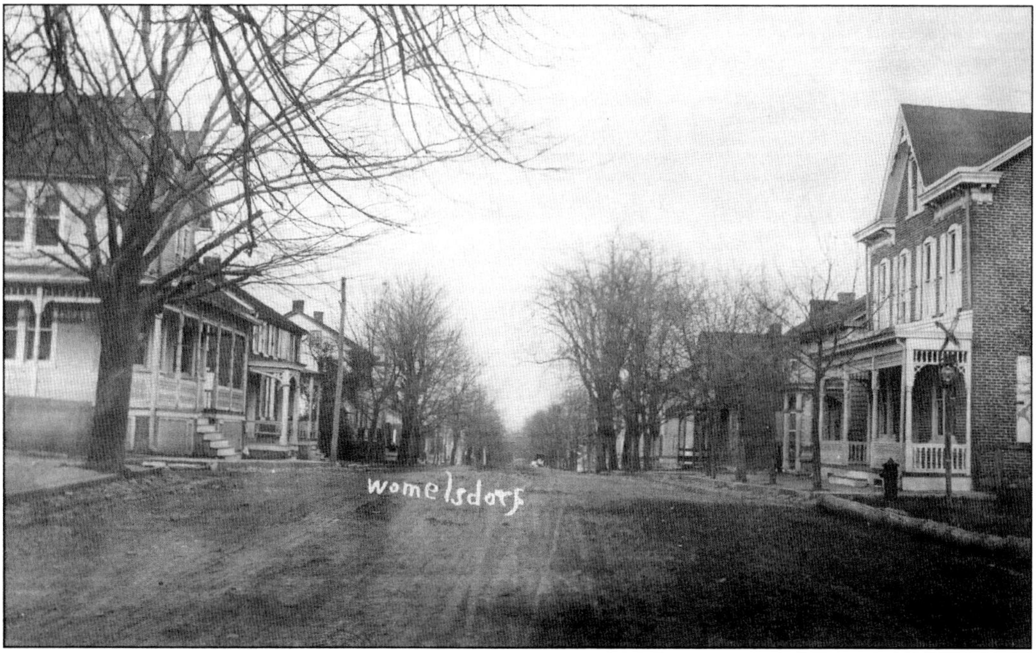

This 1908 view of Womelsdorf was taken on South Second Street, looking north. Second Street is present-day Route 419 coming from Newmanstown. Note the fire hydrant on right and the wide, clean street. (Courtesy of Ryan A. Zerbe.)

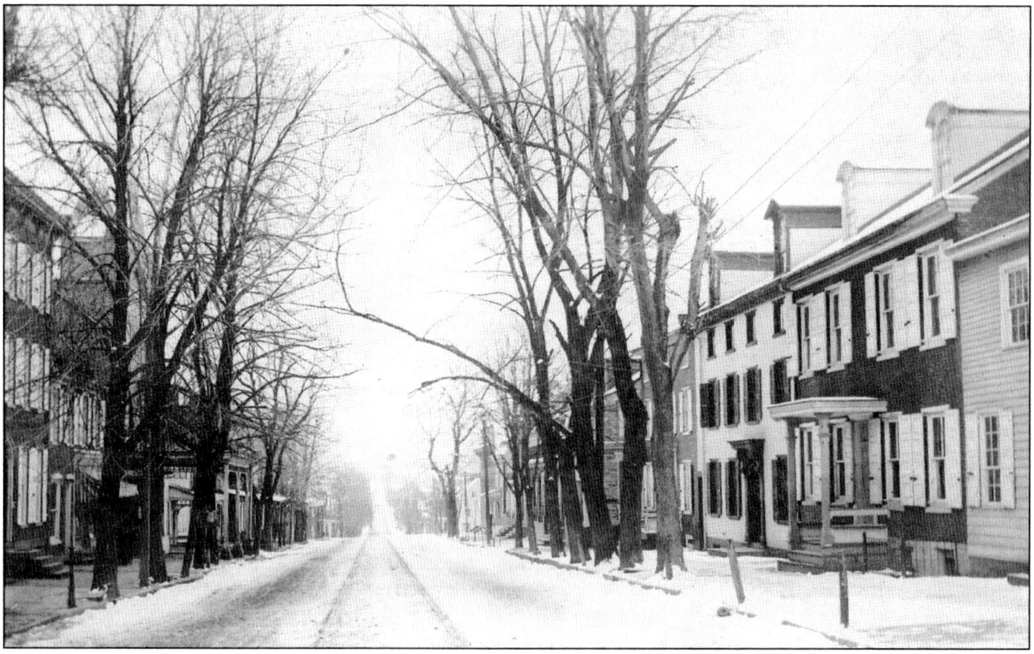

Looking east toward the square, this winter scene captures High Street in the early 1900s. Both trolley tracks and hitching posts line the avenue. In this block were a lot of businesses: on the left were the St. Elmo Hotel, later known as the Conrad Weiser Inn, and a drugstore; on the right were Stouch Tavern, Dr. Livengood's office, and Charlie Wise's barbershop. Even today, this block is home to most of the businesses on High Street. (Courtesy of Ryan A. Zerbe.)

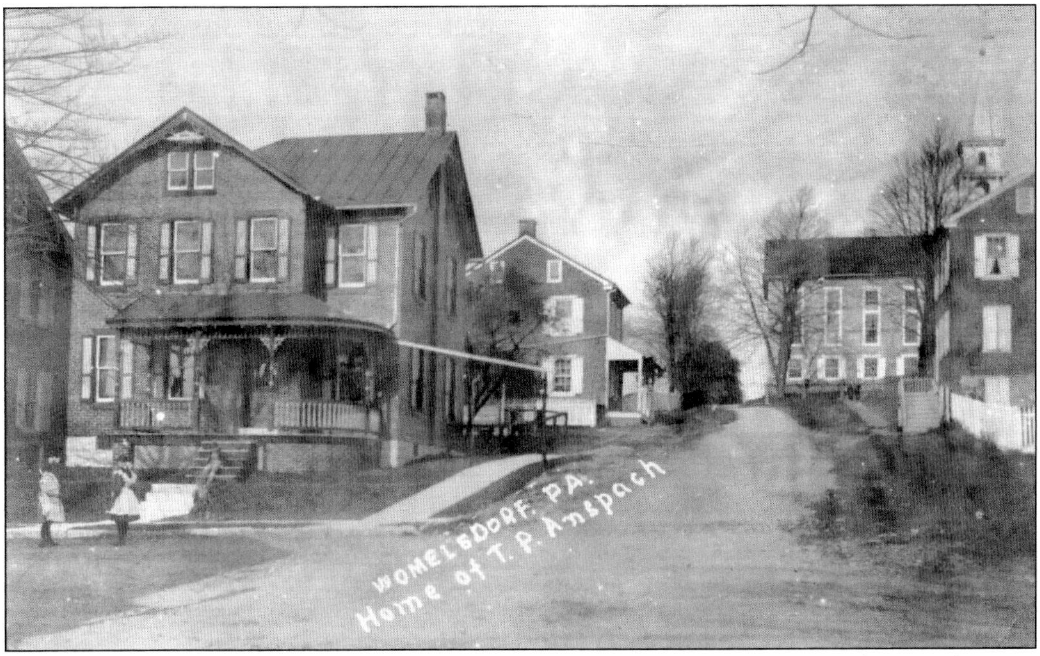

The home of T.P. Anspach at Front and Franklin Streets is pictured here around 1905. The 1792 Zion Church is atop the hill on the right. (Courtesy of Ryan A. Zerbe.)

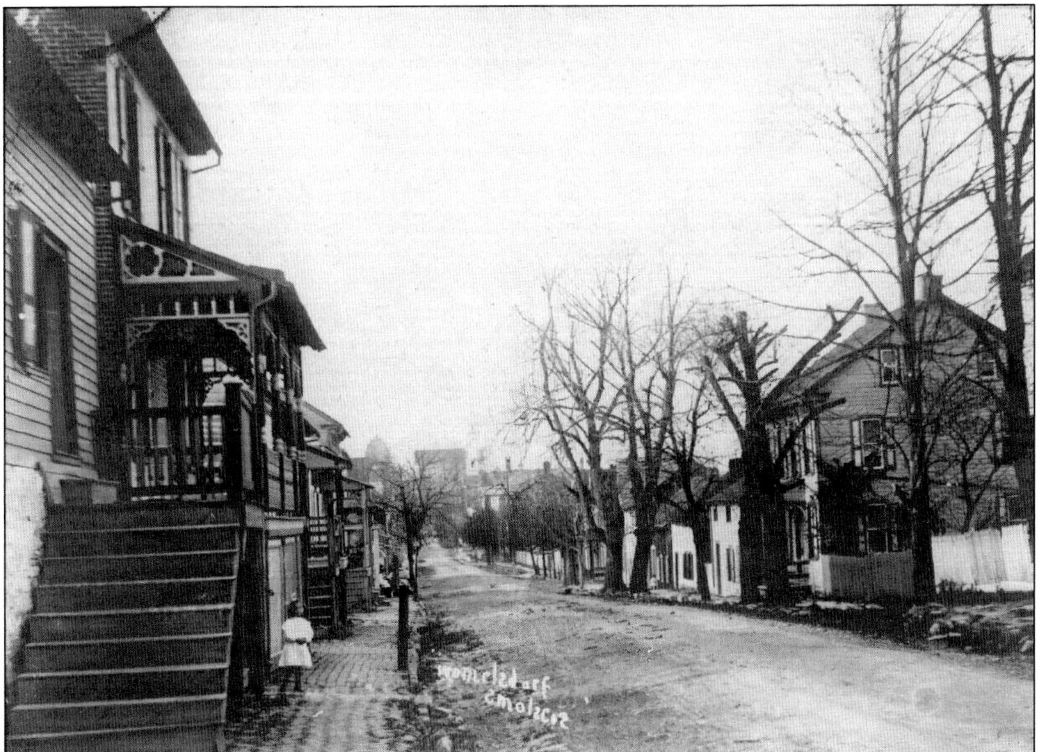

This is a c. 1905 view of South Front Street, looking north. Note the brick sidewalk and the 1792 Zion Church at the north end of Front Street. (Courtesy of Ryan A. Zerbe.)

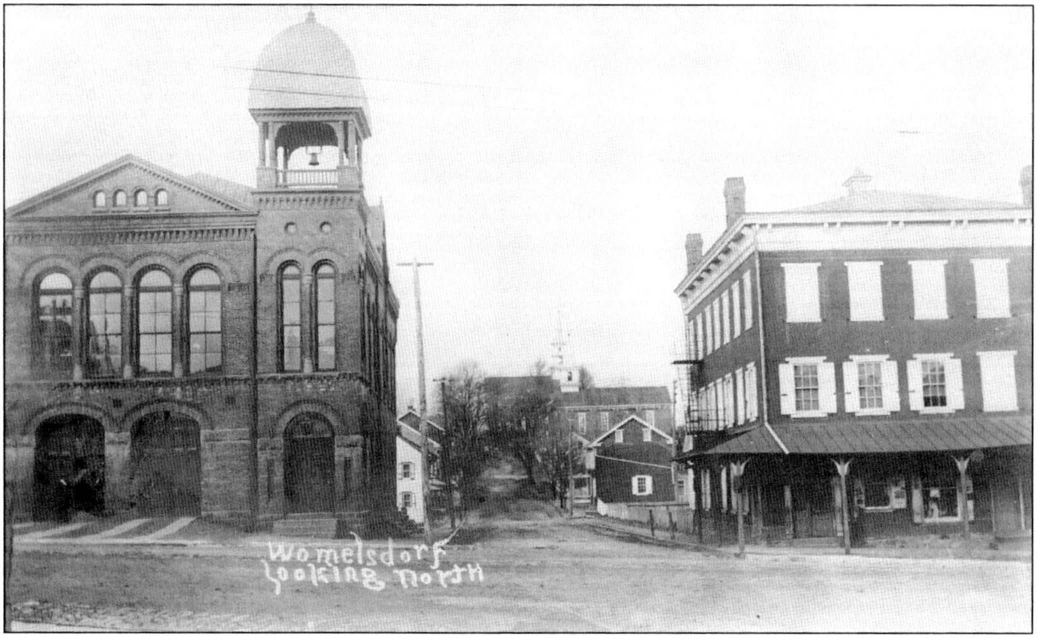

The Womelsdorf Fire Company is seen at left in this c. 1905 image of Diamond Square, looking north on Front Street. A.M. Lengle erected this building on lot No. 47, according to the original town plan, in 1897. The fire company used this building until 1977, at which time it was remodeled and now serves as the borough hall. The fire company built a new engine house at Sixth and High Streets in 1978. The Independent Order of Odd Fellows constructed the building at right. Later, it was acquired by the Masons, who would use it until a new hall was built on Mill Road. The bottom portion of the building housed different businesses over the years. (Courtesy of Ryan A. Zerbe.)

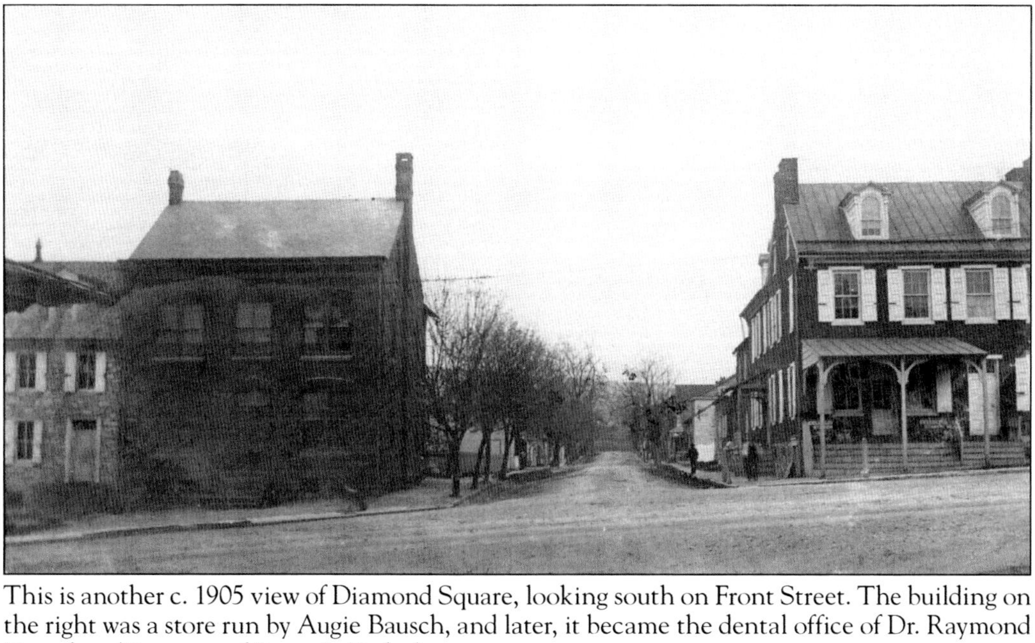

This is another c. 1905 view of Diamond Square, looking south on Front Street. The building on the right was a store run by Augie Bausch, and later, it became the dental office of Dr. Raymond Hamaker. (Courtesy of Ryan A. Zerbe.)

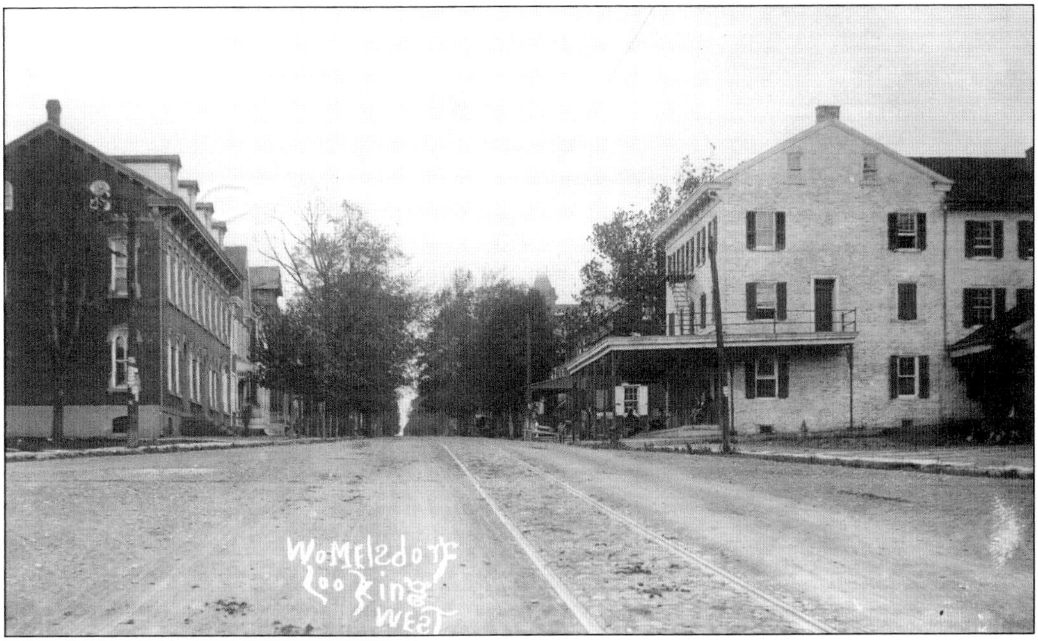

The 1800 Seltzer House is seen at right in this western view of Diamond Square from about 1905. Note the trolley tracks on High Street. Diamond Square once had a red light in the center, and the original plans for Route 422 involved travel on High Street. However, a bypass was built around town in the early 1950s. (Courtesy of Ryan A. Zerbe.)

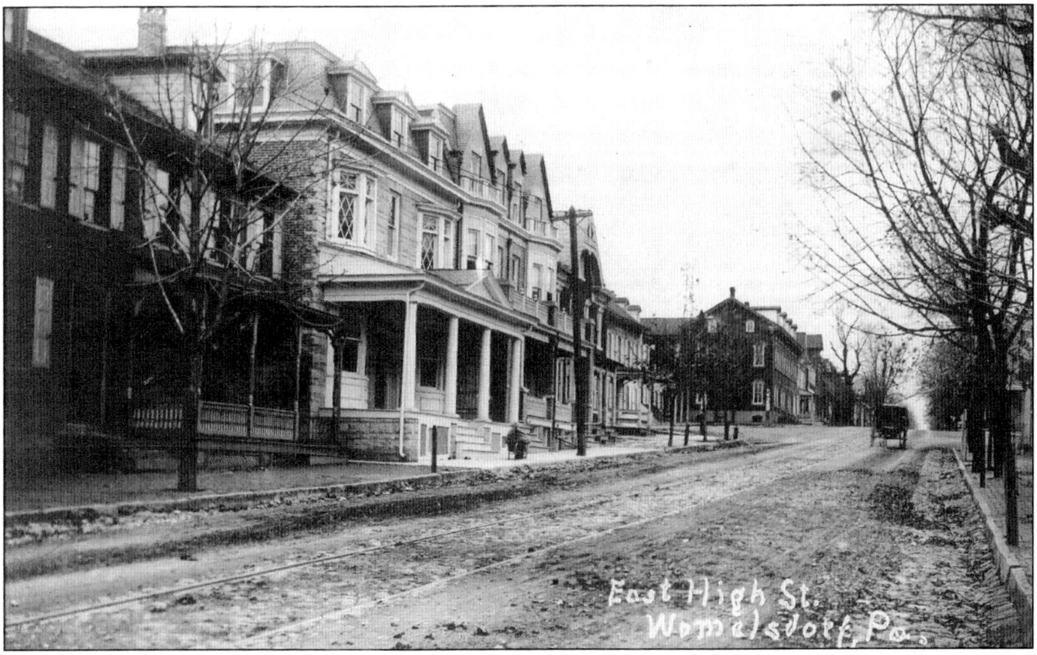

Looking west toward Diamond Square, this image depicts High Street in 1909. Jacob H. Mays, owner of Mays Seed Company at Weiser Park, lived in the second house on the left from 1906 to 1929. Mays was also a Democratic leader at the national, state, and local levels. (Courtesy of Ryan A. Zerbe.)

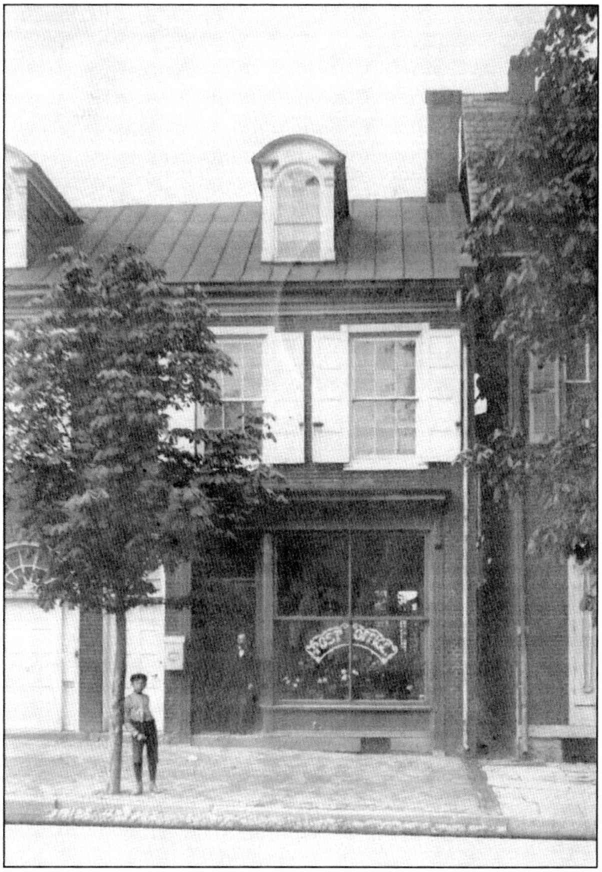

This building at 159 West High Street served as the Womelsdorf Post Office from 1897 to 1914. Standing in the doorway is Wallace Oberly, who was postmaster at the time of this 1906 photograph. (Courtesy of Ryan A. Zerbe.)

In 1855, R. Penn Smith built this Womelsdorf farmhouse, pictured around 1930. From 1920 to 1950, Lyman G. Schaum operated a dairy farm here and bottled his own milk. In 1970, Charles Anspach converted it into a fine restaurant called the Old House. In 1994, the building underwent yet another transformation when Lynn Kreider opened a fitness center, which continues to operate today. (Courtesy of Carl Ganster.)

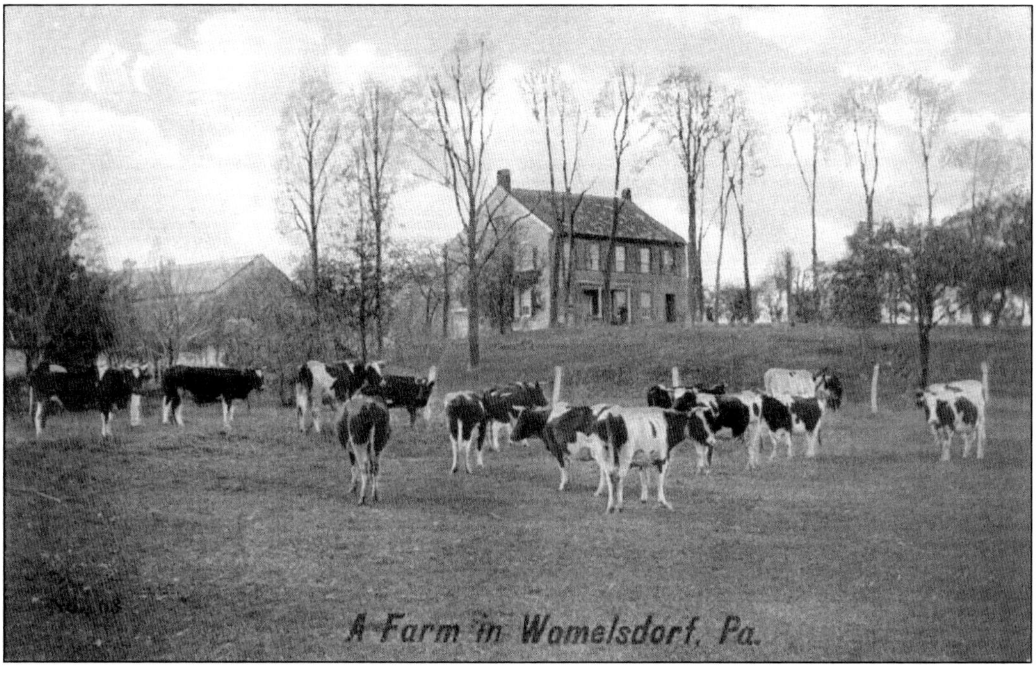

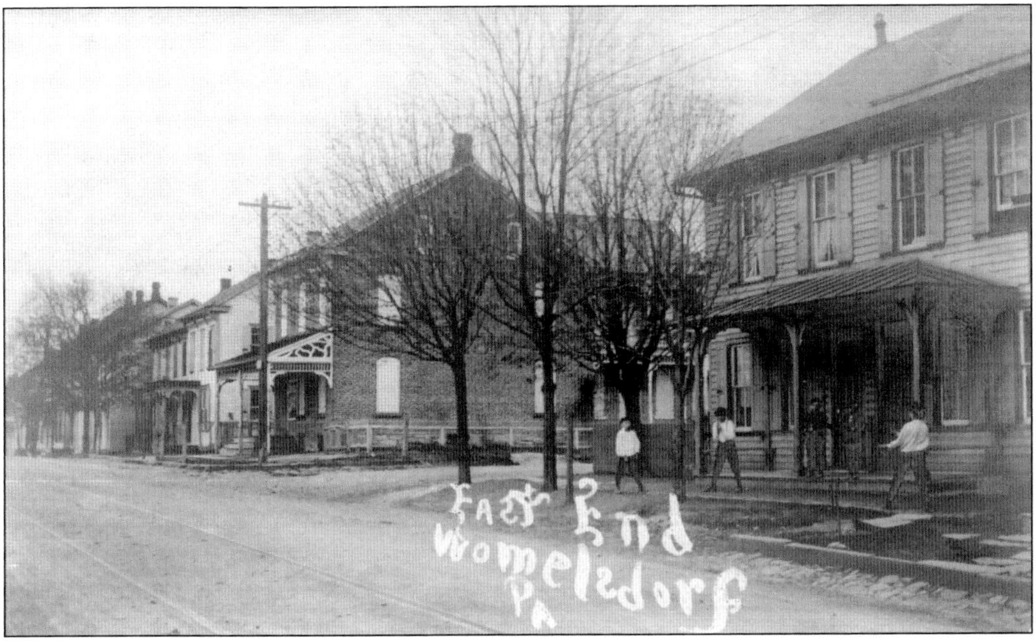

The east end of Womelsdorf is pictured here around 1905. The first house on the right was destroyed in a gas explosion in 1971, and the house that replaced it burned in 2010. The second house on the right served as the Brooklyn Hotel from 1877 to 1914. After 1914, the house was converted into a private residence. (Courtesy of Ryan A. Zerbe.)

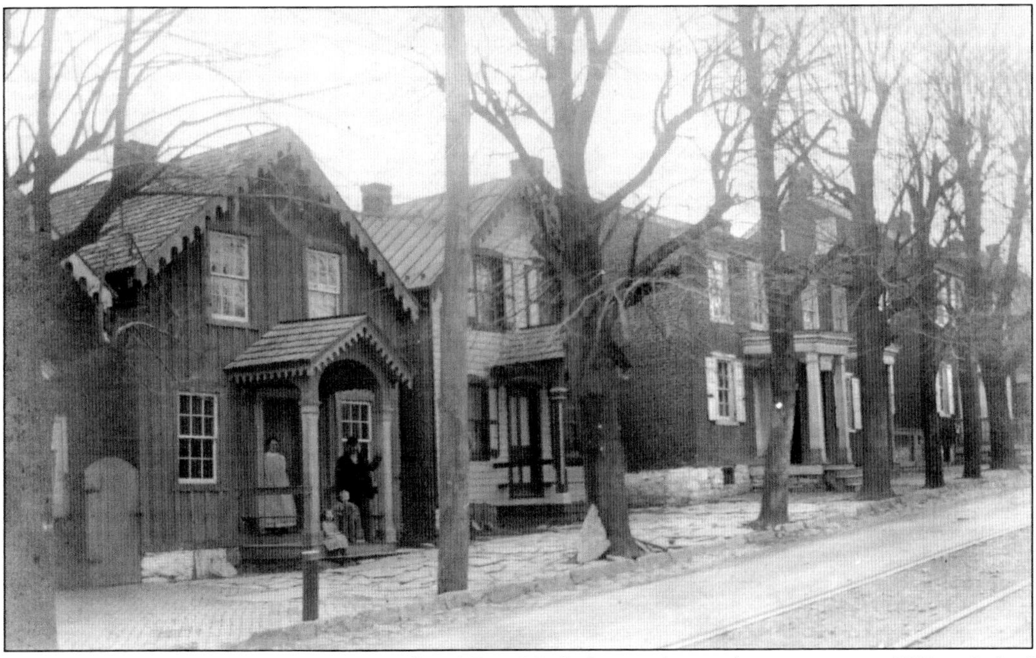

Pictured here around 1905 are 133 and 135 East High Street, located in a section of Womelsdorf called Brooklyn. These gingerbread homes have undergone major renovations over the years. The two children on the porch are Mary and George Yiengst. Note the flagstone pavement. (Courtesy of Ryan A. Zerbe.)

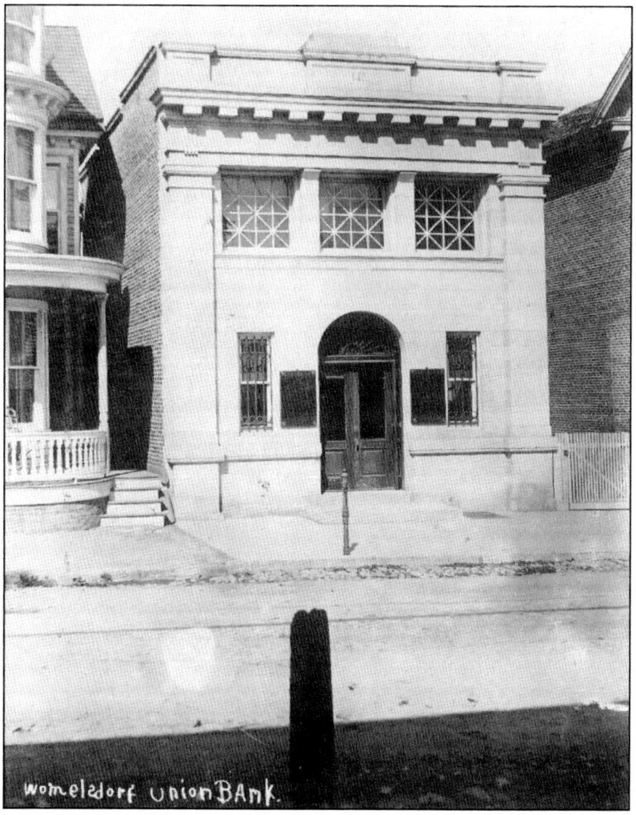

With $50,000 in capital, the Womelsdorf Union Bank, pictured here in 1909, was the first bank to be chartered west of the Schuylkill River, in Berks County. John M. Schonhour was the first president when the bank opened for business on March 9, 1903. This institution became the Bank of Pennsylvania for many years and presently serves as part of the Womelsdorf Library. (Courtesy of Ryan A. Zerbe.)

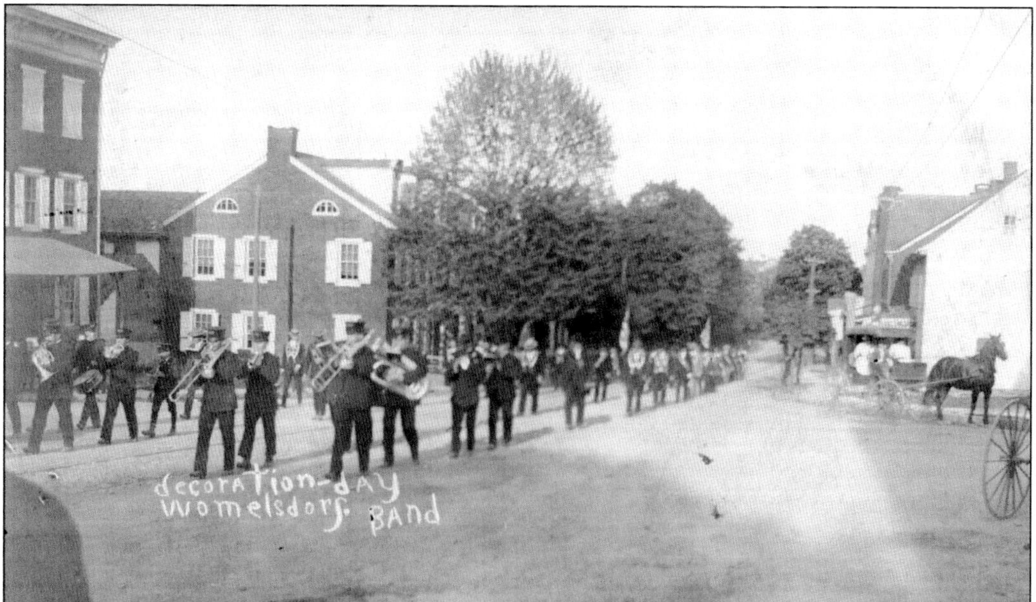

The Womelsdorf Band is pictured here in a Decoration Day parade on Diamond Square around 1910. Womelsdorf has seen many parades over the years, mostly firefighters' and Memorial Day parades, which continued into the 1960s. (Courtesy of Ryan A Zerbe.)

Three

Heidelberg Township

Once the home of famous interpreter Conrad Weiser, Heidelberg Township is the oldest township in the Conrad Weiser area. The original township was formed under Lancaster County because Berks was not a county until 1752. Heidelberg is named after the Heidelberg area in Germany, from where many of the 1723 settlers emigrated.

Until the mid-1800s, Heidelberg Township consisted of everything south of Tulpehocken Creek at the Lebanon County line to the confluence with Cacoosing Creek and everything west of it. In today's terms, that means from Stouchsburg, south of the Tulpehocken, to Lower Heidelberg Township and Sinking Spring Borough. Every municipality in the Conrad Weiser area had land carved out of Heidelberg.

The first church, St. Daniel's, was organized in 1750 and built in 1754. The original township is also the site of the Bethany Children's Home, which relocated from Philadelphia in 1867. Route 422 is the only major road that runs east and west through Heidelberg, and it has seen many businesses over the years. While the Twin Kiss and Mays Seed Company have come and gone, Murdough's Christmas Barn, which has been in business since 1954, still remains, along with auto repair, insurance, and powder-coating companies dotting the highway. The Conrad Weiser Homestead is situated at the western end of the township.

The township is mostly rural, with some of the best farmland found in Berks County. In 2012, David Wolfskill, a township farmer, had the best corn yield in the nation. The southern section of the township is mountainous and contains South Mountain.

When the Conrad Weiser School District was formed in 1954, Heidelberg was chosen as the site for the high school because of its central location. The township's population numbered 1,734 in 2010.

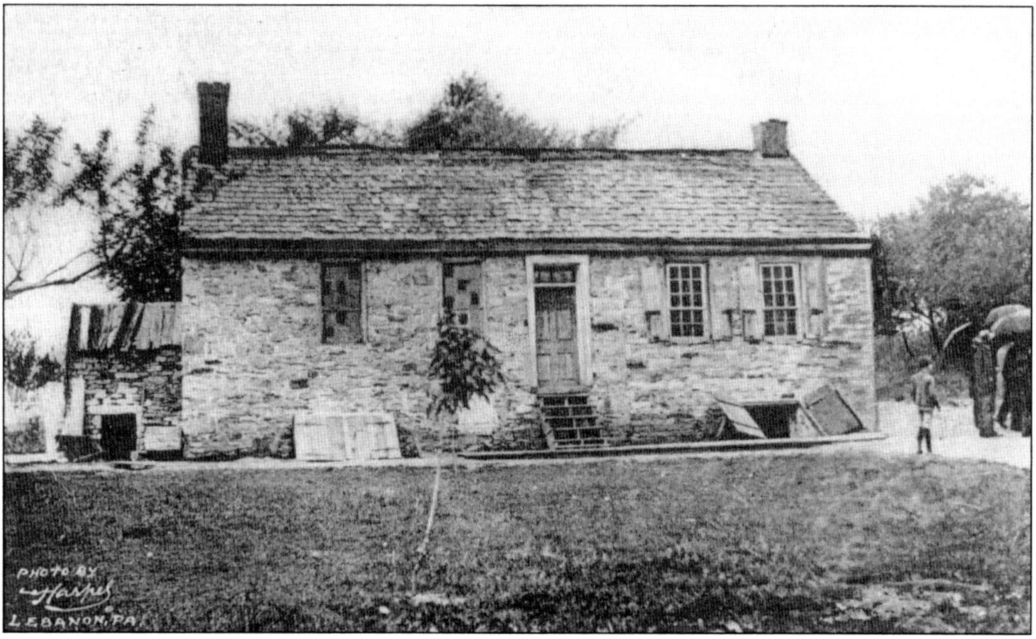

The Conrad Weiser Homestead is pictured here around 1907. Conrad Weiser came to Heidelberg in 1729 and built this home soon after his arrival. It is said that he operated a store, tannery, and farm from this location. Many important people of the mid-1700s met here, including Indian chiefs. Conrad died in 1760, and his son took over the property. The left side was built first, and the portion to the right of the door was built later. (Courtesy of Carl Ganster.)

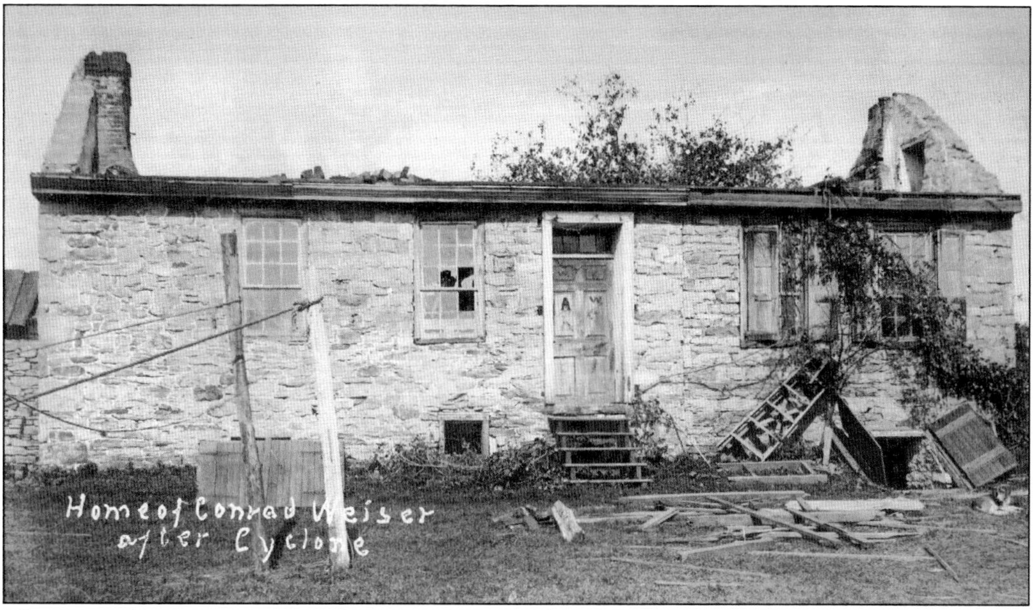

The Conrad Weiser Homestead is seen after a cyclone hit the area in 1904. This home and its surrounding land was turned into a park through private funds and dedicated on September 1, 1928, with over 25,000 in attendance. In 1935, it became a state park. Then, in 1953, it was turned over to the Pennsylvania Historical Commission and remains under the control of the state today. (Courtesy of Carl Ganster.)

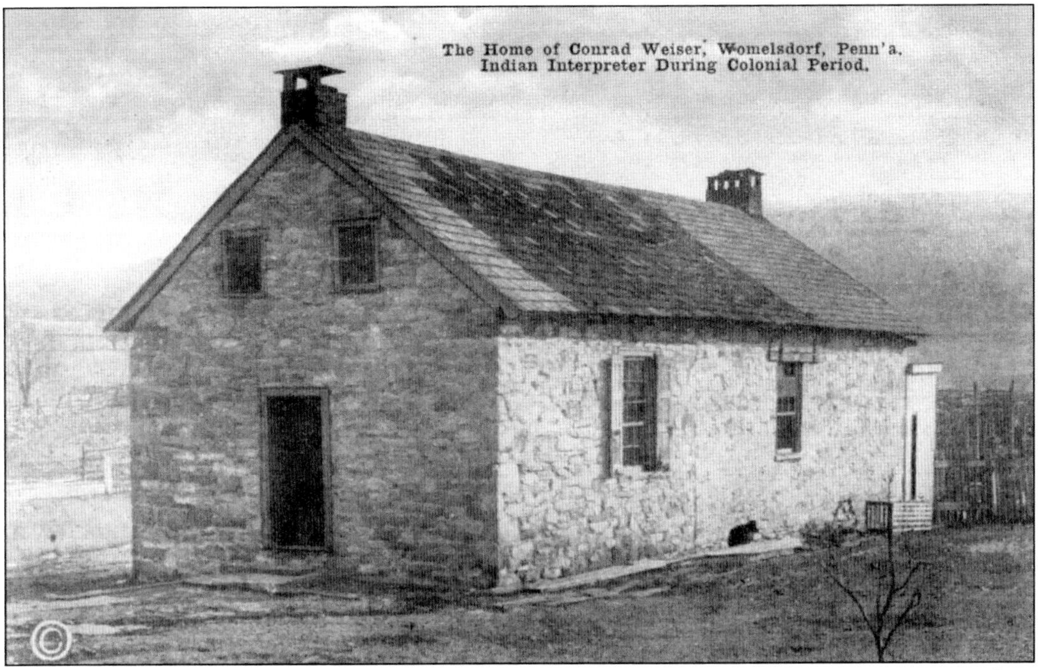

Here is the back side of Conrad Weiser Homestead around 1930. (Courtesy of Carl Ganster.)

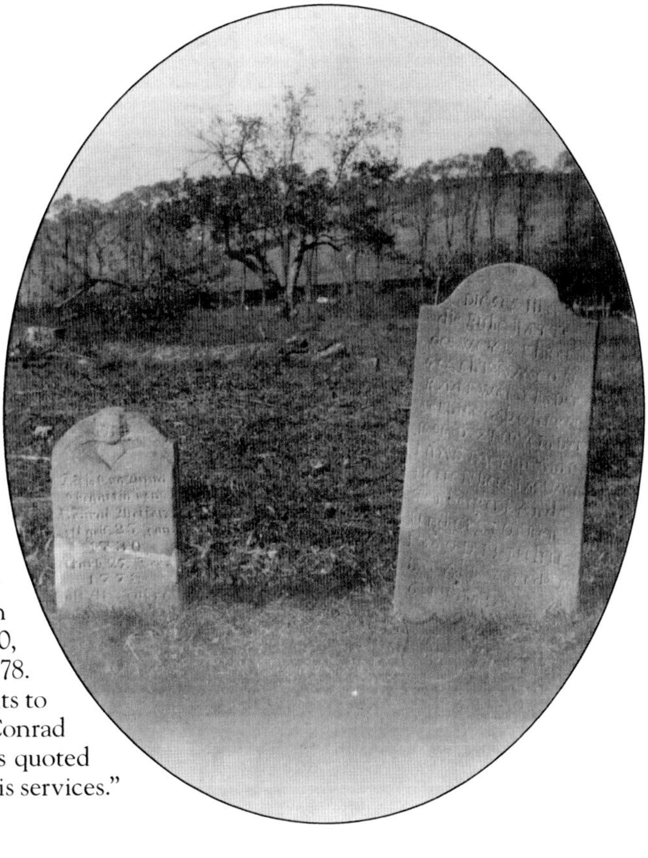

The gravestones of Conrad Weiser and his wife, Anna, are seen here in 1906. Conrad died on July 13, 1760, and Anna passed on December 27, 1778. On one of George Washington's visits to Womelsdorf, a detour was made to Conrad Weiser's gravesite. Washington was quoted as saying, "Posterity cannot forget his services." (Courtesy of Carl Ganster.)

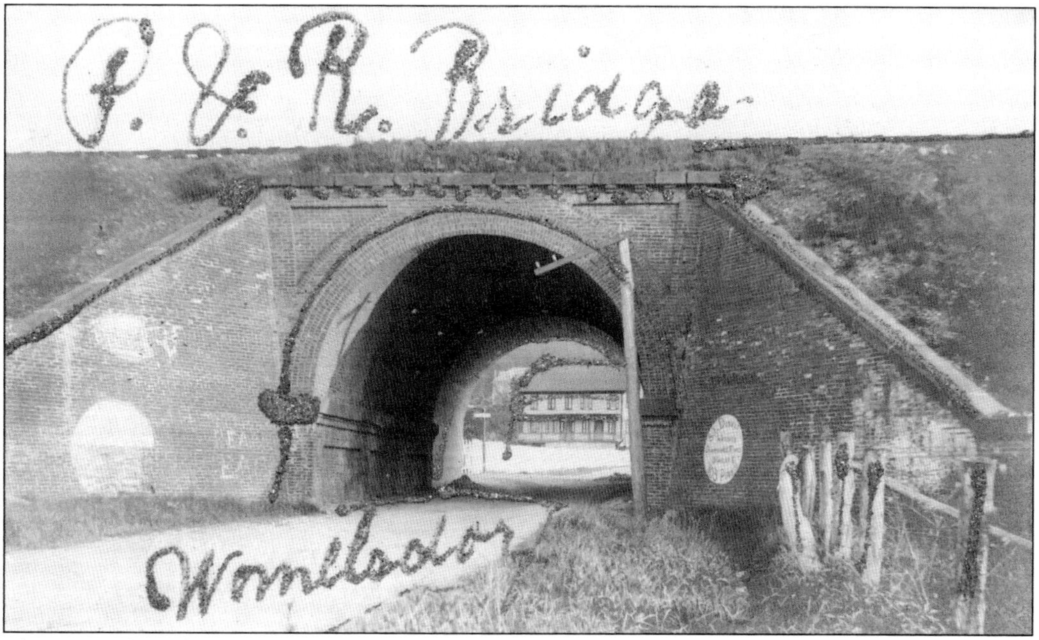

This view of South Water Street shows the tunnel railroad bridge south of Womelsdorf around 1910. The railroad line from Reading to Harrisburg was built in the 1850s, and the first train made the trip in 1858. The house on the other side of the bridge was the Manderbach Springs farmhouse, where the Bethany Children's Home now stands. The house was built around 1860 and torn down in 1959. (Courtesy of Carl Ganster.)

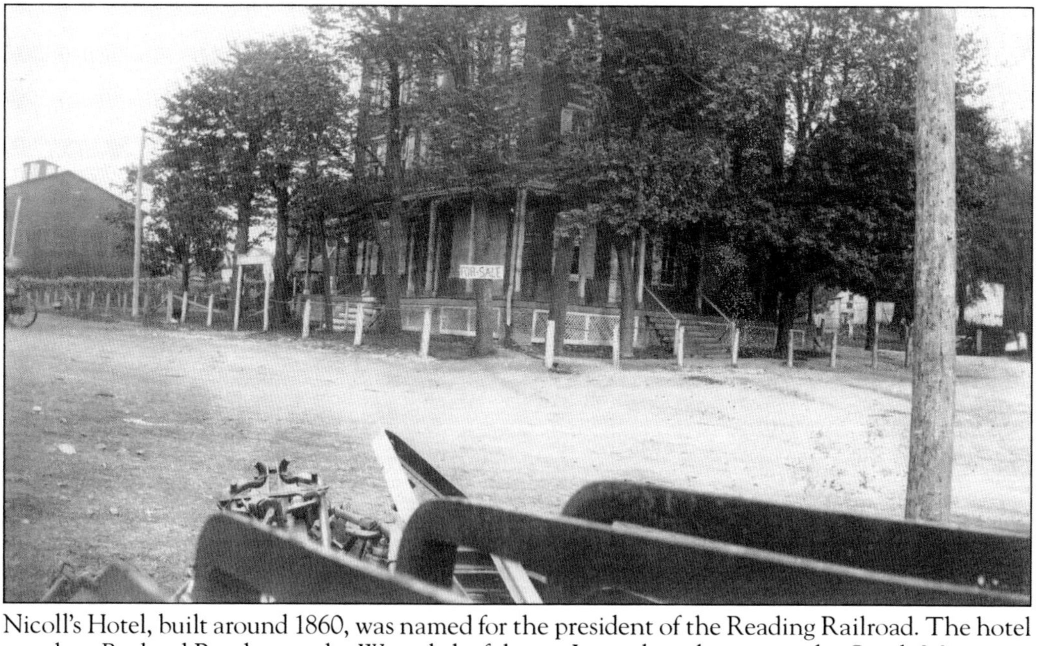

Nicoll's Hotel, built around 1860, was named for the president of the Reading Railroad. The hotel stood on Ryeland Road, near the Womelsdorf depot. It was later known as the South Mountain Hotel. The Bethany Children's Home purchased the property around 1928 and tore down the structure around 1931. The building in the background of this c. 1910 image was used by the railroad. (Courtesy of Carl Ganster.)

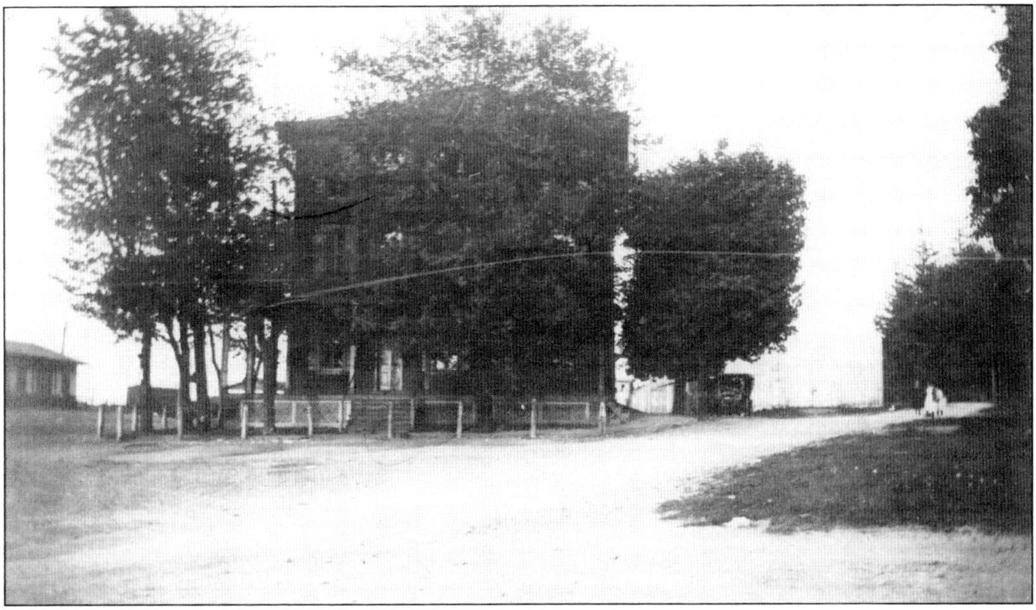

Pictured here is another view of the Nicoll's Hotel around 1915. The building seen at left in the background was part of the Womelsdorf depot; note the old car on the right. (Courtesy of Carl Ganster.)

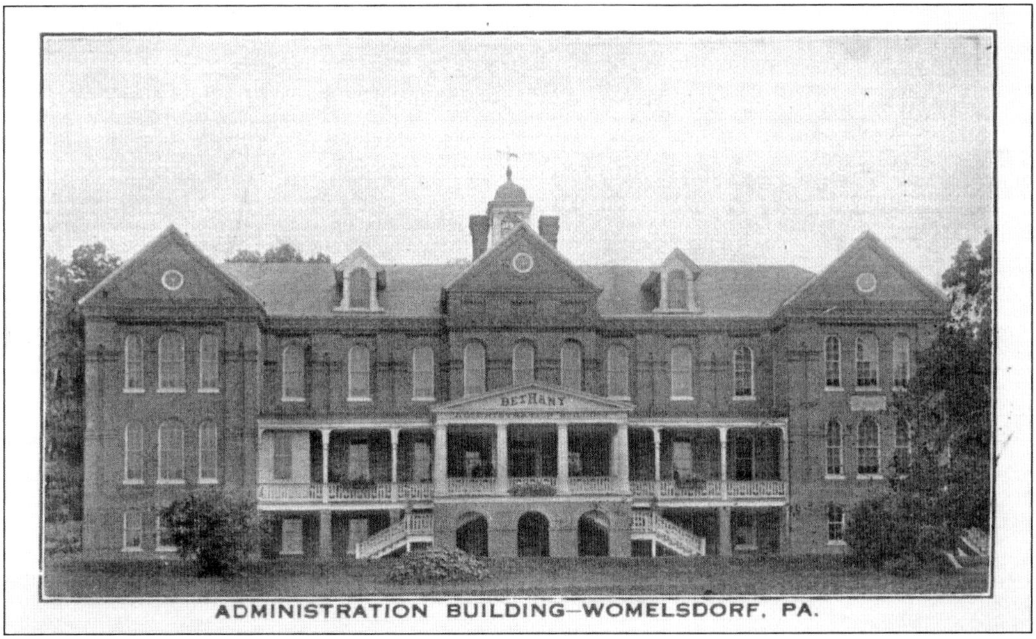

This is the administration building at the Bethany Children's Home, pictured here before 1920. When Bethany came to Heidelberg in 1867, the home used the old Manderbach Springs Resort, built in the 1850s. The old hotel burned in 1881, and Bethany built this administration building in 1882. It is said that the fire equipment was housed under its porch. This building, along with Santee Hall, was torn down in 1973 to make way for the present-day administration building. (Courtesy of Carl Ganster.)

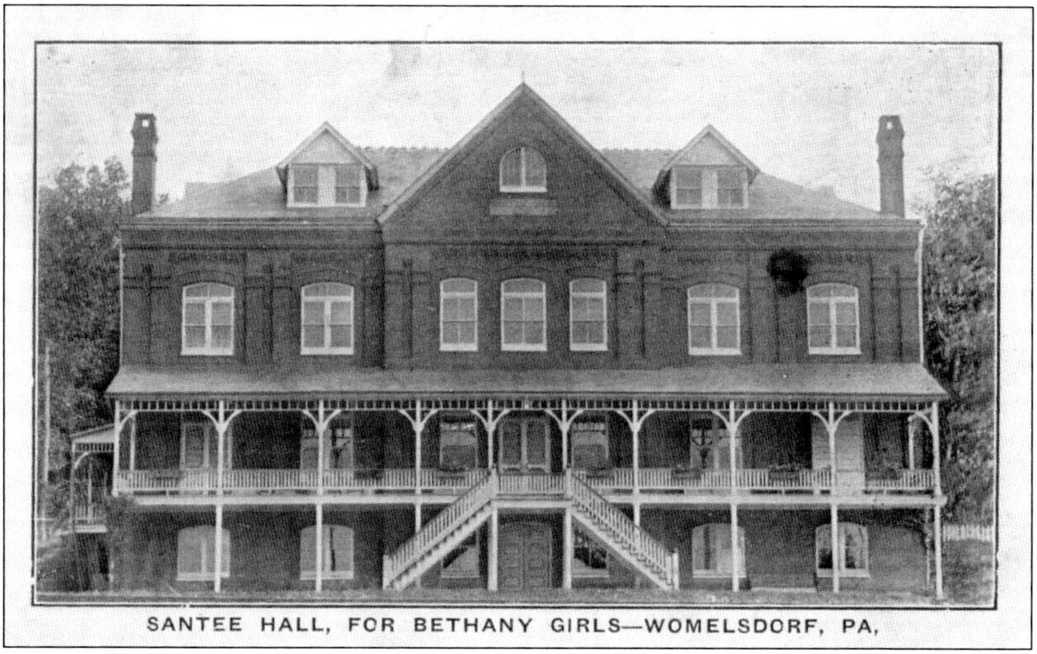

Santee Hall, named in honor of Joseph H. Santee, was built in 1891 and torn down in 1973. It housed the girls of the orphan home and had a centralized kitchen. (Courtesy of Carl Ganster.)

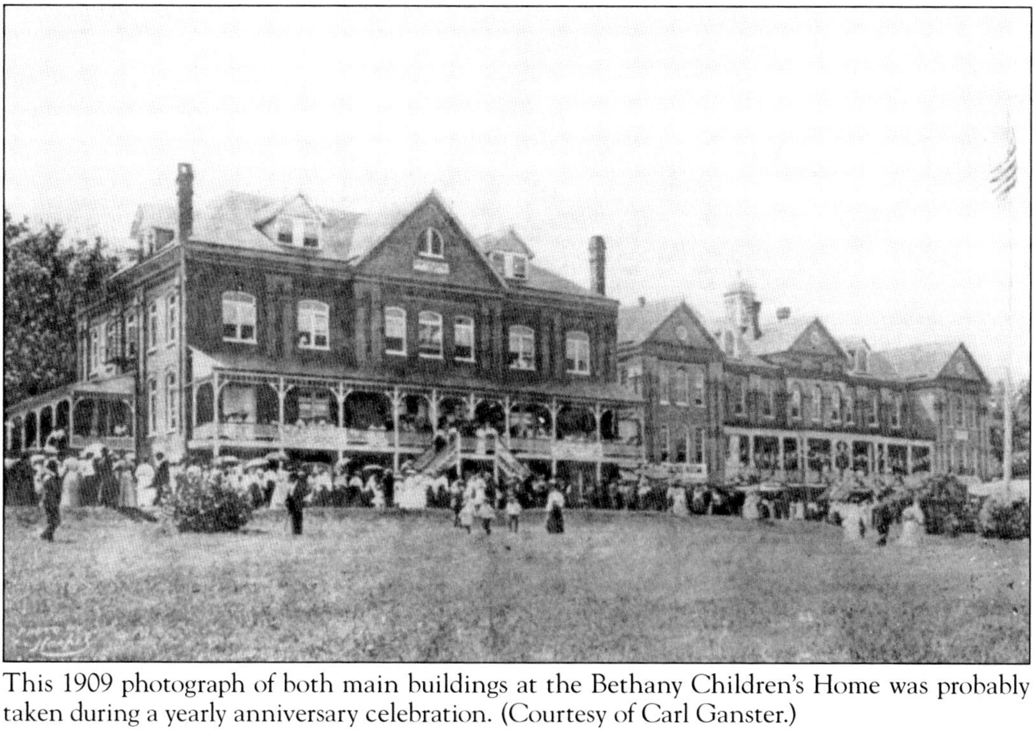

This 1909 photograph of both main buildings at the Bethany Children's Home was probably taken during a yearly anniversary celebration. (Courtesy of Carl Ganster.)

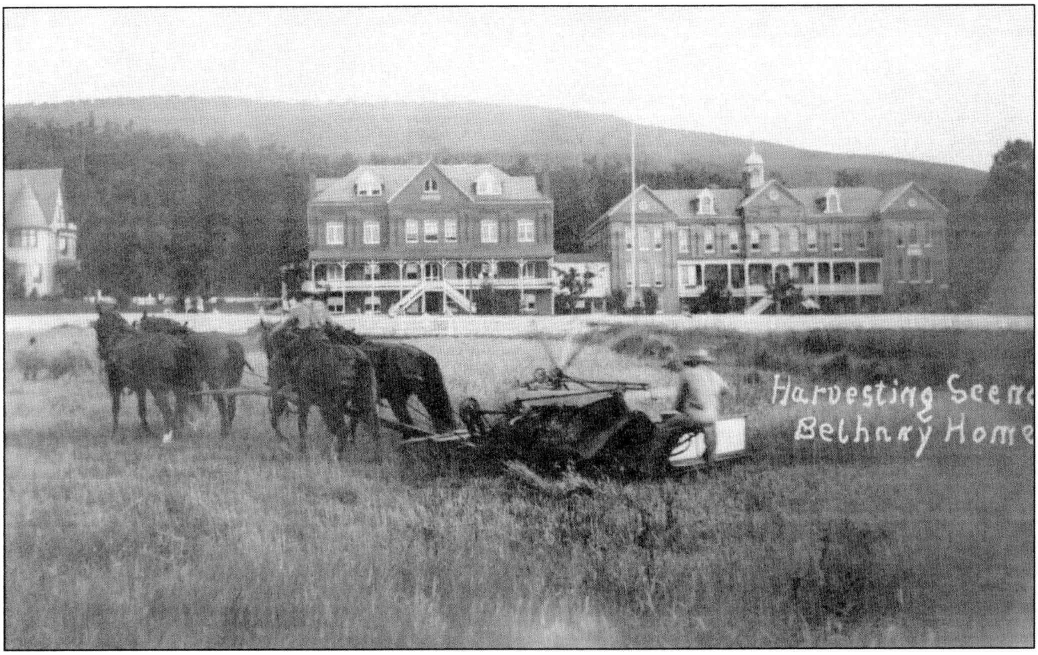

This c. 1905 harvesting scene shows the main buildings of the Bethany Children's Home, along with the side of Frick Cottage, built in 1896. Frick Cottage housed children under the age of six. Note the four-horse team making hay with two farmers. (Courtesy of Carl Ganster.)

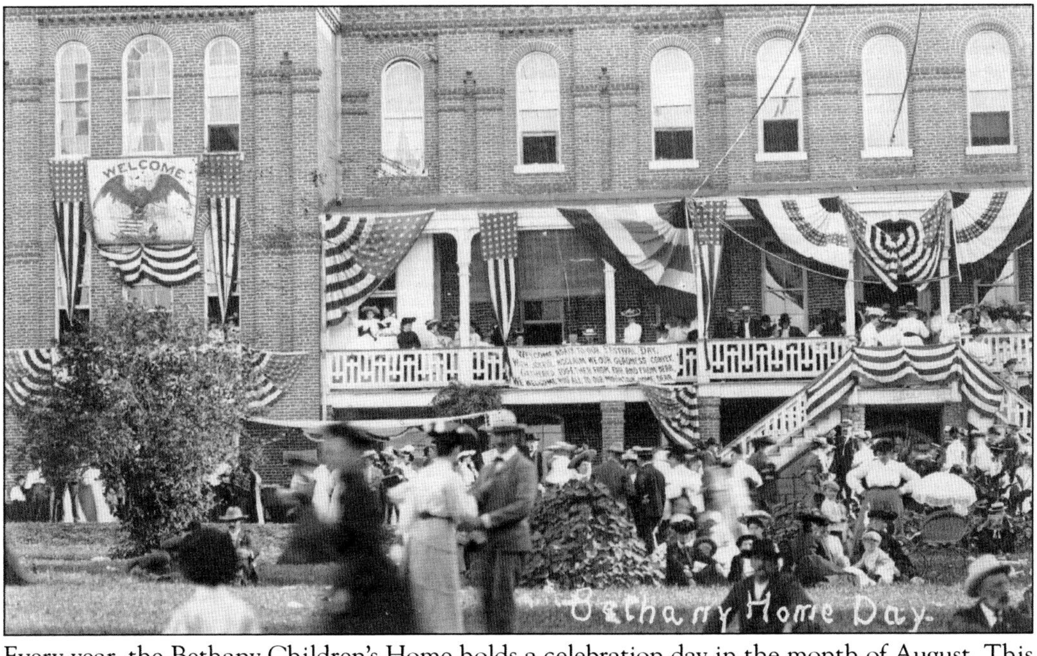

Every year, the Bethany Children's Home holds a celebration day in the month of August. This Bethany Home Day was held outside the administration building on August 23, 1906. (Courtesy of Carl Ganster.)

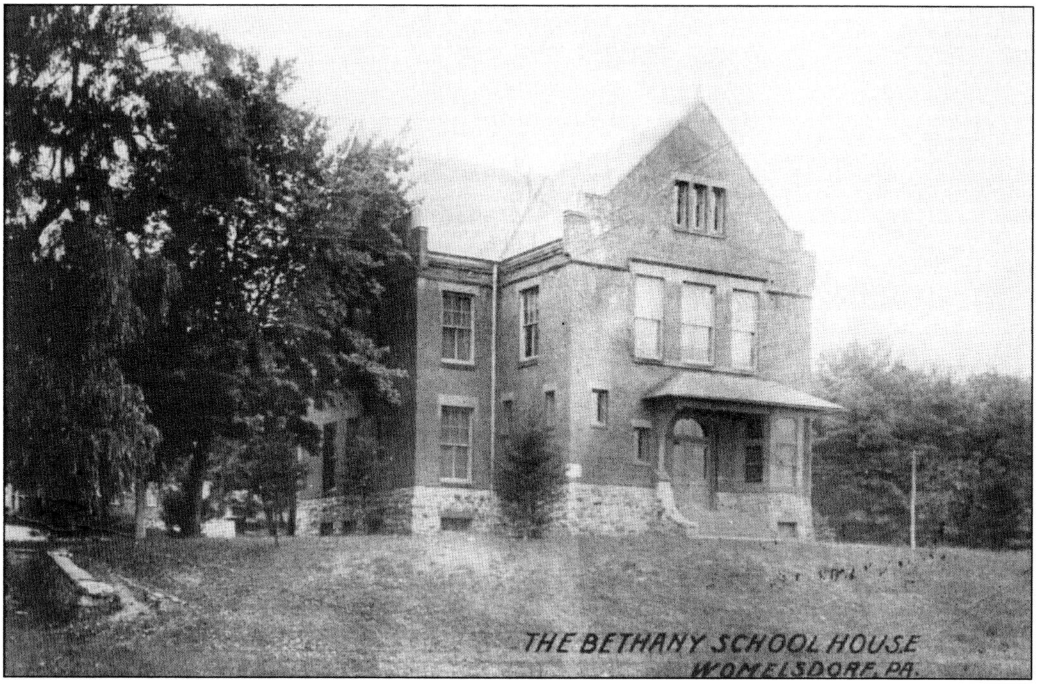

The Bethany School House, pictured around 1930, was built in 1902 to serve as an elementary school for first grade to eighth grade. After 1929, students attended the Womelsdorf High School for grades nine through twelve. The building was torn down in 1970s. (Courtesy of Carl Ganster.)

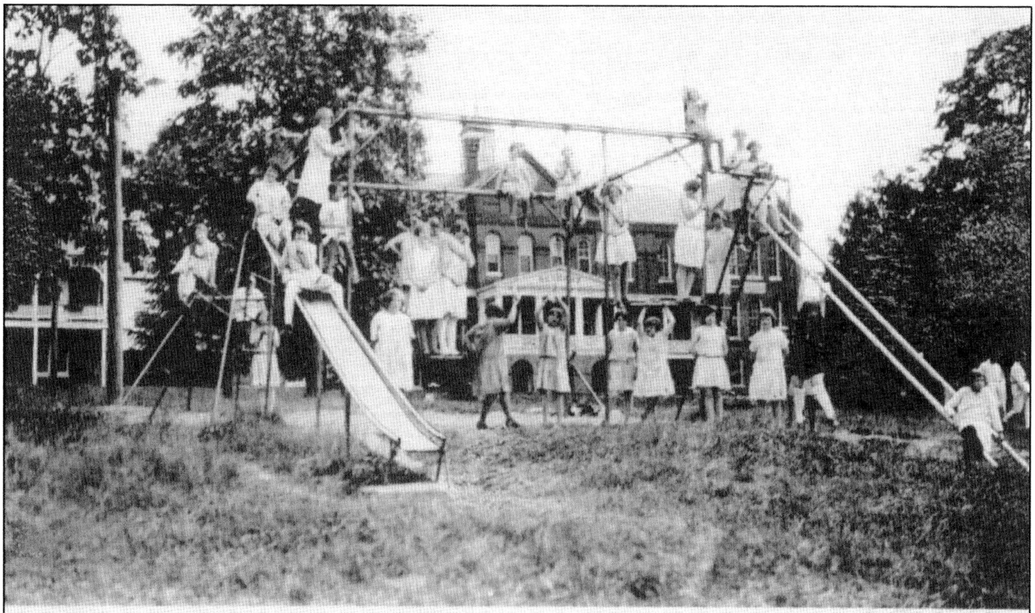

Here, children play in front of the main buildings at Bethany sometime after 1917. Note the slide on the right constructed from two parallel poles. (Courtesy of Carl Ganster.)

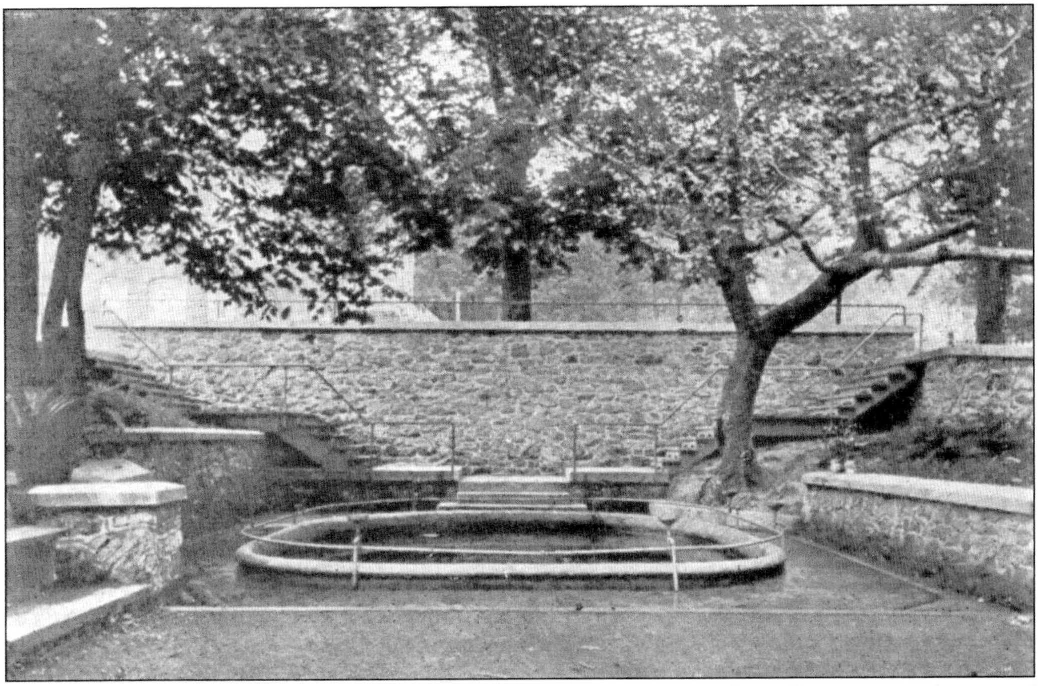

Originally called the Indian White Sand Spring, the spring at Bethany has a circumference of 20 feet. Conrad Weiser used this spring, pictured around 1905, to entertain the Indians. After meeting the Indians here, they would climb the mountain to Eagles Peak, south of this location. The mountain land between the home and Eagles Peak was called Weiser's Mountain. (Courtesy of Carl Ganster.)

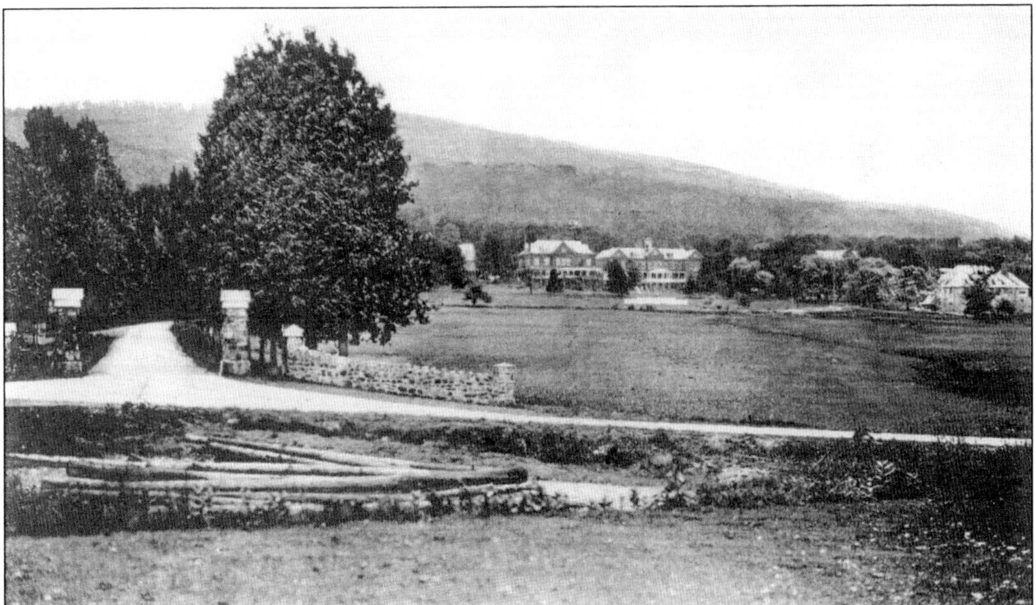

YUNDT MEMORIAL GATEWAY, BETHANY ORPHANS' HOME WOMELSDORF, PA.

This c. 1928 view from the Womelsdorf depot captures the overall landscape of the Bethany Children's Home. (Courtesy of Carl Ganster.)

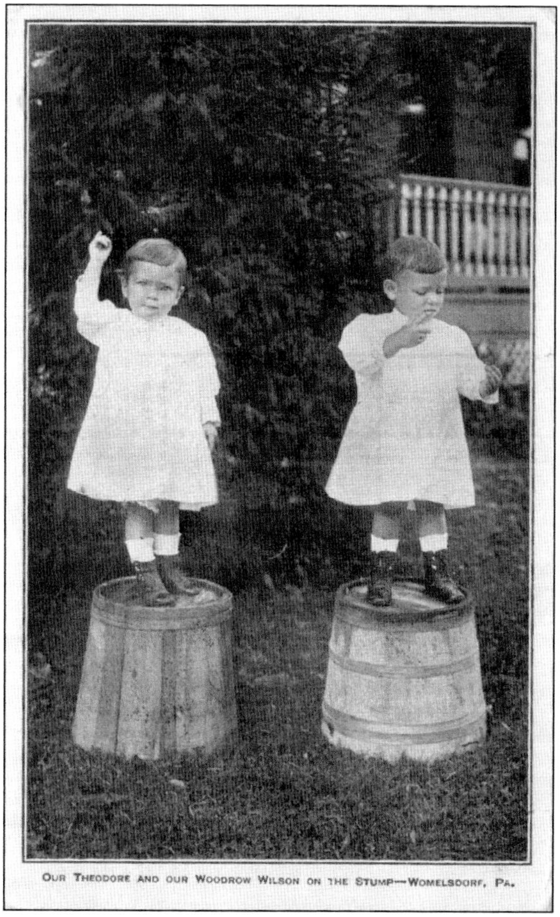

Two young boys, Theodore and Woodrow Wilson, are pictured "on the stump" at Bethany. They look like brothers. Note their style of dress and black button shoes, which were typical of the time period. (Courtesy of Carl Ganster.)

The is an aerial view of Bethany taken around 1935. The grounds of the home and school could pass as a college campus. (Courtesy of Bethany Children's Home.)

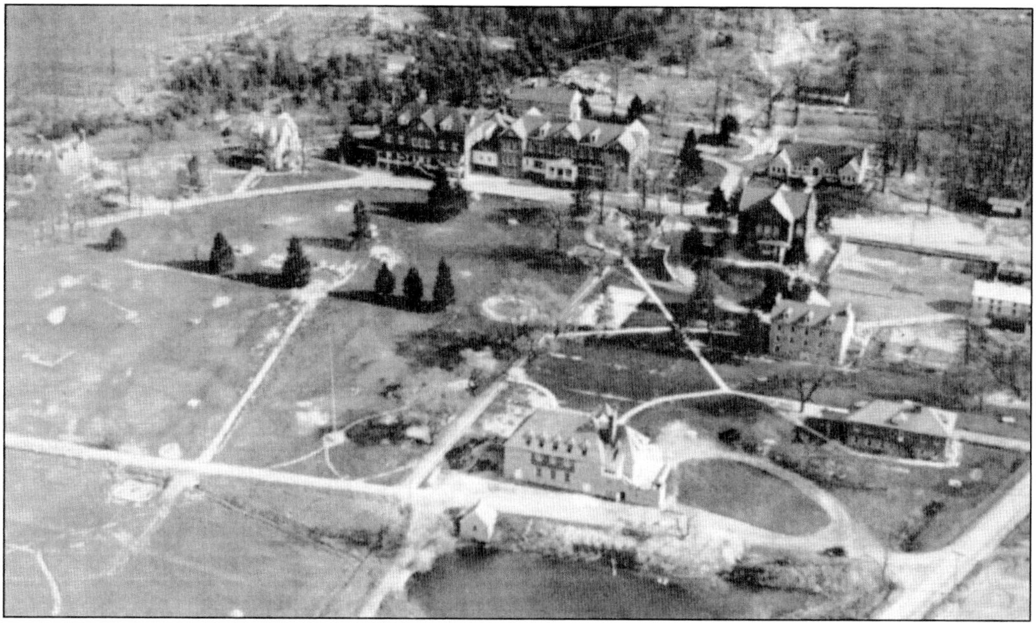

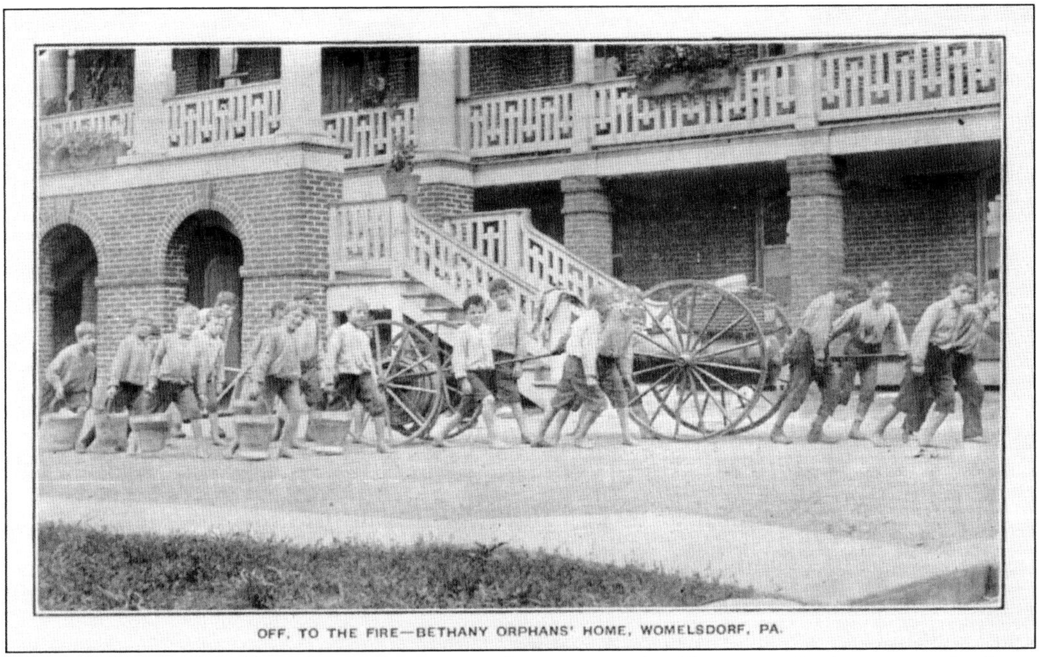

Bethany had its own firefighting equipment for its many buildings, as the home was far from Womelsdorf. It is said that Womelsdorf donated the equipment, including a hose reel and chemical wagon. Note the young bucket brigade, most of whom appear barefoot. (Courtesy of Ryan A. Zerbe.)

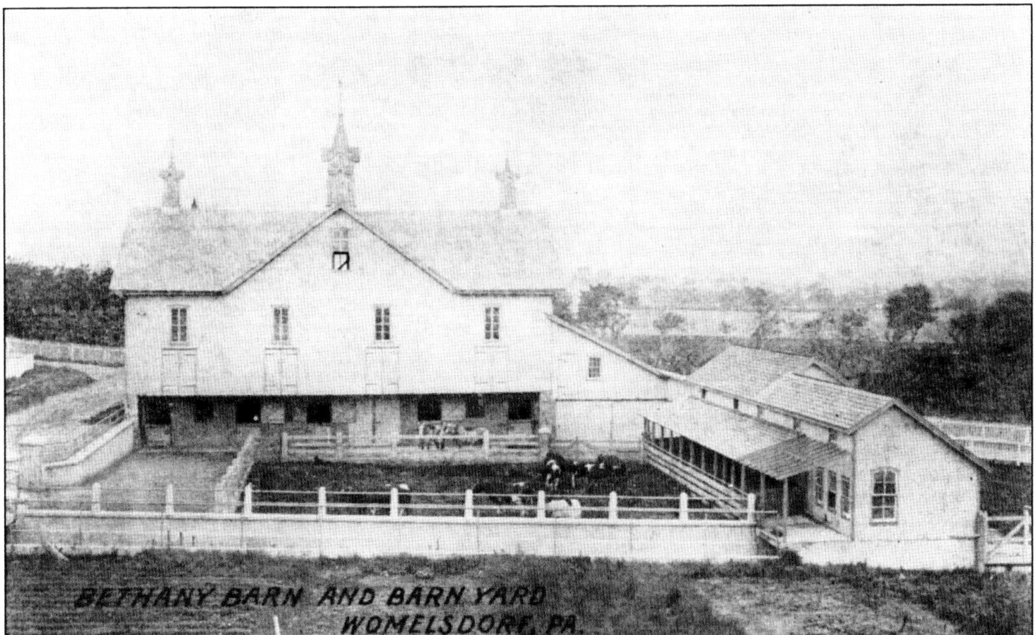

The Bethany chicken house and barn are pictured around 1920. This barn was built in 1895 and torn down in the 1950s. (Courtesy of Bethany Children's Home.)

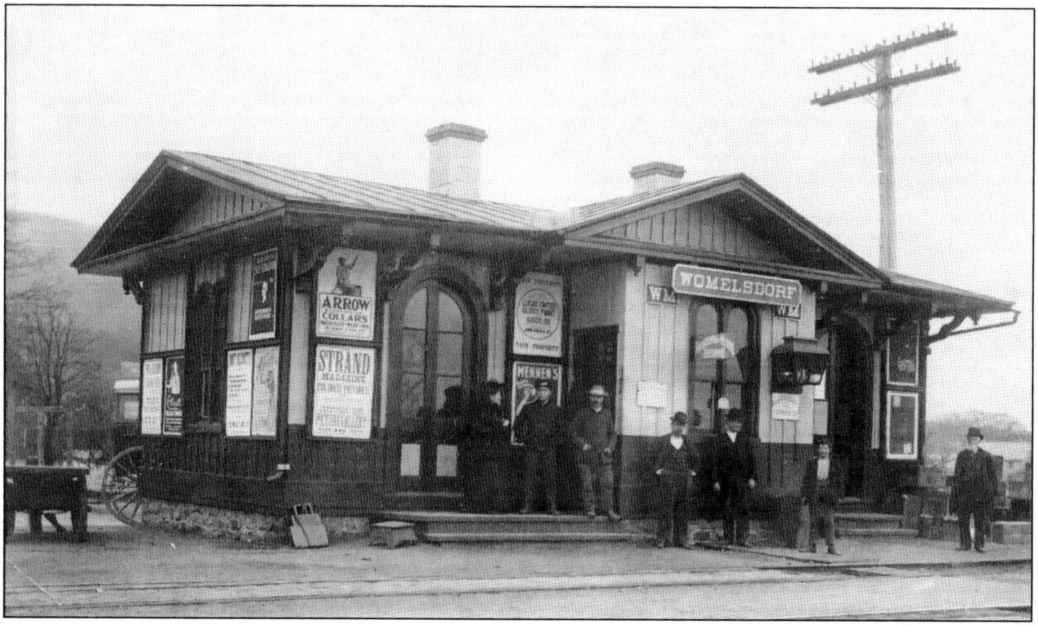

Pictured here is the Womelsdorf train station around 1915. The Lebanon Valley Line of the Reading Railroad was laid in 1850, and the first train ran in 1858. This was bad news for the Union Canal that ran along Tulpehocken Creek because it was much slower than trains. The tracks never entered Womelsdorf proper, so the rail company located the town station south of the borough. All the freight and mail for the Womelsdorf area was delivered or dispatched here. (Courtesy of Ryan A. Zerbe.)

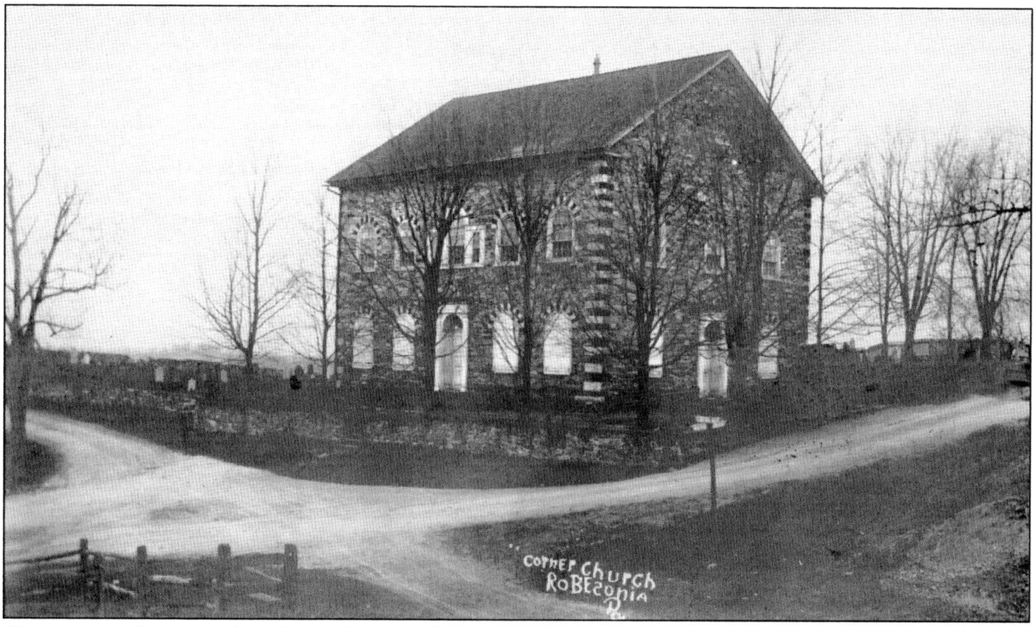

This is an early view of St. Daniel's Church, just north of Robesonia. The first church was organized in 1750 and built in 1754. The second church, pictured here, was built in 1814 and remodeled in 1912. It served as a union church from 1876 to 1905, when it became all Lutheran. This church is known as the Corner Church. (Courtesy of Carl Ganster.)

The remodeled St. Daniel's Church is seen here sometime after 1912. In later years, a Sunday school was added to the back. In December 1976, a fire destroyed the whole structure. A new church was built up the hill from the one that burned, and the old bell that was practically melted from the fire occupies the original site. (Courtesy of Carl Ganster.)

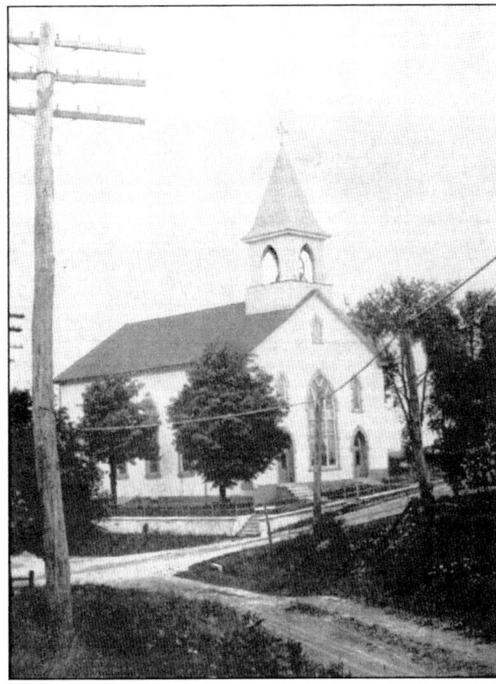

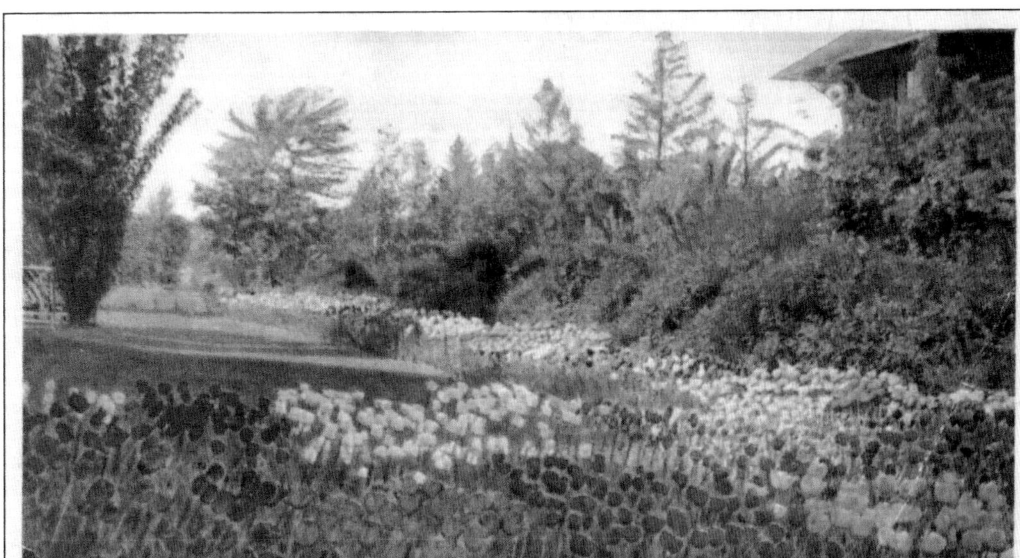

Farr's Nursery, pictured here around 1950, is located behind the Conrad Weiser Park. Founded by Bertrant Farr, the nursery began in Wyomissing, Pennsylvania, around 1908. His love of flowers became more than a hobby when people from all over the country started coming to see his gardens. In 1916, he incorporated his business, and the Wyomissing Development Company induced Farr to sell his land. He moved his business to Heidelberg Township in 1923. After his death in 1924, the business continued to grow, becoming one of the largest landscaping companies in Berks County. It is now called Outdoor Impressions. (Courtesy of Carl Reidler.)

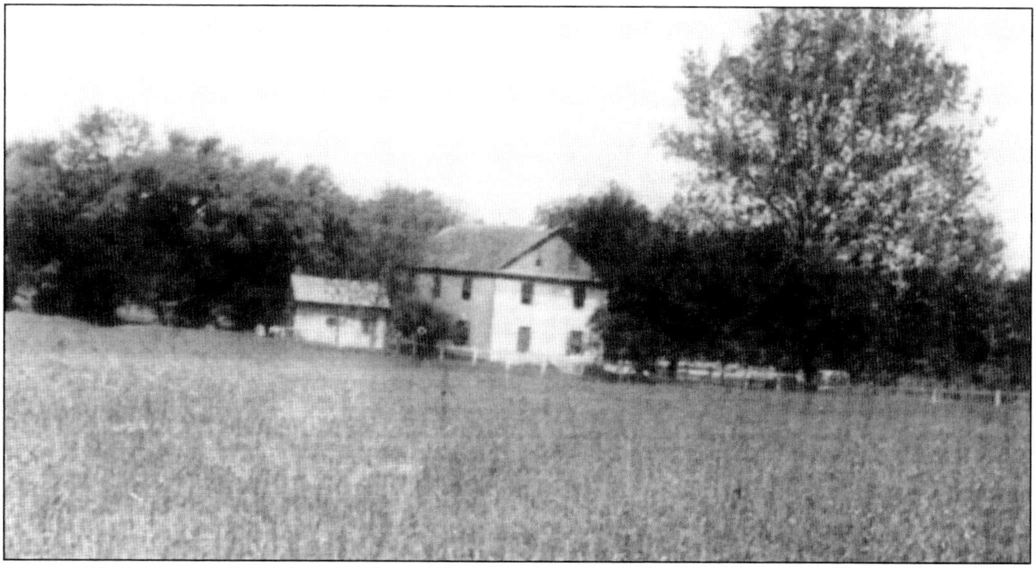

Pictured here around 1940 is the Deppen Homestead on Water Street, north of Womelsdorf. On September 16, 1736, Christian Ruchty and his son-in-law Christian Deppen arrived in Philadelphia from Europe. They ended up in Heidelberg Township alongside the Tulpehocken Creek, north of present-day Womelsdorf. The small building on the left was the site of the original cabin built by Ruchty and Deppen. In 1776, Deppen built the larger house, which still stands today. (Courtesy of Carl Ganster.)

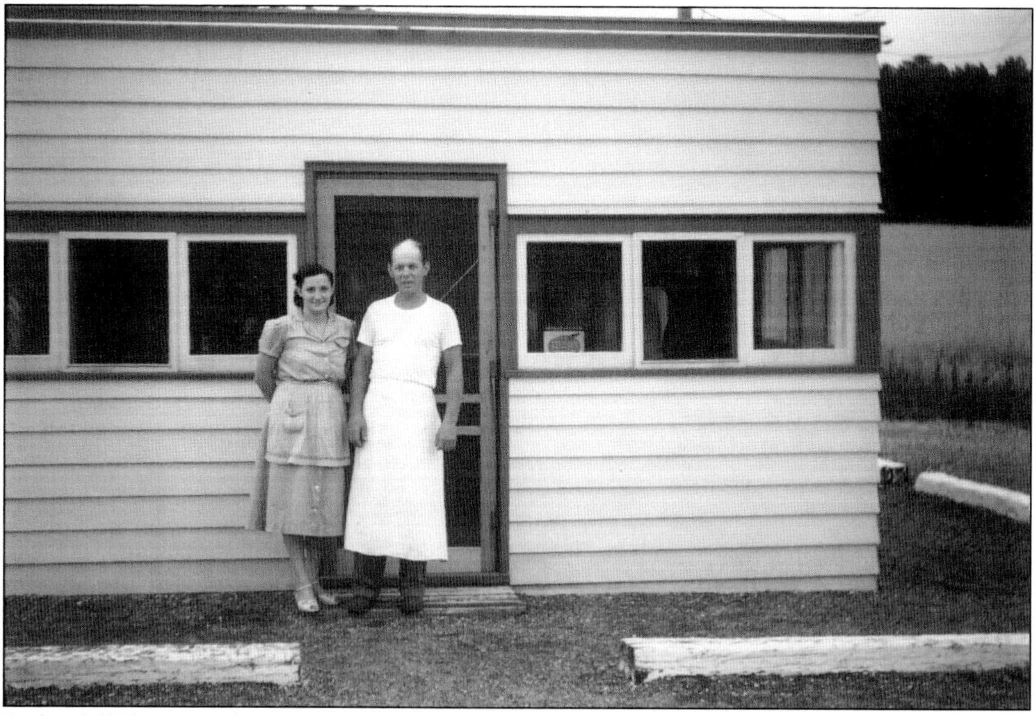

Richard "Whitey" and Margaret Boyer pose in front of the small diner he built around 1953. This diner later became part of the Twin Kiss in the early 1950s. Prior to this building, there was a smaller eatery with nine stools that was built in 1951. (Courtesy of Greg Boyer.)

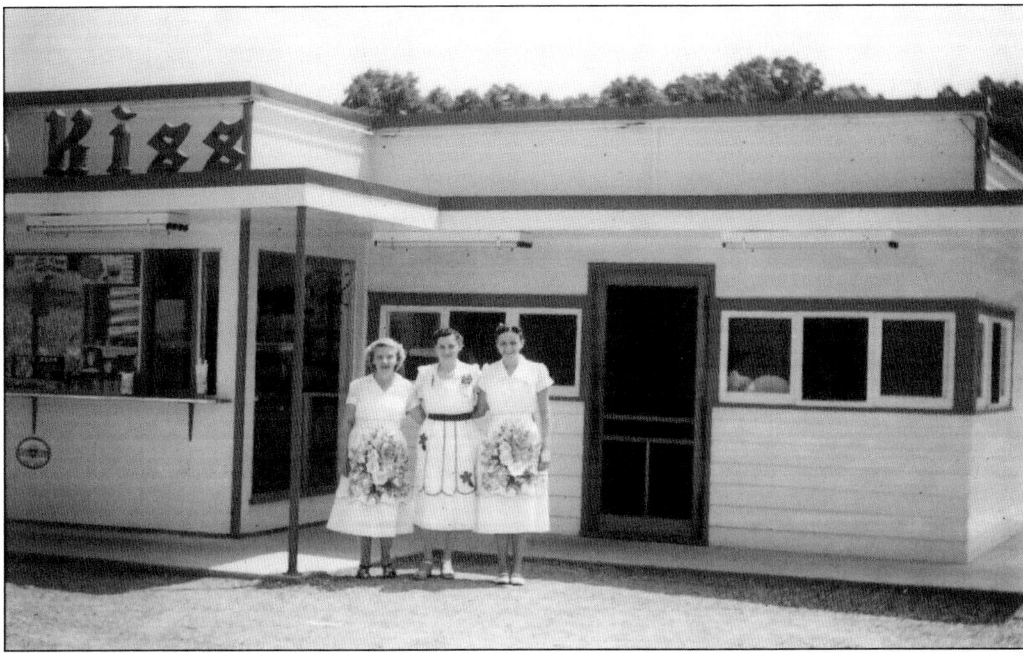

Employees pose in front of the Twin Kiss on Route 422 in the early 1950s. The Twin Kiss was added to the side of the small diner that was built around 1953. Whitey Boyer sold the business to Jane and Harry Wolf from Stouchsburg in 1959. (Courtesy of Greg Boyer.)

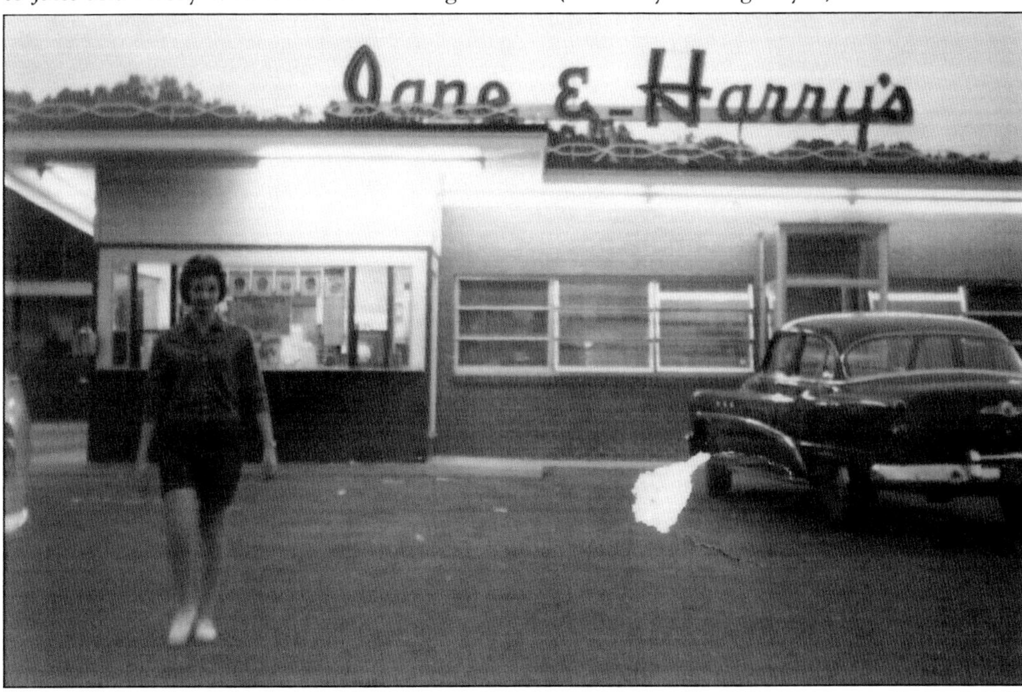

Jane & Harry's Twin Kiss is seen here in October 1960. The Wolfs sold the place in the mid-1970s to Charles Eckert, who converted it into the Heidelberg Restaurant. Eckert's son was murdered outside the restaurant in 1987. In 1999, Elsayrd "Steve" Elmarzouky purchased the Heidelberg Restaurant, known for its fine food. (Courtesy of the Heidelberg Restaurant.)

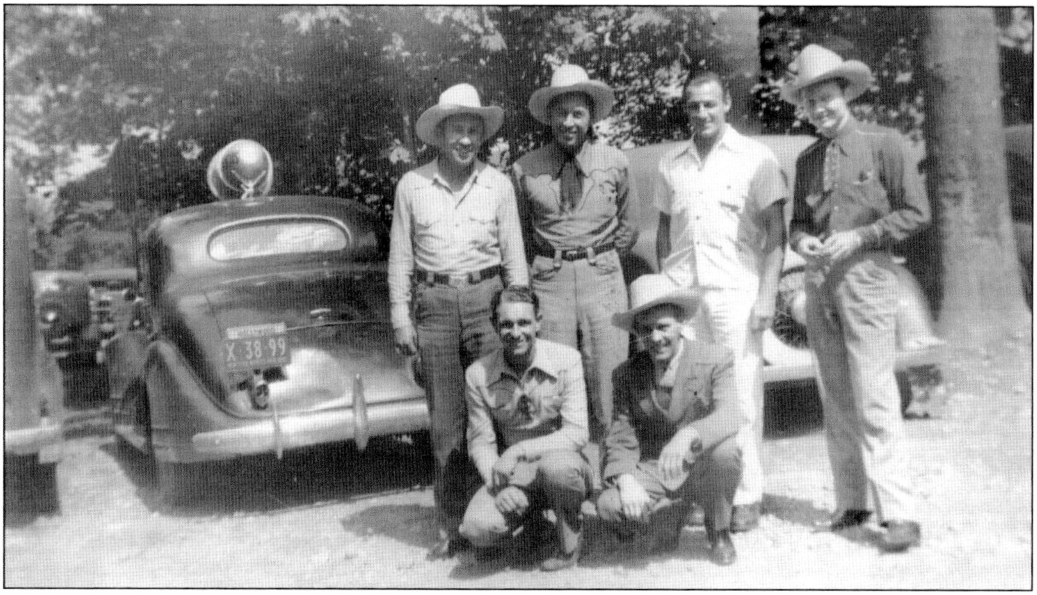

Himmelreich's Grove, pictured here in the 1940s, sat at the corner of Ryeland and Hill Roads. The entertainment capital of Berks County, it started in the 1930s and lasted into the early 1960s. Here is a snapshot of the Sons of the Pioneers, a well-known country and western music group that started in 1934 and appeared in more than 90 movies. This group performed the hit song "Cool Water." They were inducted into the National Cowboy Hall of Fame and the Grammy Hall of Fame. Note the old car with a loudspeaker on the roof. (Courtesy of Earl W. Ibach.)

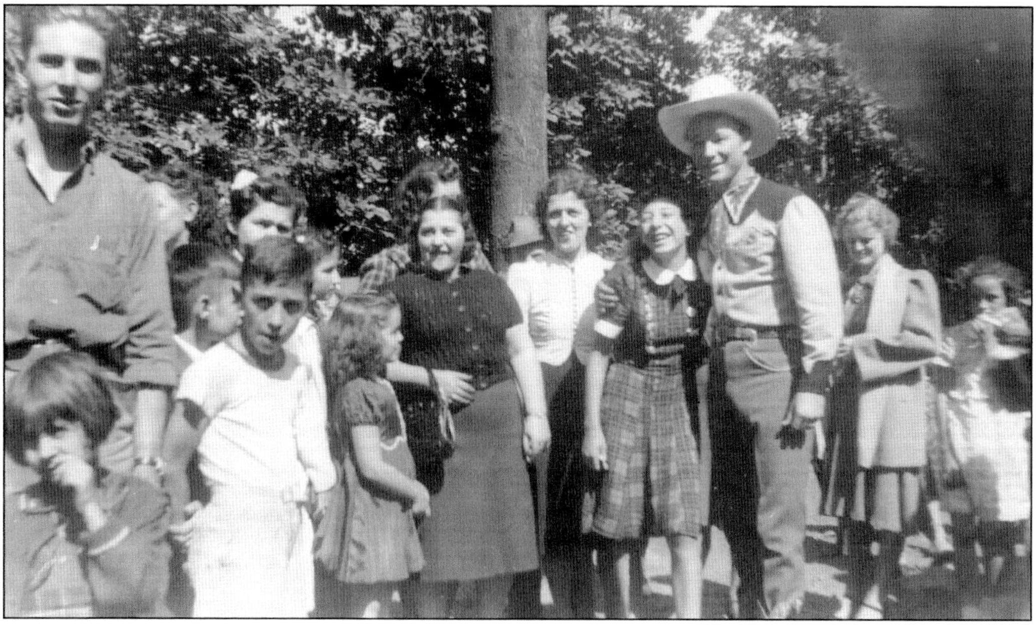

Roy Rogers (1911–1998), born Leonard F. Slye, founded the Sons of the Pioneers. He began his acting career in 1934, appearing in more than 100 films. He also had his own radio and television show for many years. Rogers was the only person to be elected twice to the Country Music Hall of Fame, first in 1980 with the Sons of the Pioneers, then in 1988 as a solo artist. In this photograph, he meets with local fans at Himmelreich's Grove in the 1940s. (Courtesy of Earl W. Ibach.)

Four

North Heidelberg Township

North Heidelberg Township was part of Heidelberg Township until 1845, when local taxpayers filed a petition to the county court to set aside 7,200 acres under the name of North Heidelberg. This new township was created to have better roads, along with a road district supervisor who would be responsible for them.

Some of the first settlers in the township were the Klopps and the Zerbes. Tulpehocken Creek, which forms the northern boundary of the township, provided waterpower for some of the early mills. Lorentz Zerbe operated a mill as early as 1735, and another mill had been established on the North Heidelberg side of Charming Forge by 1817. Sunday's Mill was built about 1820.

In 1744, the Moravians left Reed's Church in Marion Township and built the first church in North Heidelberg, where Tobias Bickel had set aside three acres of land. At one time, the church was attended by Moravian, Lutheran, and Reformed congregations. Today, the church is affiliated with the United Church of Christ.

In the 1960s, the federal government notified the township that a flood-control dam would be built along Tulpehocken Creek and that 1,500 acres would be taken in the process. This acreage accounted for one-fifth of the land surface in North Heidelberg, and 53 farms were lost to the Blue Marsh project. Despite the initial loss, the area has gained hiking, biking, boating, and other recreational opportunities because of this property.

Today, the township is very rural, with a couple of small businesses. Barnett's Garage is the oldest, dating back to the 1930s. It is also home to the Texas Eastern Pipeline pumping station, which began as the World Emergency Pipeline. The purpose of this pipeline was to transport oil from Texas to the East Coast during World War II. Later, it was converted to natural gas. Other than Blue Marsh Lake, the township is mostly farmland. It is the smallest township in the Conrad Weiser area and has the smallest population, at 1,214 in 2010.

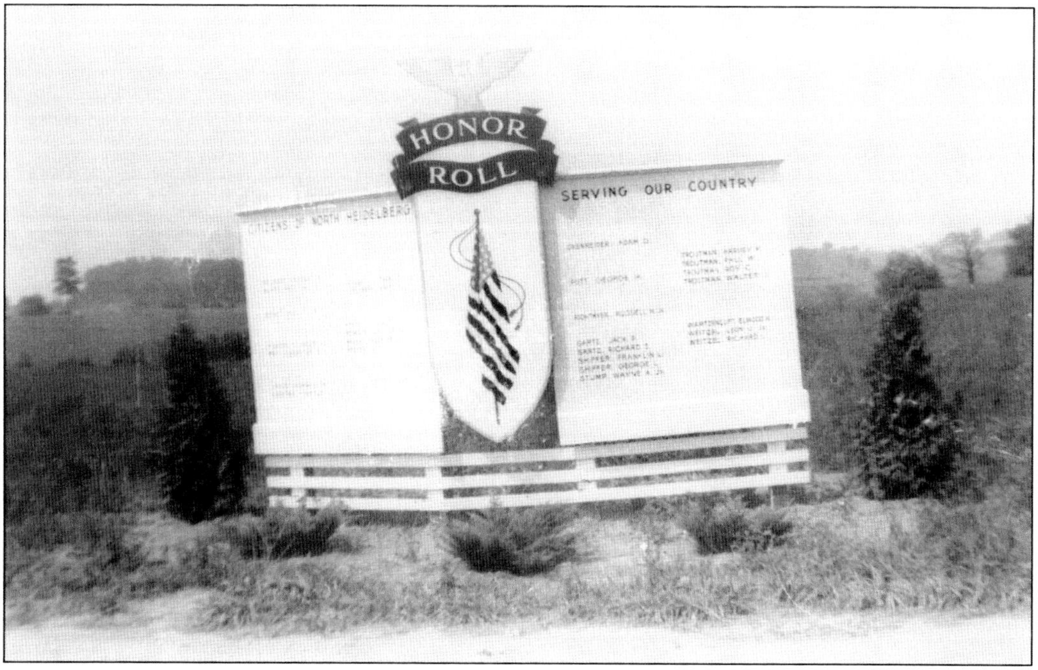

Most towns erected a Honor Roll memorial for its citizens who served in World War II. Made out of wood and not taken care of over the years, many were torn down or replaced with others carved from stone. This wooden memorial stood at the south corner of North Heidelberg and Charming Forge Roads. A stone monument was erected at the North Heidelberg Church at a later date. (Courtesy of Robert Bausher.)

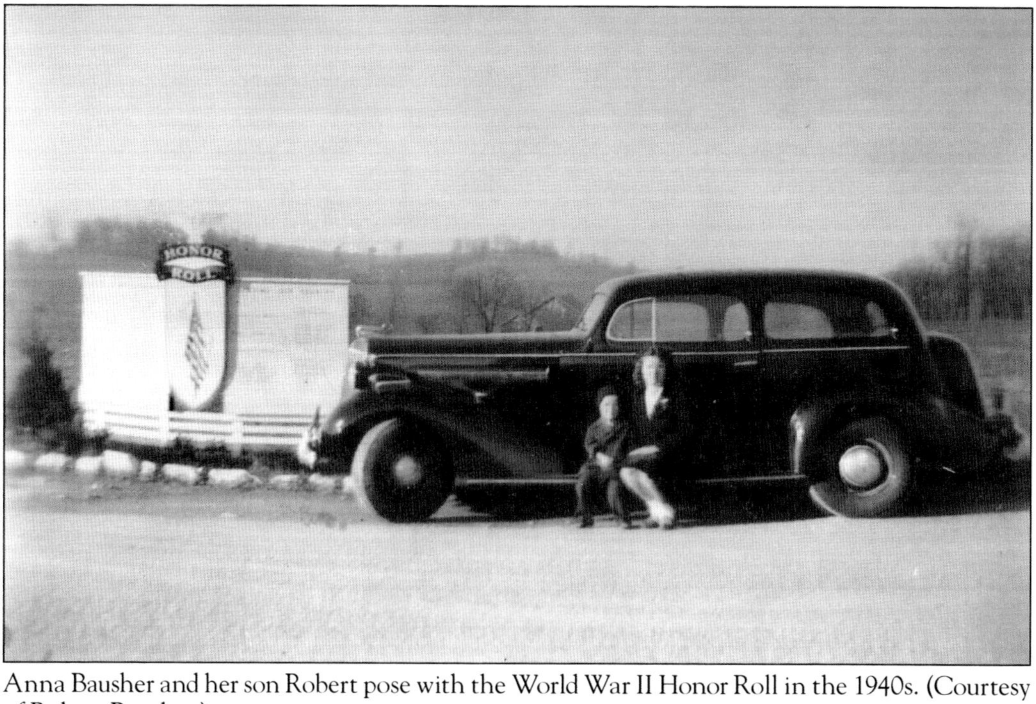

Anna Bausher and her son Robert pose with the World War II Honor Roll in the 1940s. (Courtesy of Robert Bausher.)

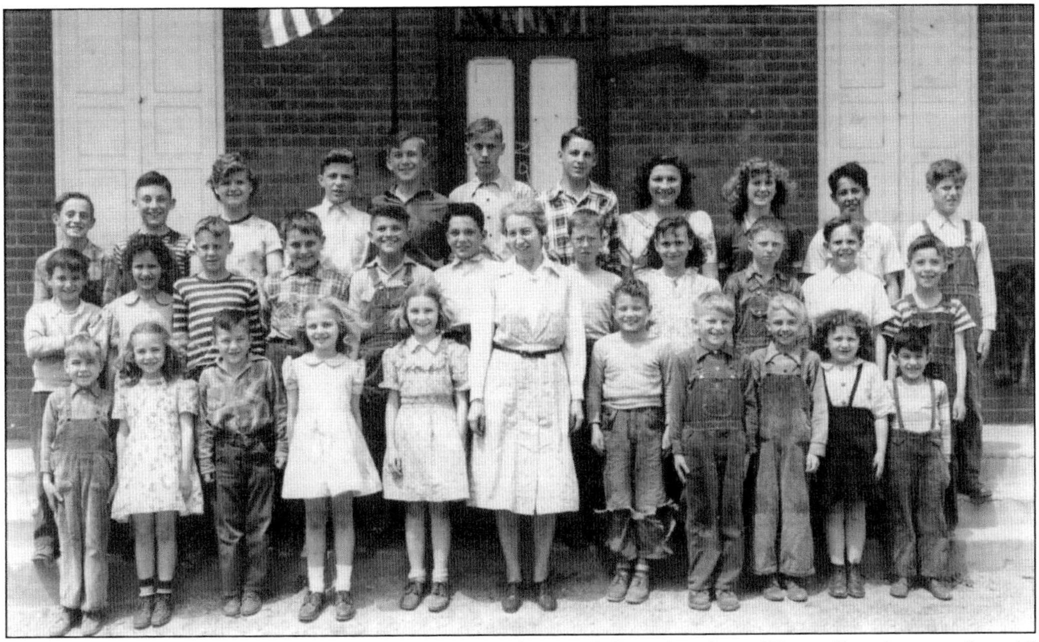

Klopp's School students of 1948–1949 pose in front of the school on Klopp Road, near the old Klopp's Store on Charming Forge Road. From left to right are (first row) B. Feeg, B. Blatt, J. Blatt, F. Nye, N. Feeg, Elsie Stine (teacher), D. Yokem, H. Moyer, R. Feg, A. Oxenreider, and T. Martin; (second row) B. Graupp, D. Fisher, H. Kramer, D. Wartluft, J. Forry, M. Yokem, R. Bausher, J. Yokem, R. Kritz, B. Graupp, and B. Bausher; (third row) C. Neuin, J. Feeg, G. Hartman, L. Barnett, B. Moyer, J. Sell, B. Fisher, E. Forry, S. Neuin, R. Klose, and R. Sell. (Courtesy of Robert Bausher.)

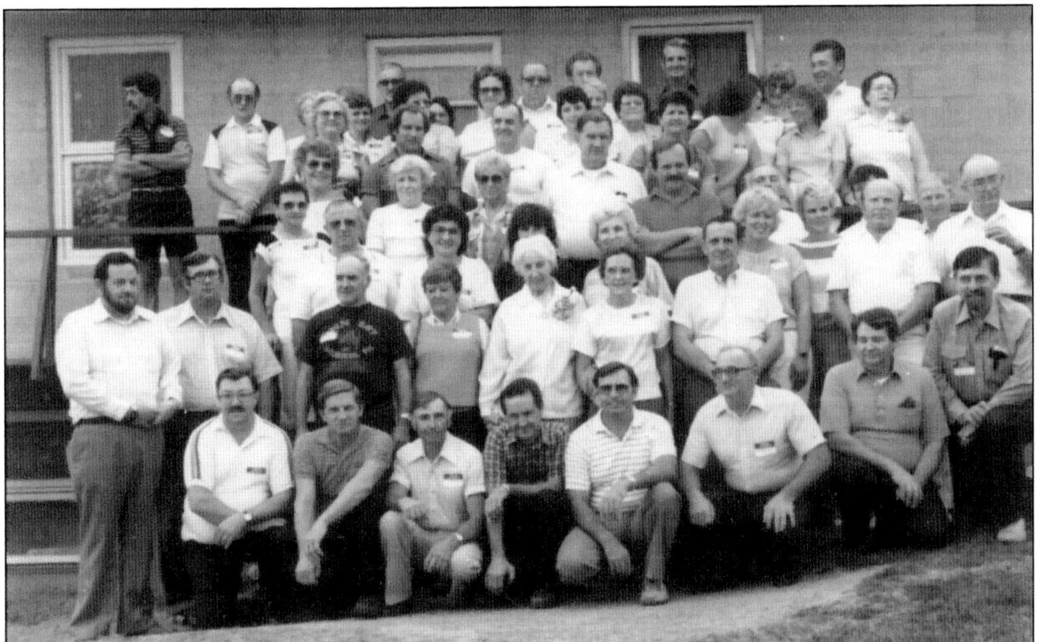

Former students of the Klopp's School gather for a reunion in 1985. Their teacher Elsie Stine stands in the center of the second row with a flower on her blouse. (Courtesy of Robert Bausher.)

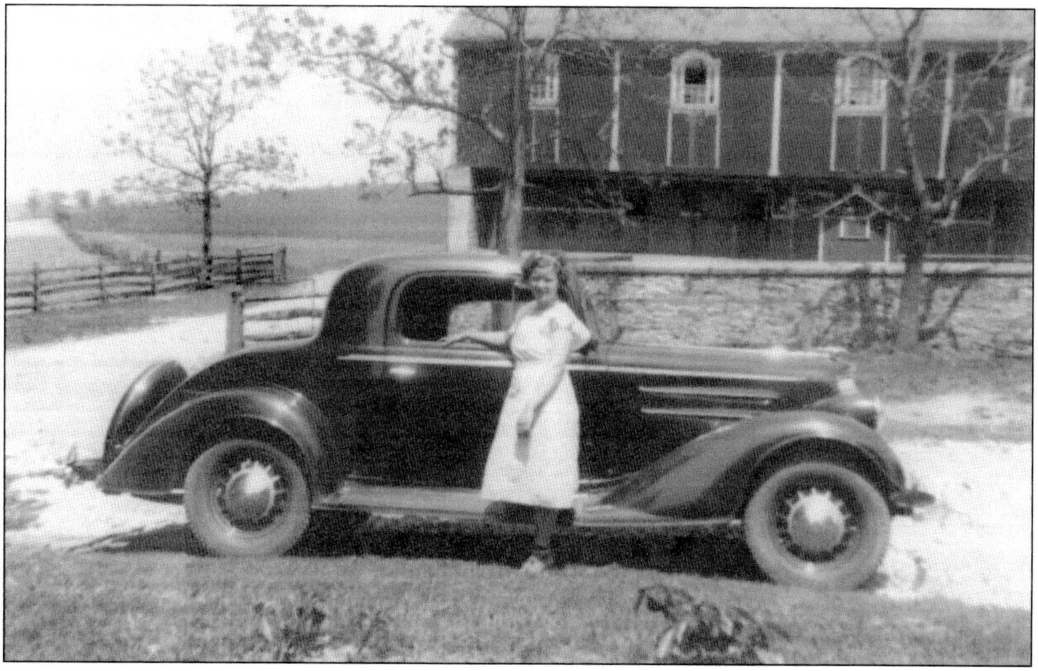

Anna (Hartman) Bausher poses with a car at Klopp Farm in 1937. (Courtesy of Robert Bausher.)

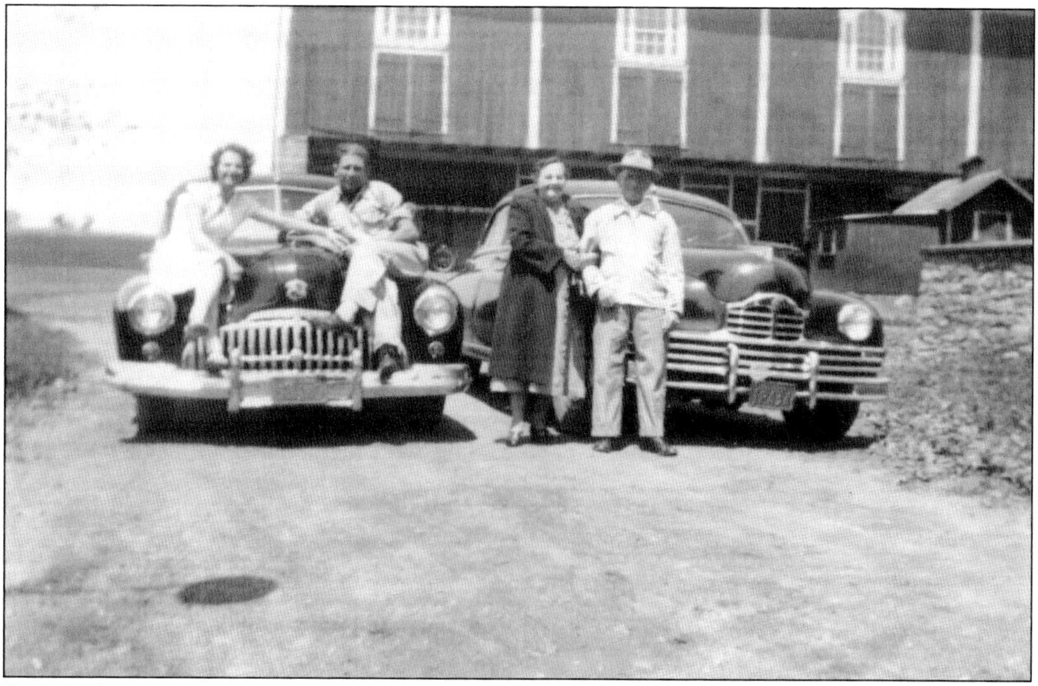

Cora and George Neuin (right) show off their car at Klopp Farm in 1930. The couple on the left is unidentified. (Courtesy of Robert Bausher.)

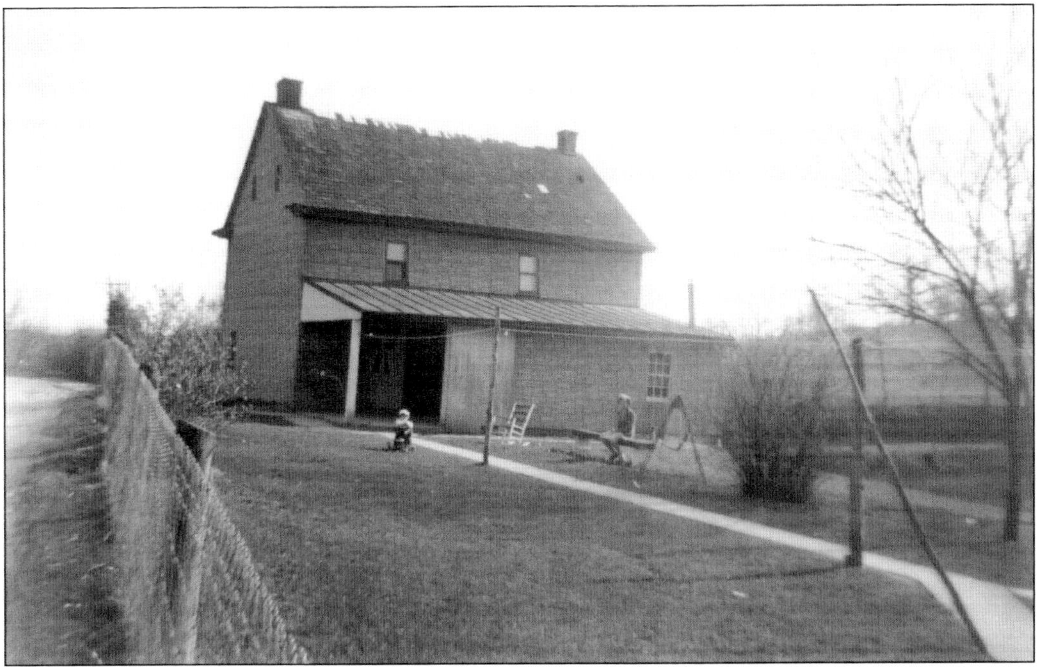

This is a 1946 photograph of Lester Bausher's log farmhouse. In the 1940s, the surrounding 67-acre farm was self-sufficient. This land was originally warranted to Michael Bush in 1743. (Courtesy of Robert Bausher.)

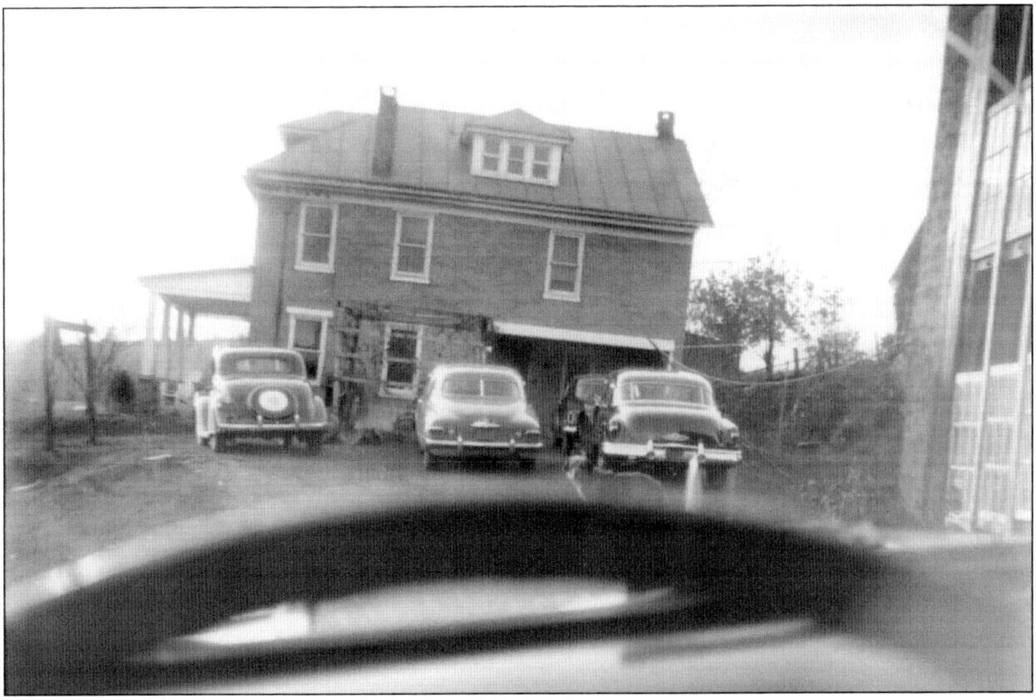

The Graupp House, which is now the property of Clover Hill Winery, is pictured here in 1954. This site is a satellite retail location of the vineyard, established in 1986 in Breinigsville, Lehigh County. (Courtesy of Robert Bausher.)

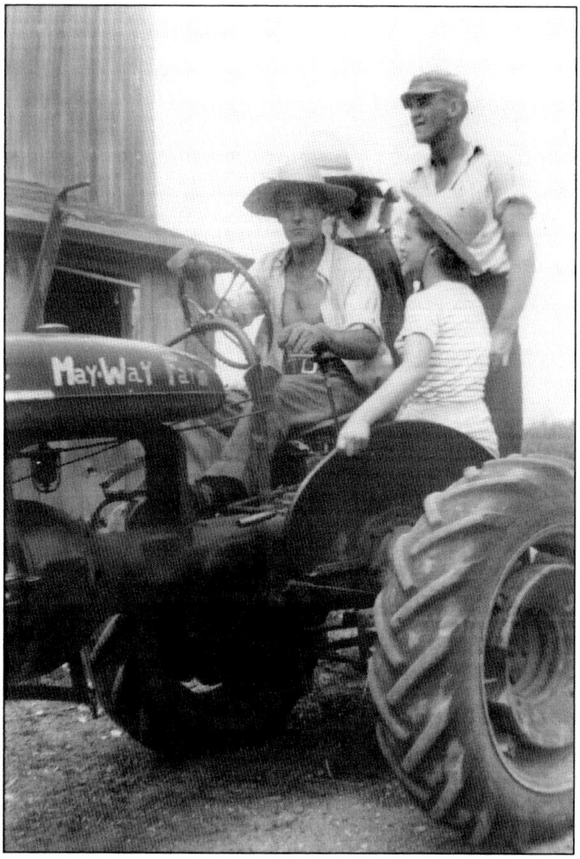

From left to right, Lester Hartman, Grace Hartman, and Robert Seese are pictured on a Farmall Model A tractor at the Bausher farm in 1940. (Courtesy of Robert Bausher.)

Lester Bausher works with a team of two horses attached to a manure spreader at Klopp Farm in 1925. (Courtesy of Robert Bausher.)

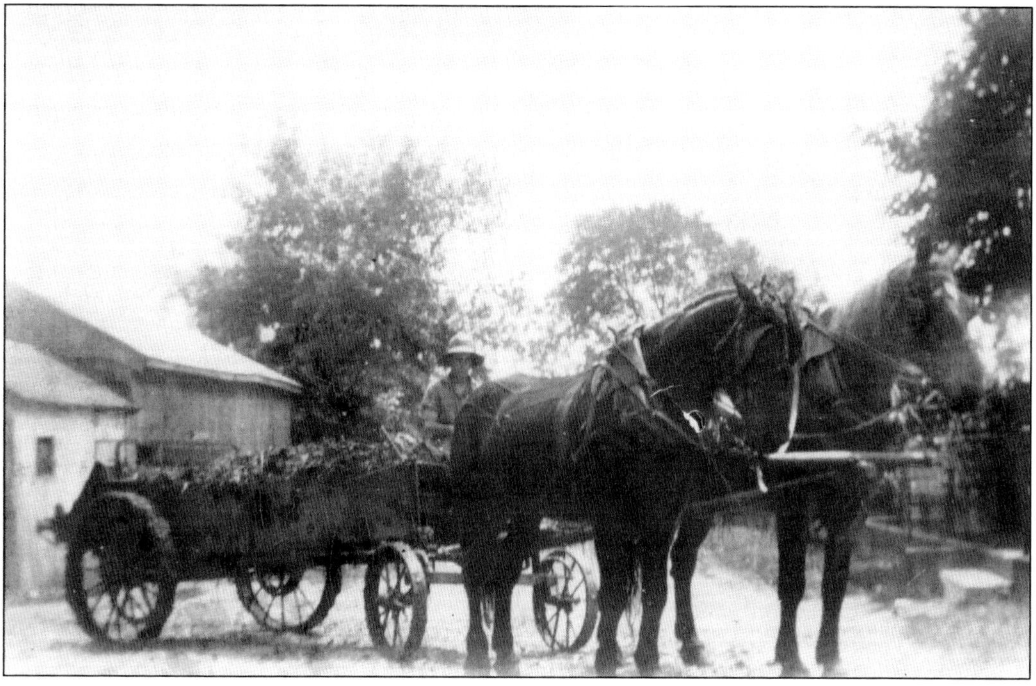

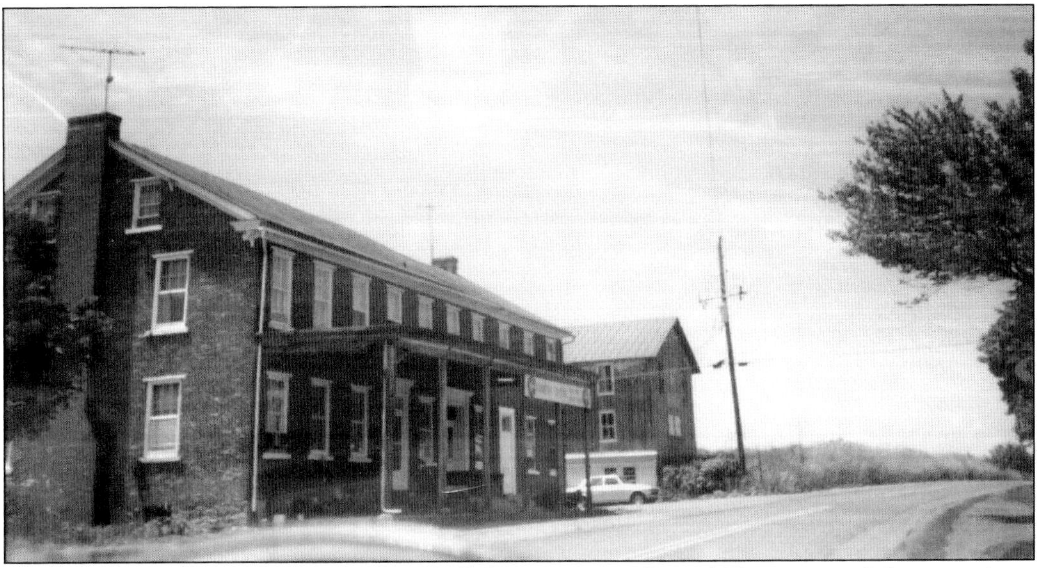

Klopp's Store, pictured around 1970, sold all the necessities. Daniel Klopp erected the store about 1850. Jonathan Klopp expanded the business with a hotel about 1857. The store also housed the North Heidelberg Post Office from 1867 to 1907. In 1881, Morgan Klopp formed Klopp's Cornet Band, which was active here in the 1880s. Adolphus Klopp served as postmaster in 1887. Finally, in the 1920s, the Klopps sold the business, which continued until the 1950s. (Courtesy of Robert Bausher.)

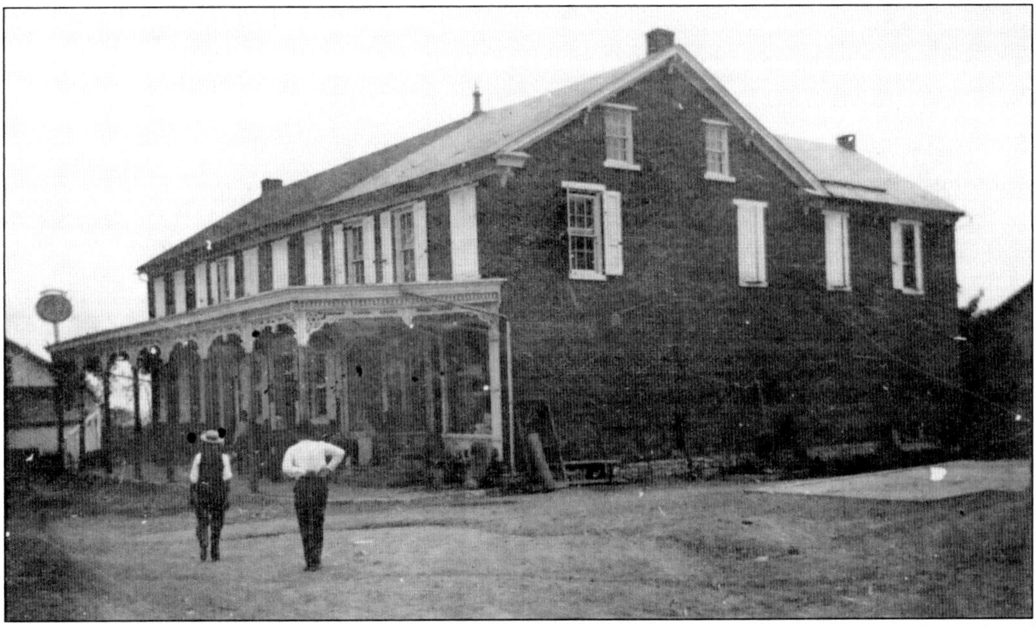

In September 1924, the local area had a series of robberies and other strange events. On the night of September 26, 1924, three men entered Klopp's Store and made their way to the bedroom of Adolphus and Mary Klopp. Their son Jonathan, who had just returned from his honeymoon, intervened and was shot to death. He died in the arms of his bride. After the murder, Adolphus sold the store to John A. Lengel. This ended the Klopps' ownership, but the name remained the same. Klopp's Store is pictured here around 1900. (Courtesy of Carl Ganster.)

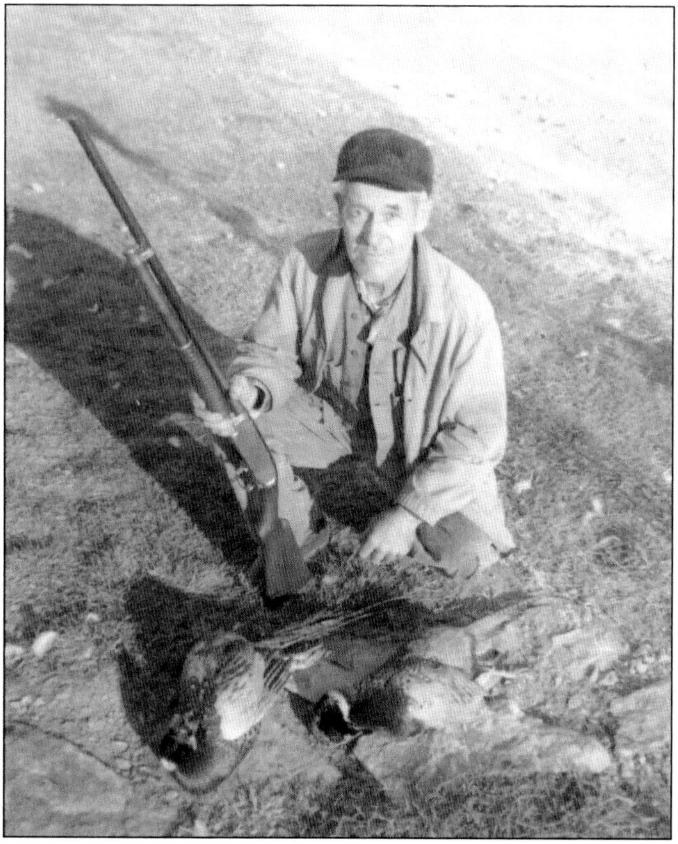

Lester Bausher poses with his Winchester Model 12 shotgun and two cock birds while hunting in 1967. Small-game hunting was popular in rural areas until the 1970s. Now pheasant sightings are rare in the Conrad Weiser area. (Courtesy of Robert Bausher.)

The Bausher brothers, Robert (left) and Lee (right), pose on their North Heidelberg farm in the winter of 1957. (Courtesy of Robert Bausher.)

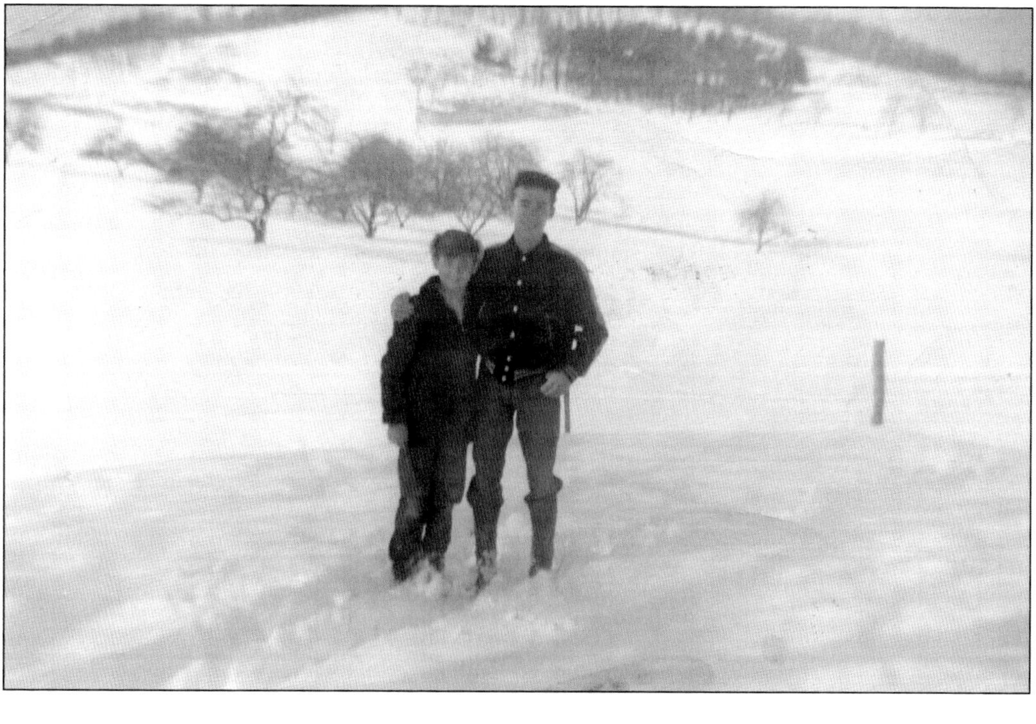

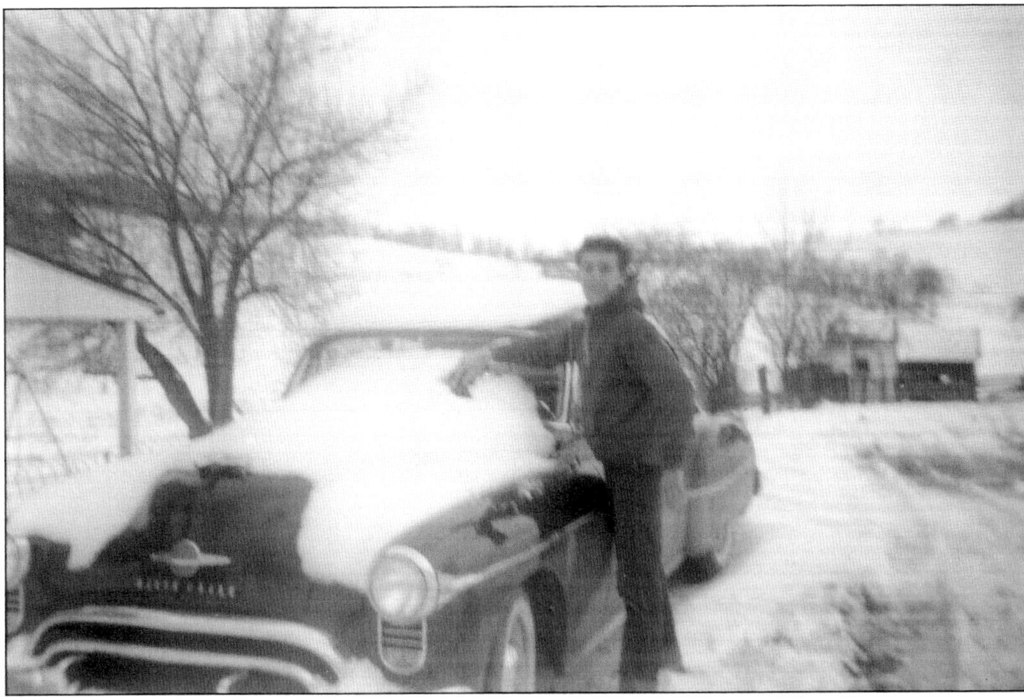

Pictured here is another 1959 snow scene in North Heidelberg. This 1950 two-door Oldsmobile was one of the fastest cars in the area, according to Robert Bausher. (Courtesy of Robert Bausher.)

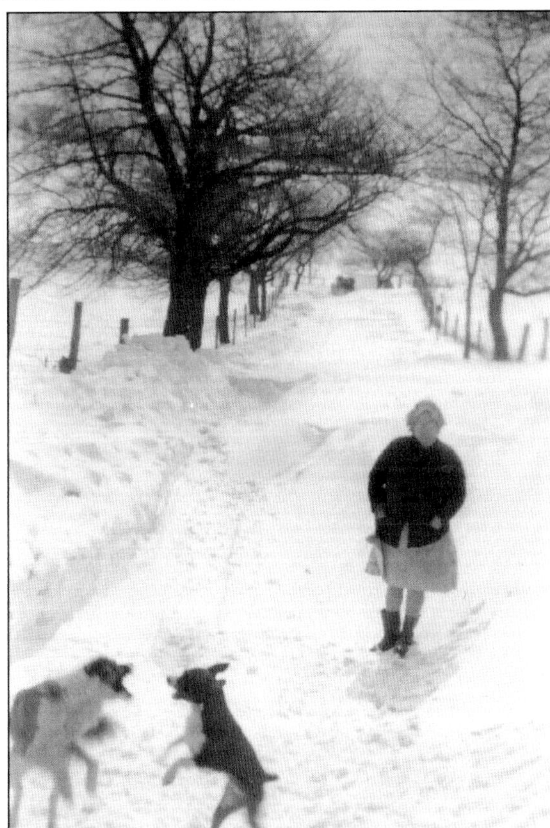

Margaret Fromm is pictured here with two playful dogs on Hillview Road in North Heidelberg. The road had drifted shut following a winter storm in the 1950s. Sometimes it was a week before the roads were completely open after a large snowfall. (Courtesy of Robert Bausher.)

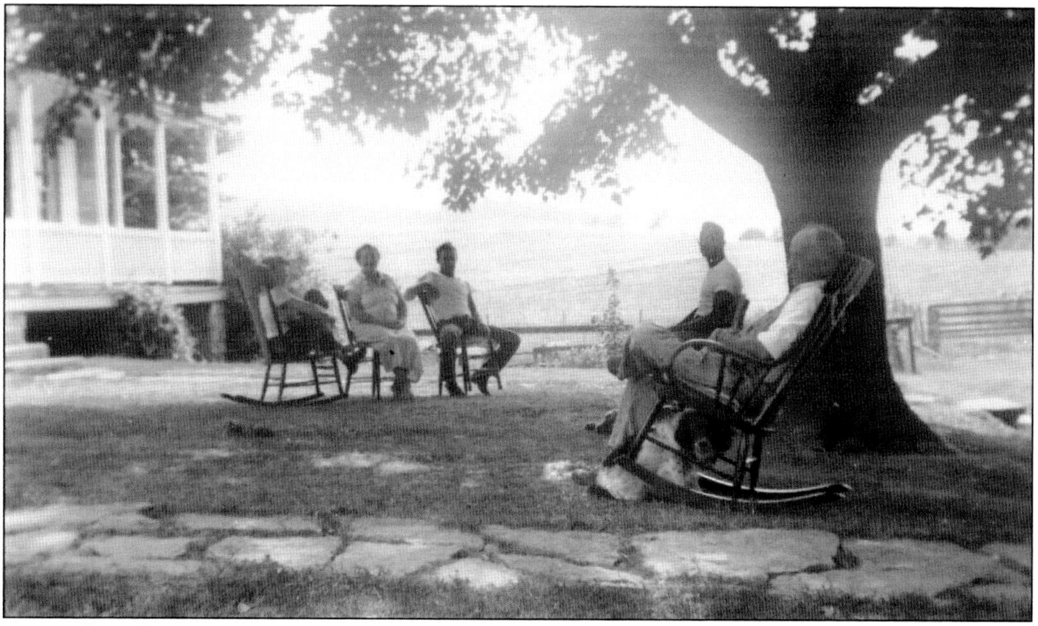

It must have been a Sunday or a holiday when this photograph was taken in 1955. Enjoying this leisure time are, from left to right, Martha Neuin, Cora Neuin, Curtis Neuin, Harold Neuin, and George Neuin. (Courtesy of Robert Bausher.)

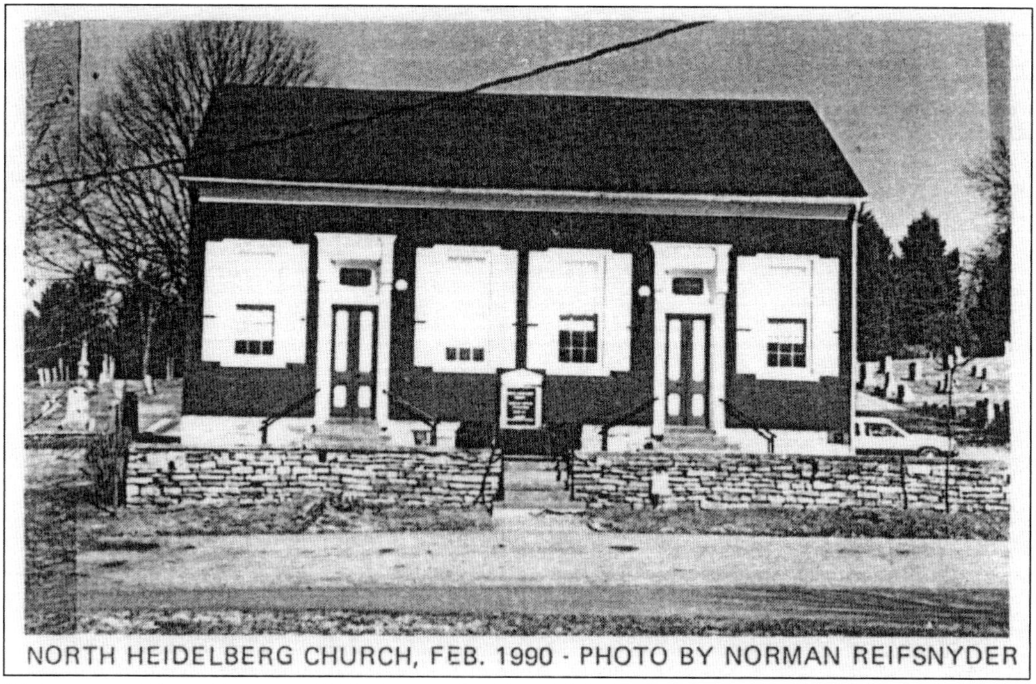

This postcard from February 1990 depicts the North Heidelberg Church, the only church in the township. Moravian, Reformed, and Lutheran congregations built this church on Old Church Road in 1846, and today, it is controlled by the Reformed church. Its cemetery has tombstones dating back to the 1740s. This church held strawberry festivals for many years. (Courtesy of the Institute of American Deltiology.)

This is an interior view of North Heidelberg Church in 1967. The church has a central pulpit flanked by two staircases. In 1894, the organ was purchased for $850 and hauled by Alvin Blatt, with the help of his horses and wagon. (Courtesy of the Institute of American Deltiology.)

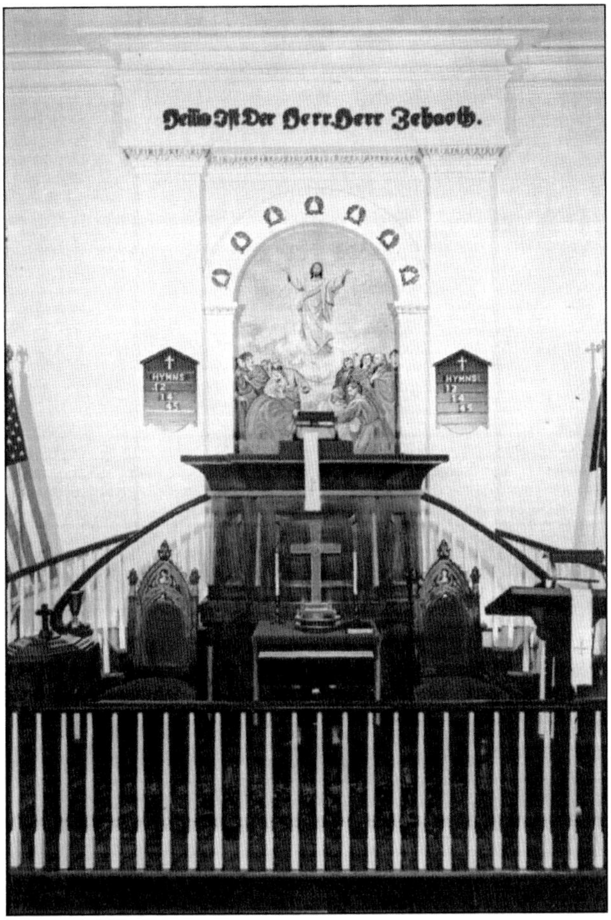

Charming Forge School was built in 1876 on the site of a school from 1848. Seen here in 1911, this school was located in North Heidelberg, near the village of Charming Forge in Marion Township. North Heidelberg Township rejected a 1952 ballot to join the Penn-Bernville School District, and in 1954, the residents voted instead to join the newly formed Conrad Weiser School District. The Anspachs lived here after the school was closed, and Helen Anspach was murdered here in the late 1970s. The Anspachs also sold Christmas trees in the 1960s. (Courtesy of Carl Ganster.)

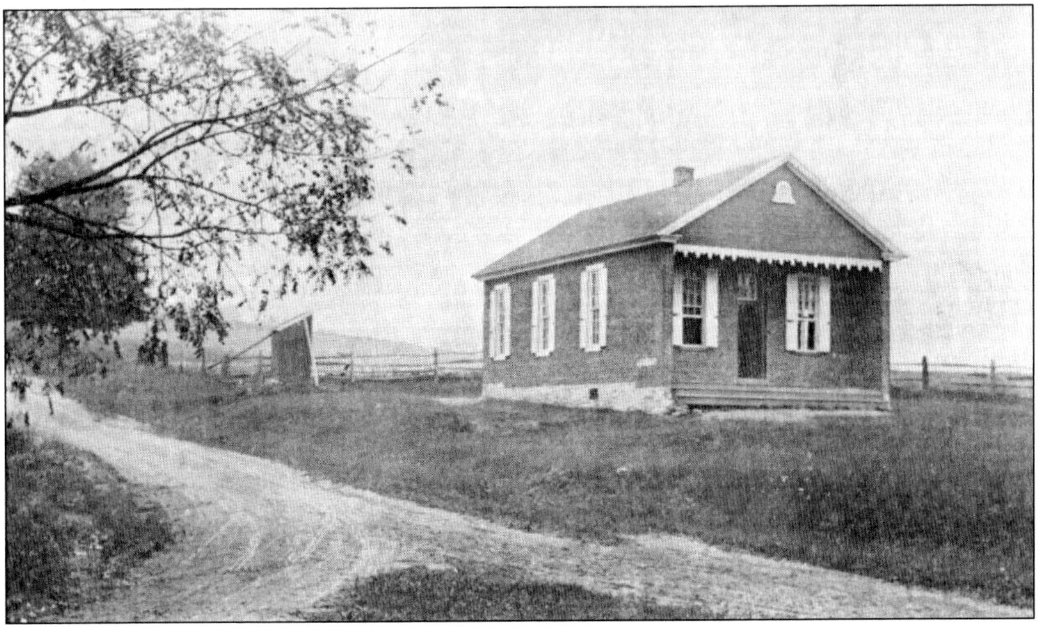

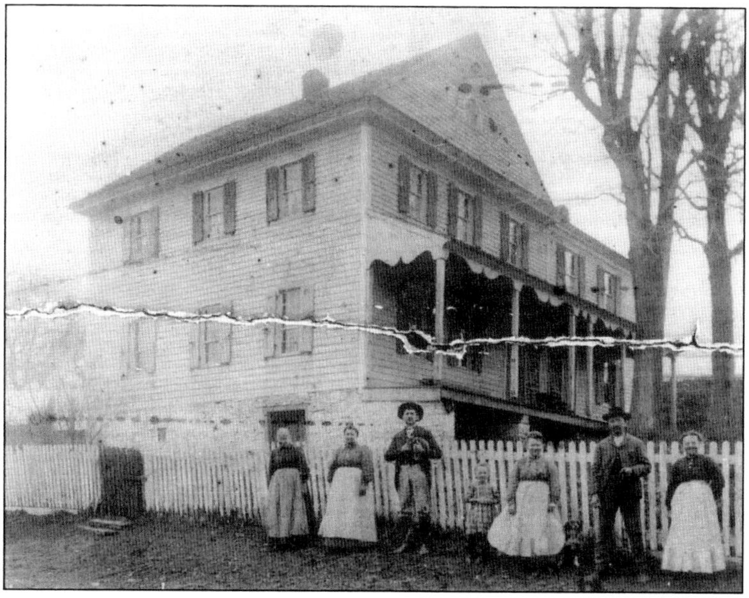

Pictured here in 1905 is a Zerbe house on the site of the Zerbe mill. J. Lorentz Zerbe built the first mill in the township in the 1730s, and it stood along the Tulpehocken Creek at Kricks Mill Road until it burned in 1897. (Courtesy of Leonard Rohrbach.)

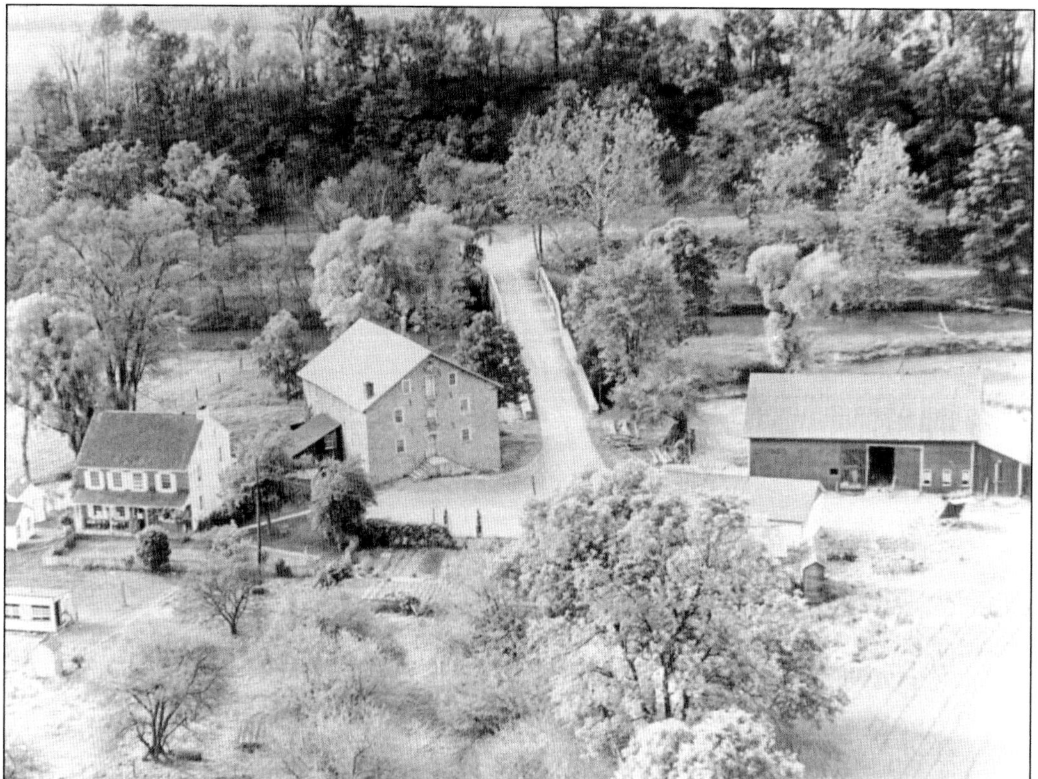

This an aerial view of Sunday's Mill on Station Road along the Tulpehocken Creek in 1954. John Zerbe built this mill in 1820, then known as Cross Keys Mill. In 1883, Jacob Sunday purchased the mill, lending his name to the business. This mill operated under members of the Lutz family until 1956. The house was built in 1852, and the barn burned in the late 1970s. (Courtesy of Leonard Rohrbach.)

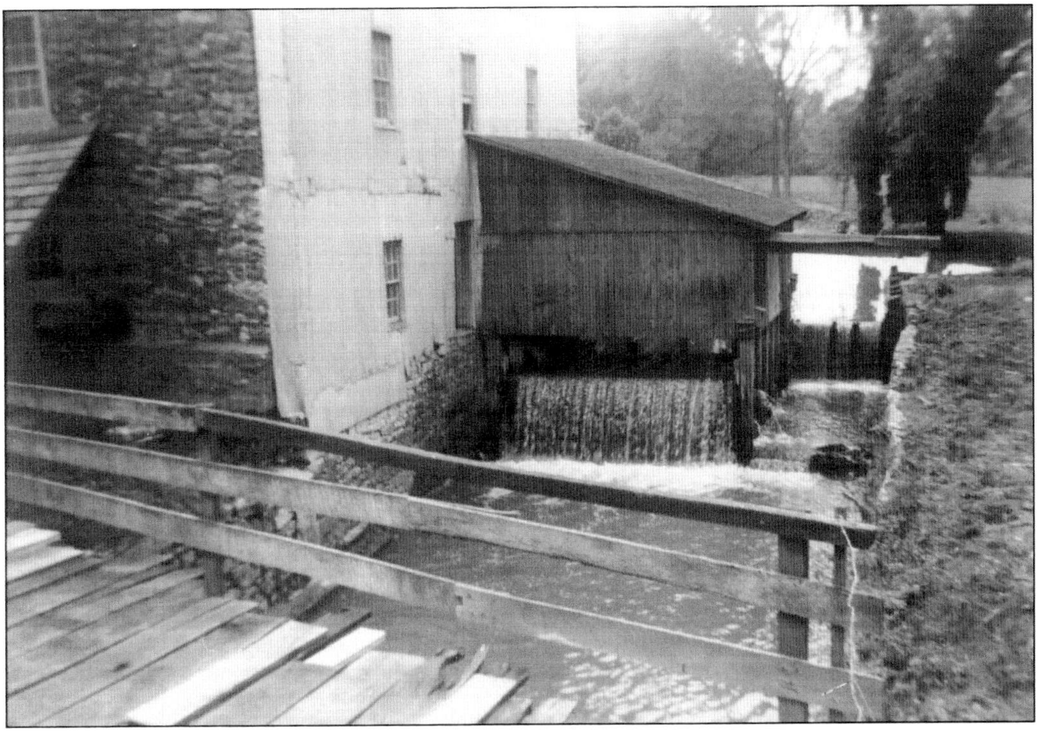

Sunday's millrace is pictured here in 1957, when the mill was no longer operating. As of 2014, the millrace was in the process of being repaired, and Leonard Rohrbach operates a small sawmill on the property. (Courtesy of Leonard Rohrbach.)

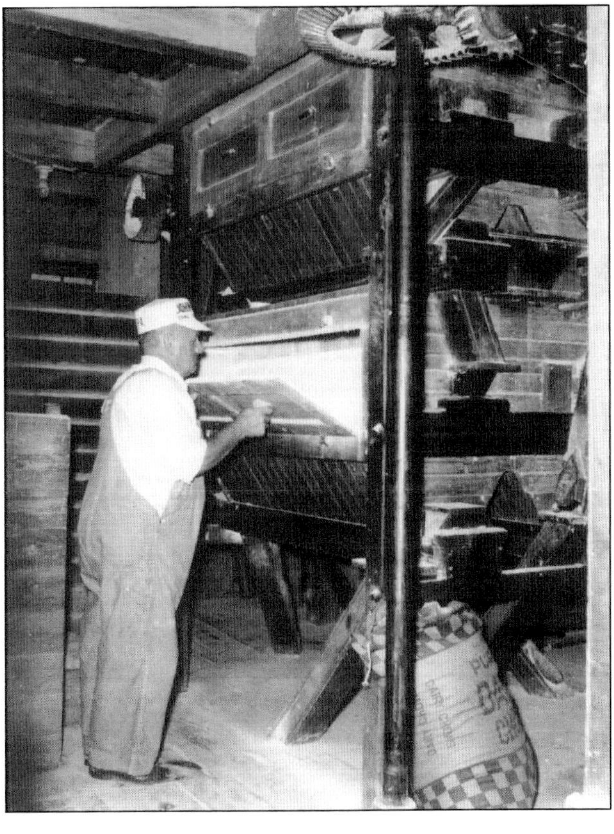

Lammas Lutz is seen working in his mill in the 1950s. He operated the mill from 1929 to 1956. Very few mills operate in Berks County today. (Courtesy of Leonard Rohrbach.)

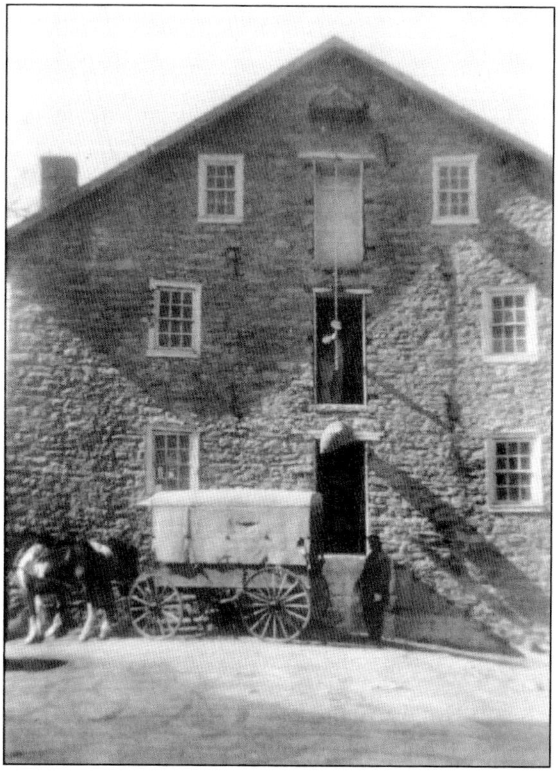

Grain bags are being loaded onto a horse and buggy at Sunday's Mill in 1920. Before the brick house was built, the miller's family lived on the upper floor of the mill. (Courtesy of Leonard Rohrbach.)

The Feeg farm at 442 Station Road is pictured here in 1896. This farm was first owned by Jacob Hochstetler, who was captured, along with his son, by hostile Indians near Shartlesville on September 19, 1757. Hochstetler was taken to Erie and later released by the Indians. He returned to Berks County and purchased this farm, which he passed on to his son. Ammon Feeg later purchased the farm, and James Feeg is the present owner. The barn was replaced about 1896, and the house is made of logs. (Courtesy of James Feeg.)

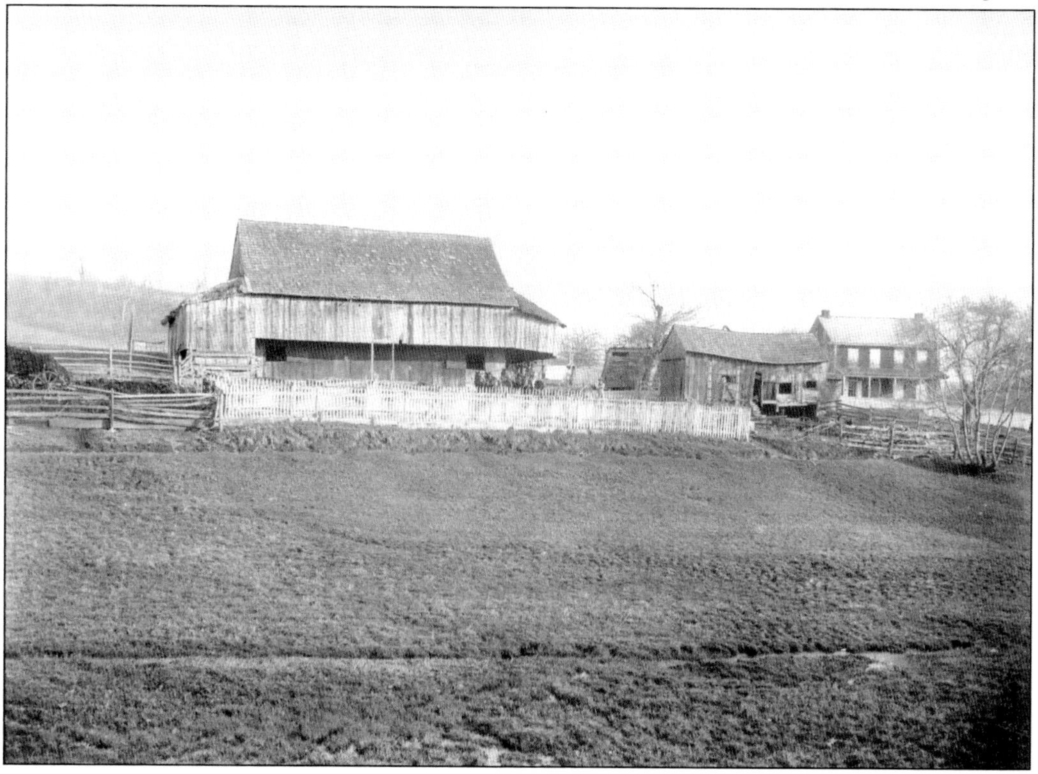

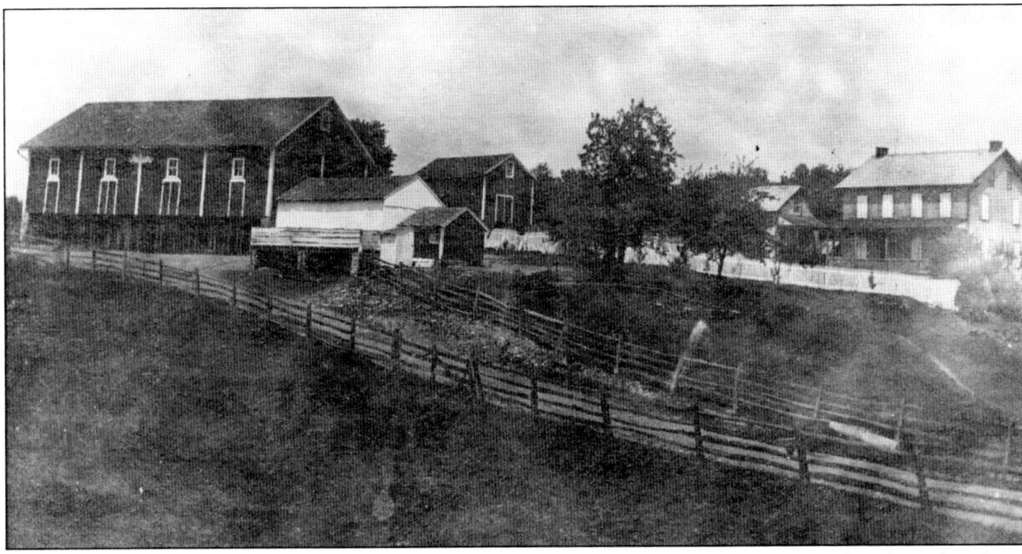

This is a later view of the Feeg farm, after the new barn was built in 1896. This farm has been in the Feeg family for over 100 years. Ammon Feeg started an apple and peach orchard about 1920, and his son James ran the orchard until about 1970. The fruit was sold at local auctions. (Courtesy of James Feeg.)

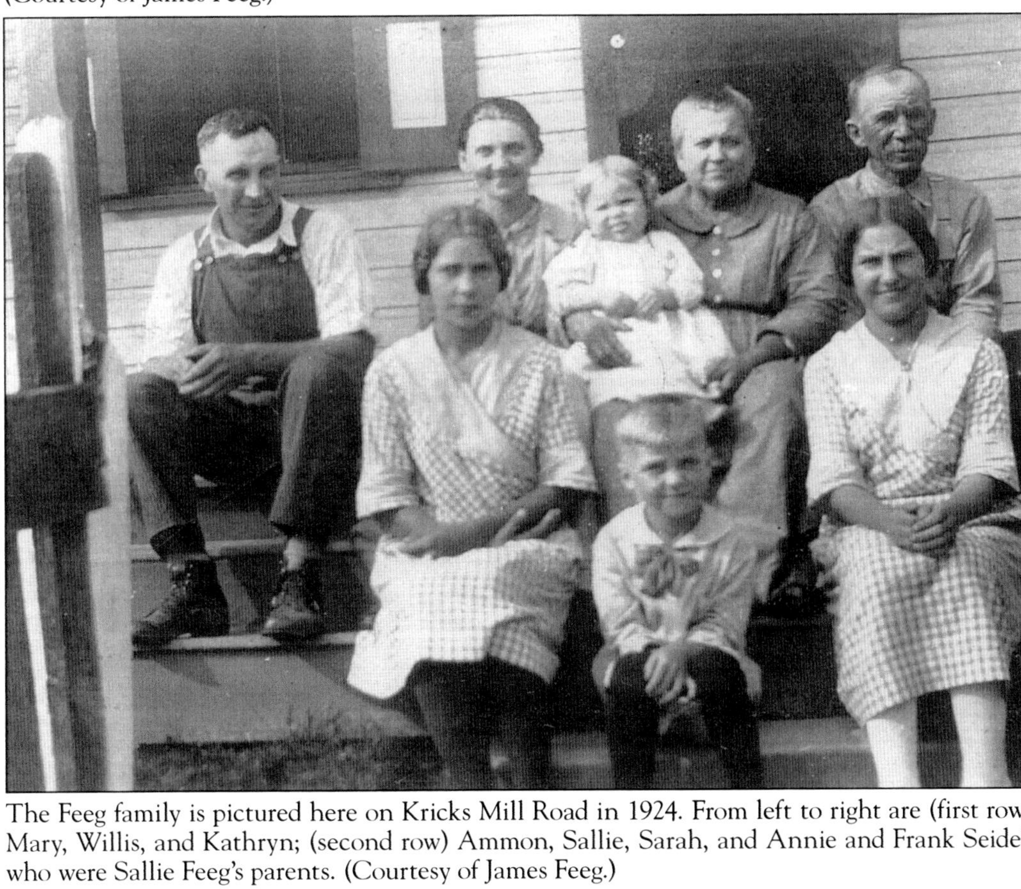

The Feeg family is pictured here on Kricks Mill Road in 1924. From left to right are (first row) Mary, Willis, and Kathryn; (second row) Ammon, Sallie, Sarah, and Annie and Frank Seidel, who were Sallie Feeg's parents. (Courtesy of James Feeg.)

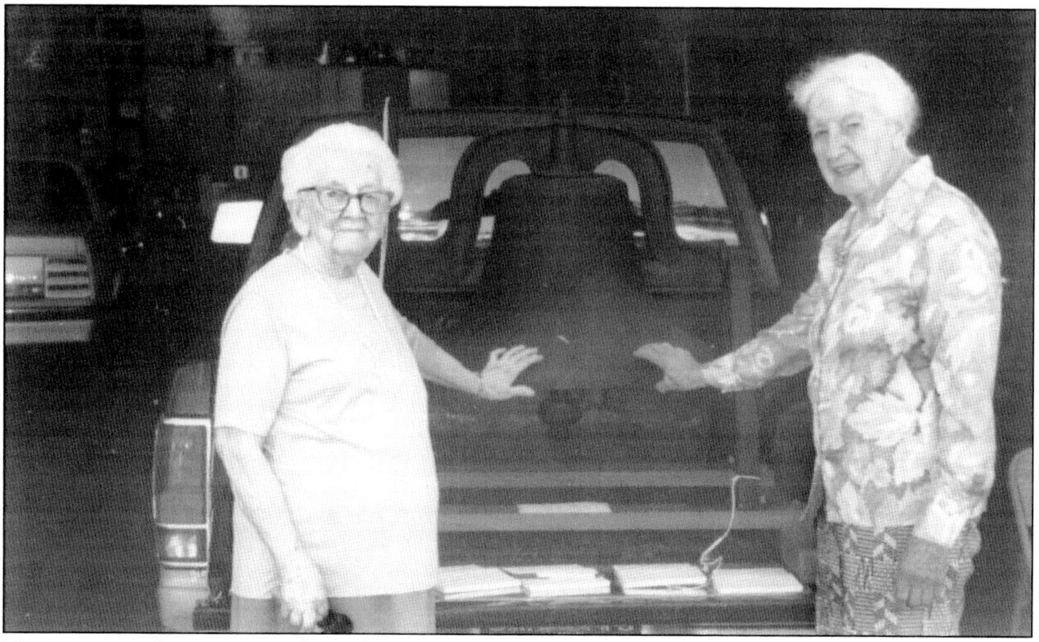

Here are two longtime teachers from one-room schoolhouses in North Heidelberg Township. Cora Feeg (left) taught at the Charming Forge School, and Elsie Stine taught at the Klopp's School. Behind them is the bell that hung at the Klopp's School. (Courtesy of James Feeg.)

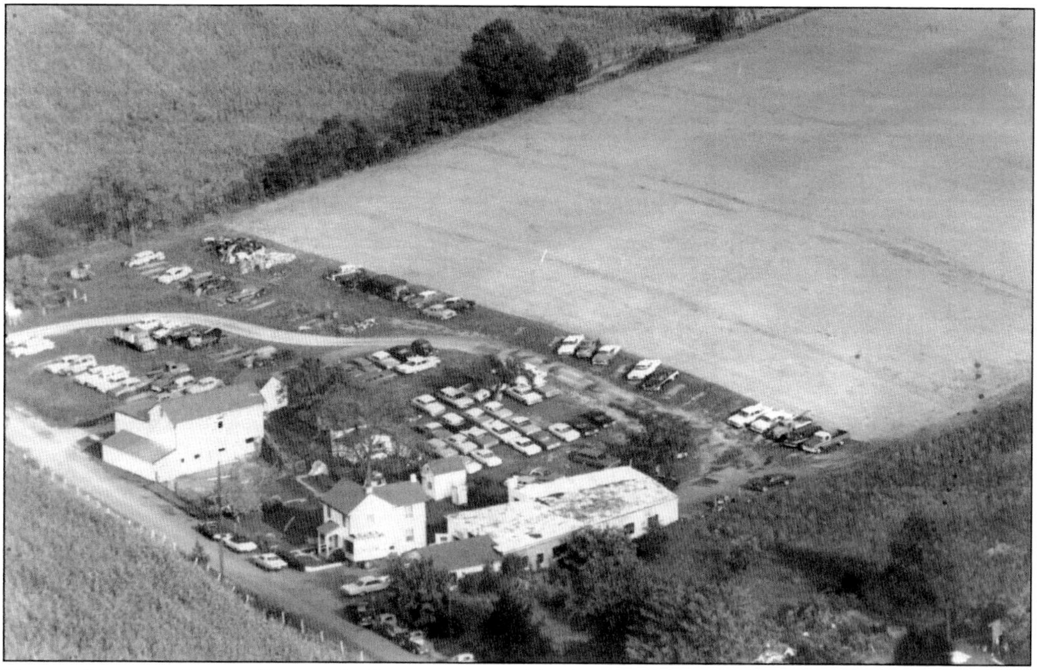

Pictured here in 1960 is Barnett's Garage, started by Earl L. Barnett about 1937. Today, his sons Lloyd and Jim Barnett run the operation, which they took over around 1970. They now offer used car and truck sales, general repairs, wrecker service, and auto body repair. The garage, located at 129 Heidel Road, is also an official Pennsylvania inspection station. (Courtesy of Barnett's Garage.)

Five

Robesonia Borough

The village of Robesonia was formed in part due to the Robesonia Furnace, which accounted for an immense area south of the village. The furnace was founded by ironmaster George Ege in 1794 as the Reading Furnace. Then, in 1845, Henry P. Robeson purchased the furnace and expanded it, leading to the creation of Robesonia in 1855. The village was incorporated as a borough in 1913.

Lester P. Breininger Jr. (1935–2011), a world-renowned redware potter who helped put Robesonia on the map, was known as the resident historian of the furnace, or "neat old place," as he referred to it. Breininger was active in founding the Friends of the Robesonia Furnace organization and preserving the historic remains of the furnace and its grounds, of which he provided walking tours. The community regrets the loss of such a local treasure.

Robesonia has always been an industrial town. It supplied jobs to many with the Gloray Knitting Mills, Caron Spinning Mill, and Rich Kraft Kitchens, all of which are gone today. However, Snap-on Tools, Sonoco Products, and Adelphi Kitchens, among many other small businesses, are still in existence.

As with all small towns, Robesonia is working to keep what businesses it has and trying to keep its community spirit alive and well. Over the years, Robesonia has hosted a number of community-oriented events, such as the Jack Frost Frolic, the Furnace Festival, firefighters' parades, a yearly carnival with fireworks displays, and many other local activities. Recently, efforts have been made to revive some of these events for its current population of 2,132. Supporting its sports teams, from the high school level to Lebanon Valley League baseball, has also been a facet of community life in Robesonia.

The town is known for its wide, tree-lined streets, for which it continues to win Tree City USA awards. Driving through town, most notably the southern part, its history is evident.

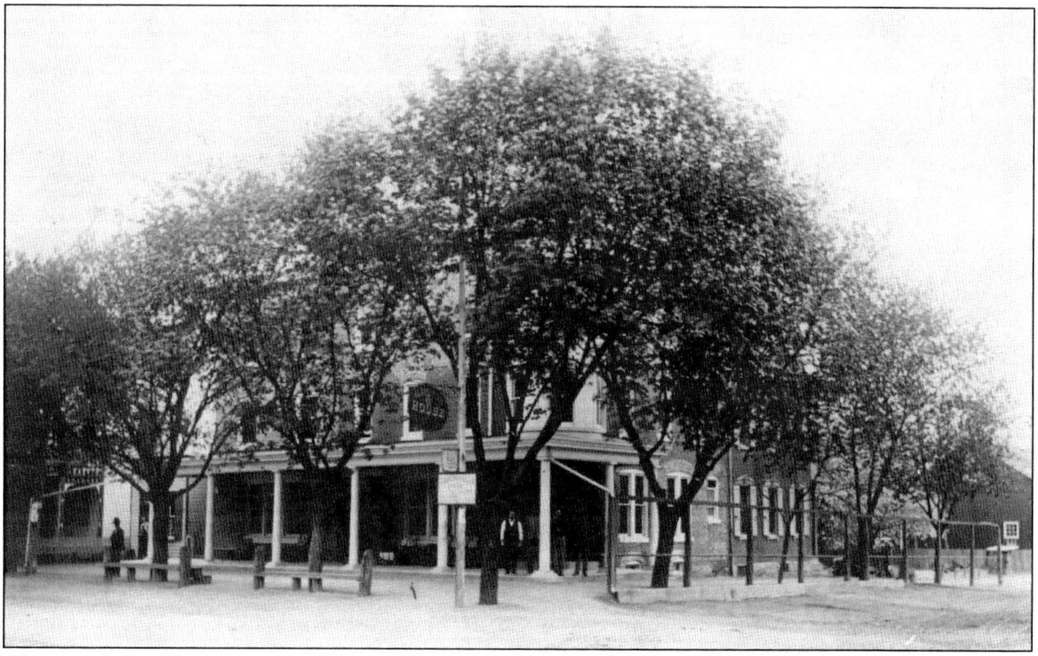

This view shows the Mansion House at Penn Avenue and North Robeson Street. Built in 1876, it served as a bar, with apartments on top and garages for rent in the rear. In 1923, the Robesonia State Bank was born, and the building was remodeled to accommodate the bank. This building also housed a barbershop and the post office. The bank ran its course until 1968, and shortly thereafter, the building was razed. The sign on the pole out front denotes the pickup location for Bernville Stage. (Courtesy of Carl Reidler.)

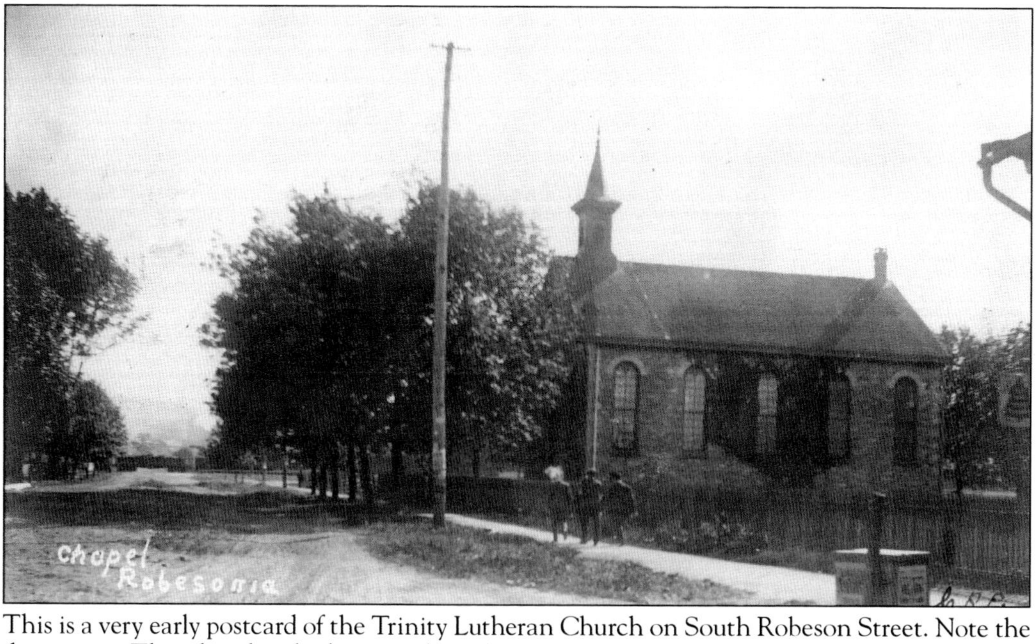

This is a very early postcard of the Trinity Lutheran Church on South Robeson Street. Note the dirt streets. This church, which was enlarged in the 1980s, has been very active over the years and still is today. (Courtesy of Carl Reidler.)

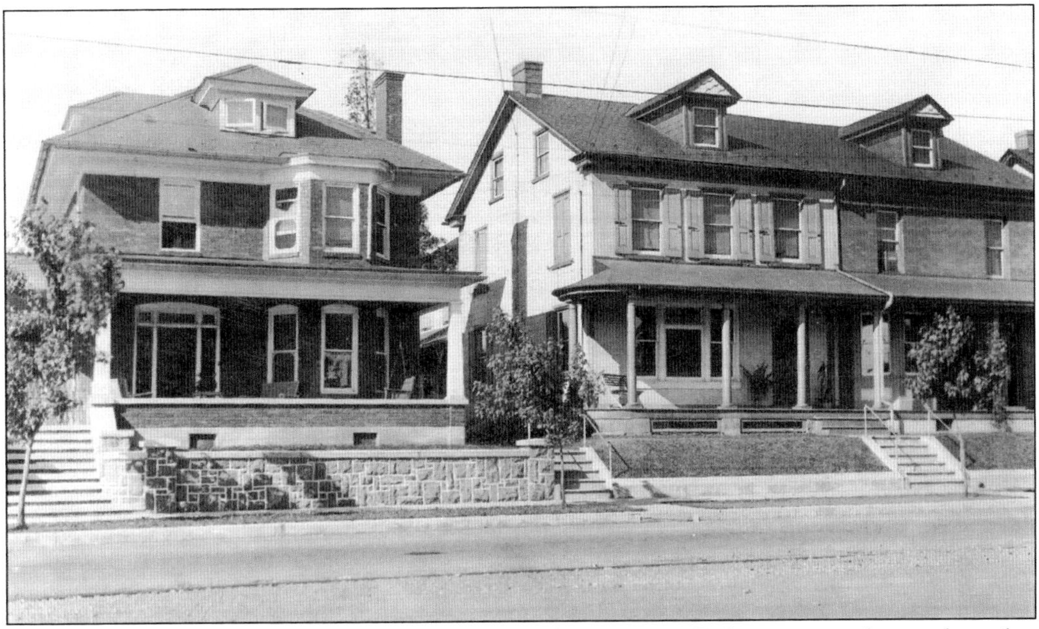

Some of the nice homes on Penn Avenue near Elm Street in Robesonia are featured on this postcard. A postmark from 1924 dates the image to the 1920s. (Courtesy of Carl Reidler.)

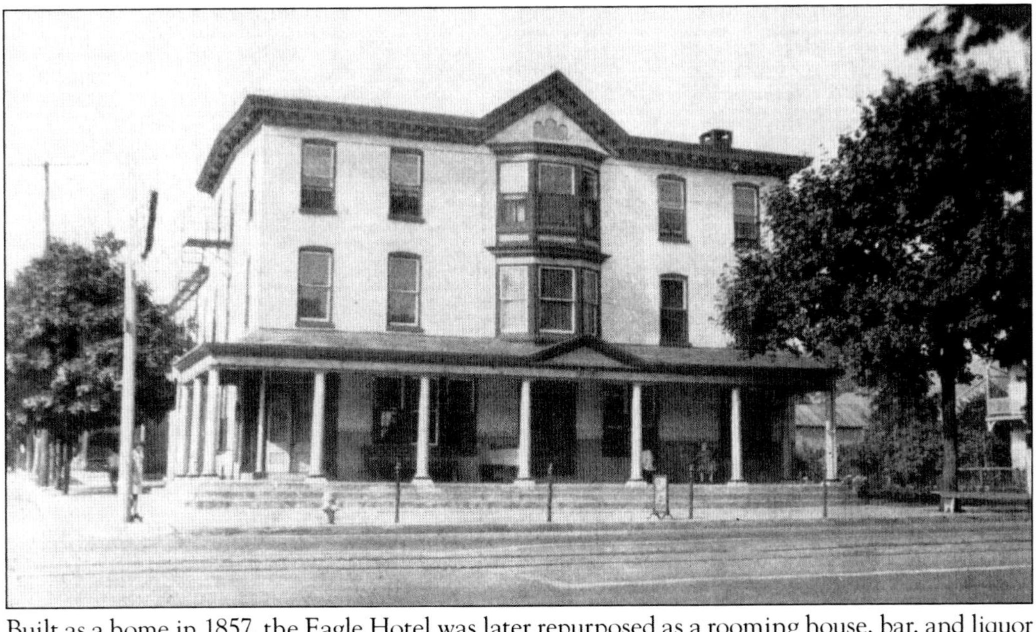

Built as a home in 1857, the Eagle Hotel was later repurposed as a rooming house, bar, and liquor store. There was also an A&P store in the west end of the building during the 1930s. Sadly, it was razed in 1967. It is difficult to save everything, but this hotel, and the Mansion House, would have been great landmarks in Robesonia today. (Courtesy of Carl Reidler.)

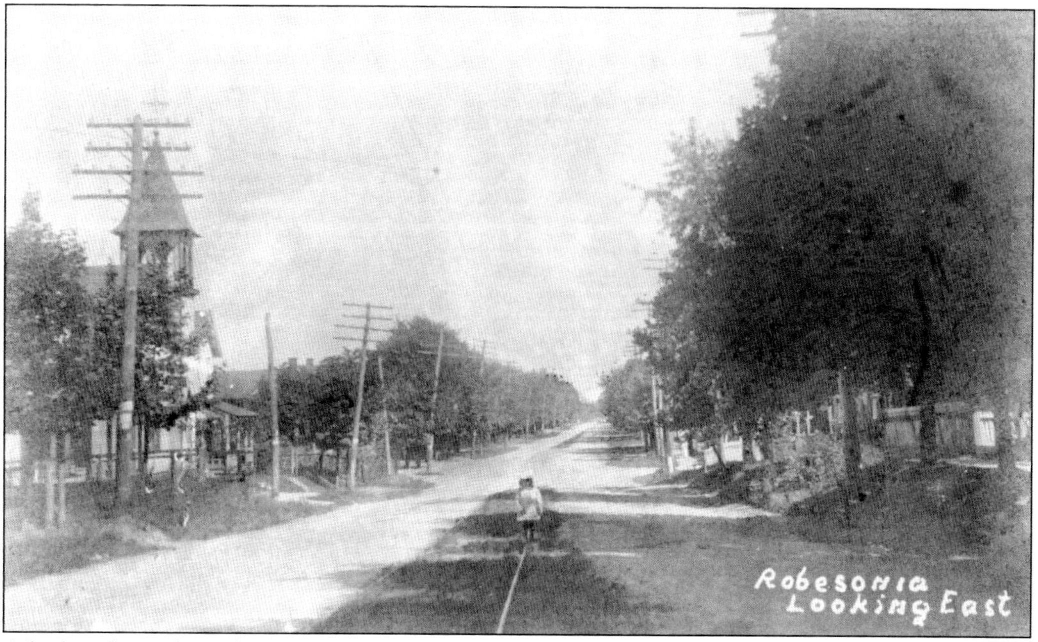

A little girl stands on the trolley rails on Centre Street (now Penn Avenue) in this view postmarked 1907. Looking east toward Wernersville, the old Evangelical Church is visible on the left, but it is no longer standing. (Courtesy of Carl Reidler.)

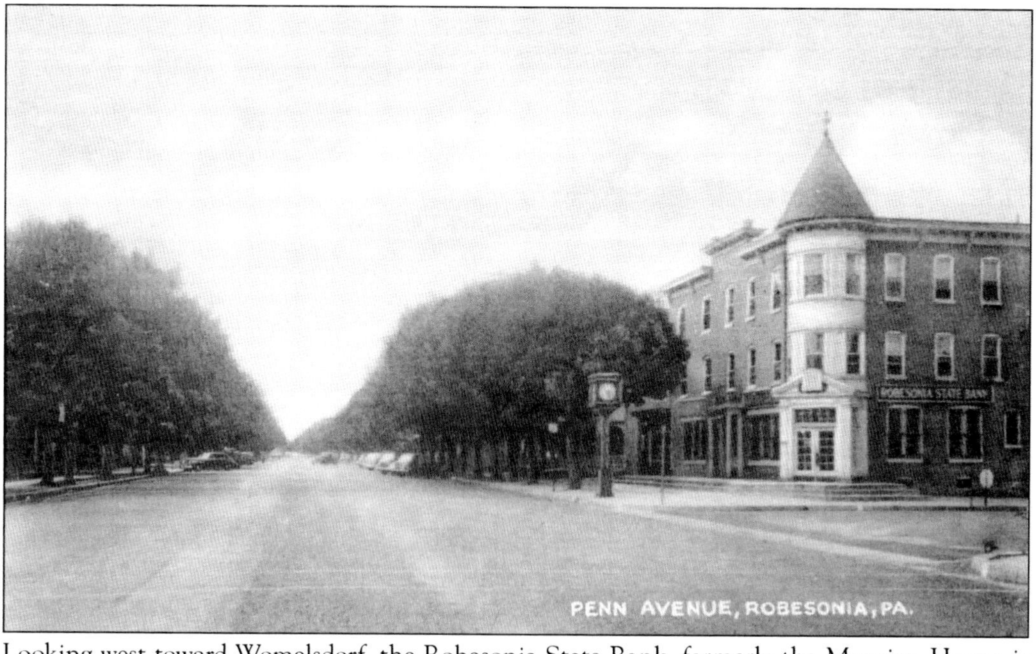

Looking west toward Womelsdorf, the Robesonia State Bank, formerly the Mansion House, is seen at right. Notice the wide streets and the cars parked diagonally along Penn Avenue and North Robeson Street. (Courtesy of Carl Reidler.)

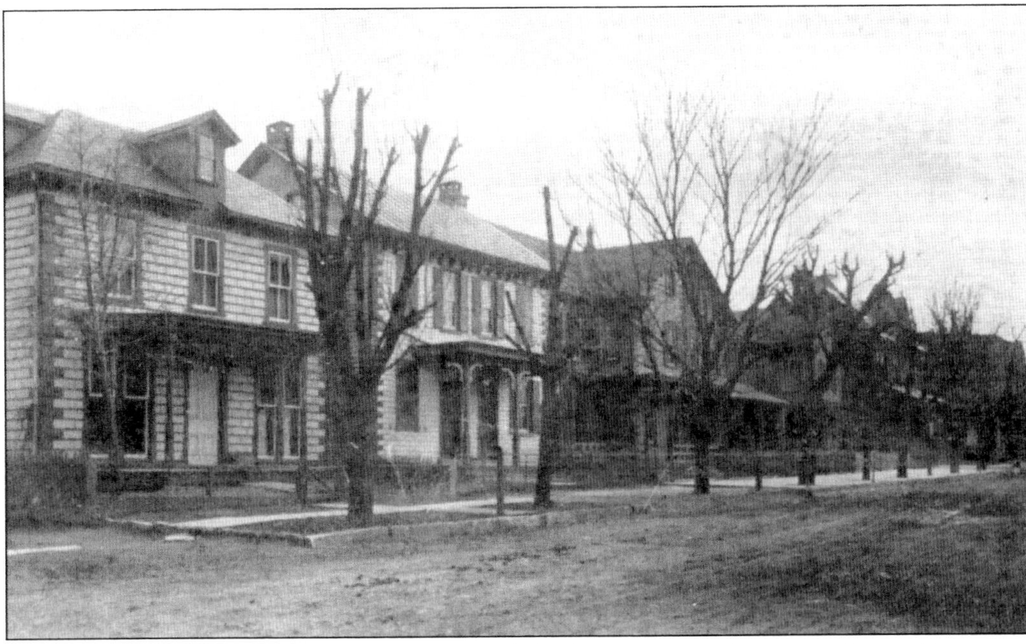

This c. 1915 view shows the homes on South Robeson Street, between Centre Street and Ruth Avenue, with dirt streets still intact. All these homes are still there today. (Courtesy of Carl Reidler.)

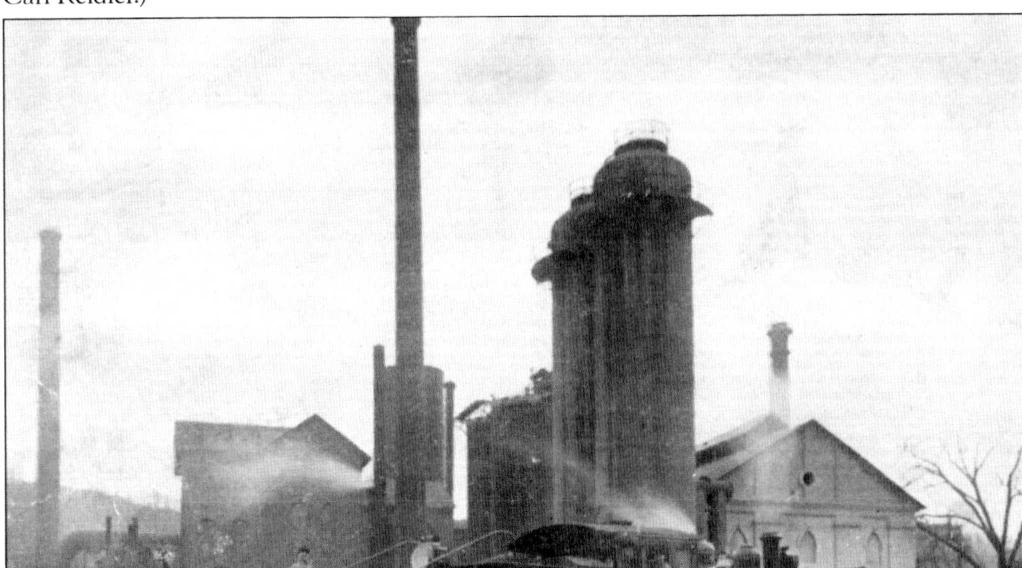

Pictured around 1900, the steam locomotive from the Robesonia Furnace (Robesonia Iron Works) stands in the vicinity of what is now the intersection of Freeman and Furnace Streets. (Courtesy of Carl Reidler.)

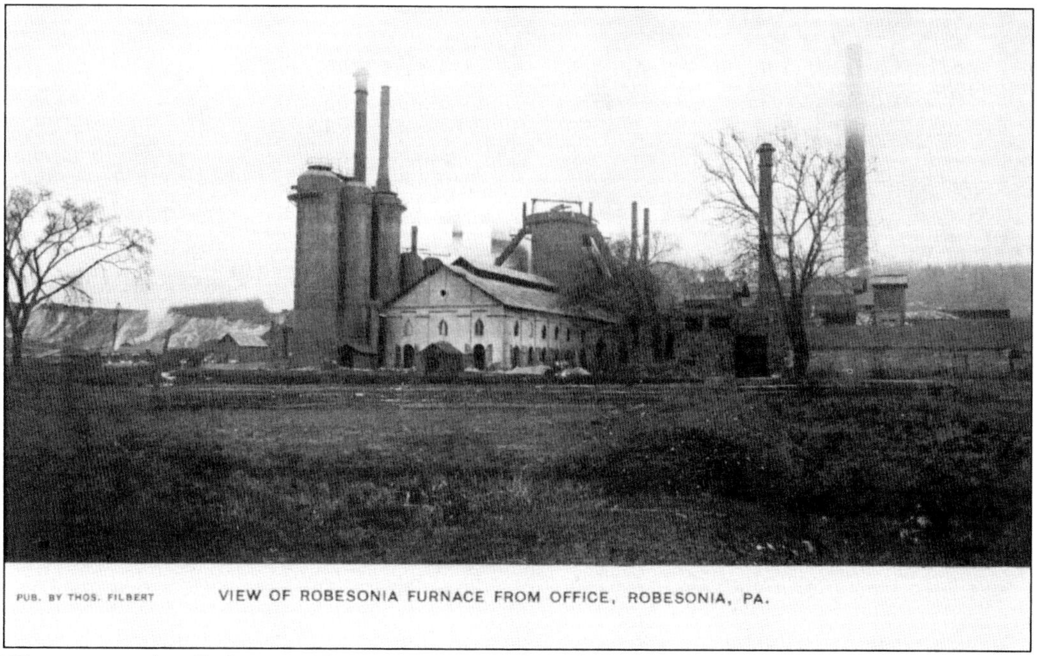

The once mighty Robesonia Furnace is captured in this view from the furnace office, which is across the street from the ironmaster's mansion. This furnace is why Robesonia exists today. Most of its infrastructure has been razed, along with a lot of history, but the Friends of the Furnace have displays on this site for educational purposes. (Courtesy of Carl Reidler.)

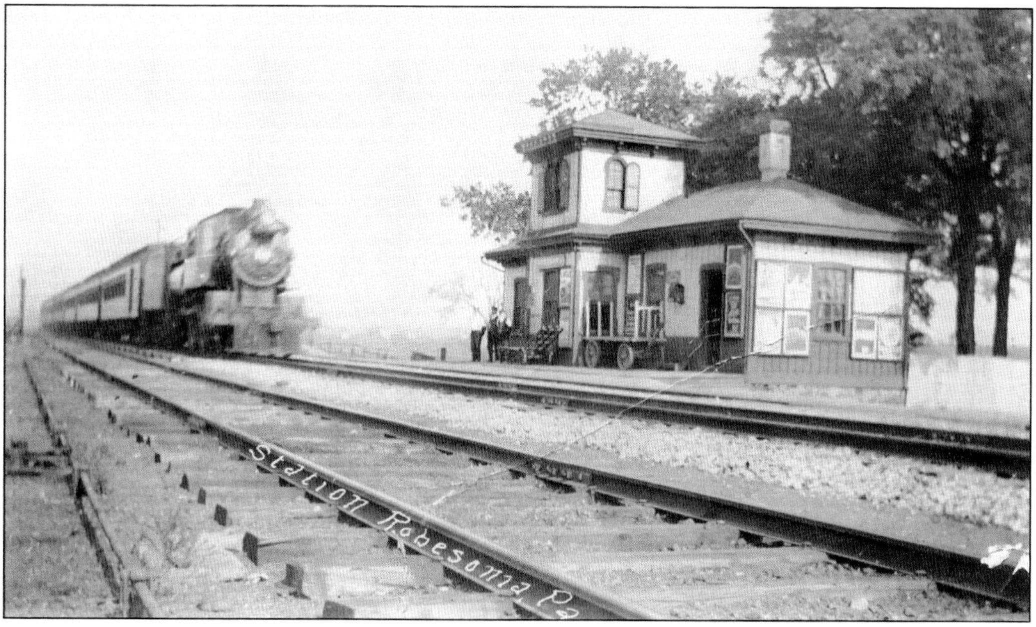

Coming from Wernersville, a locomotive arrives at the Robesonia train station in this postcard view from 1909. Closed in 1956, the station is no longer found at the end of South Robeson Street in Robesonia, but it can be visited at 211 Ninth Street in New Cumberland, Pennsylvania. It was disassembled, then rebuilt and converted into a hobby shop. (Courtesy of Carl Reidler.)

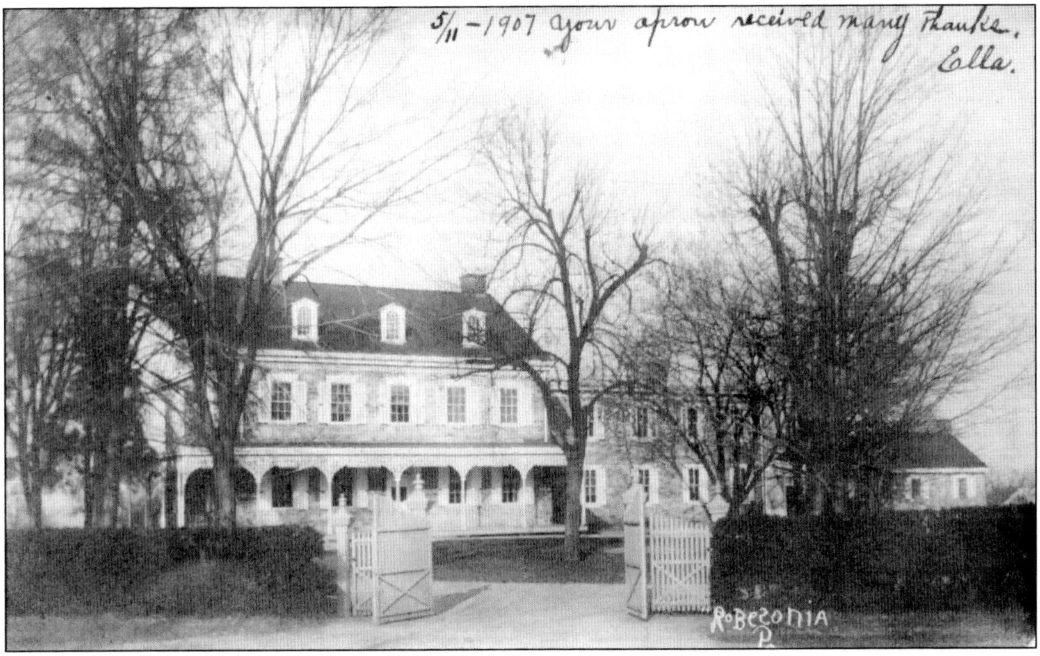

Seen here in 1911, the ironmaster's mansion on South Robeson Street at the southern end of Freeman Street still stands today, although slightly altered, as a testament to a business and art that once flourished in Robesonia. (Courtesy of Carl Reidler.)

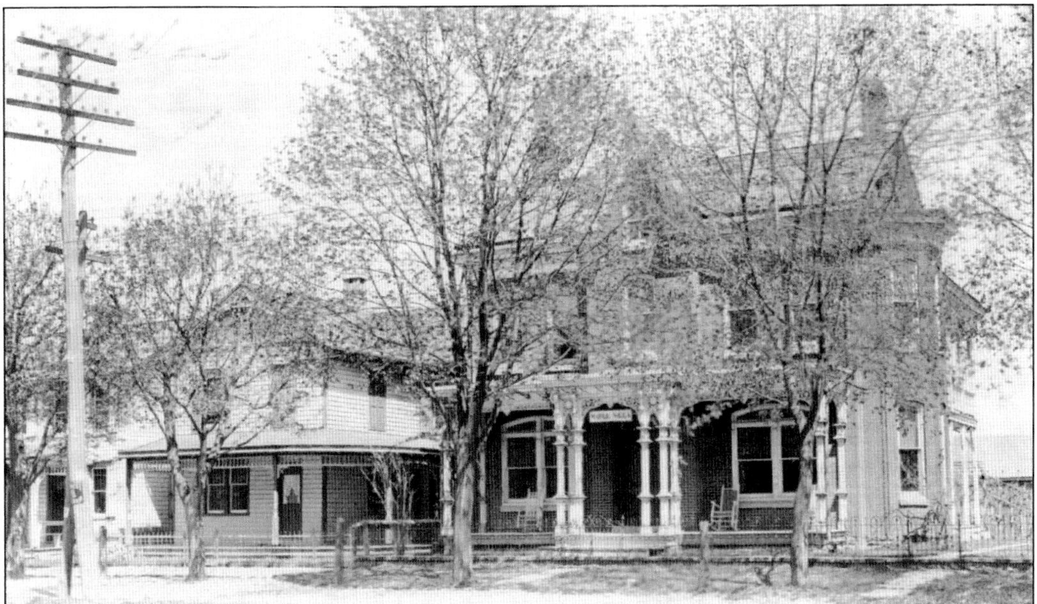

This is an image of some of South Robeson Street's older homes from back around 1900. (Courtesy of Carl Reidler.)

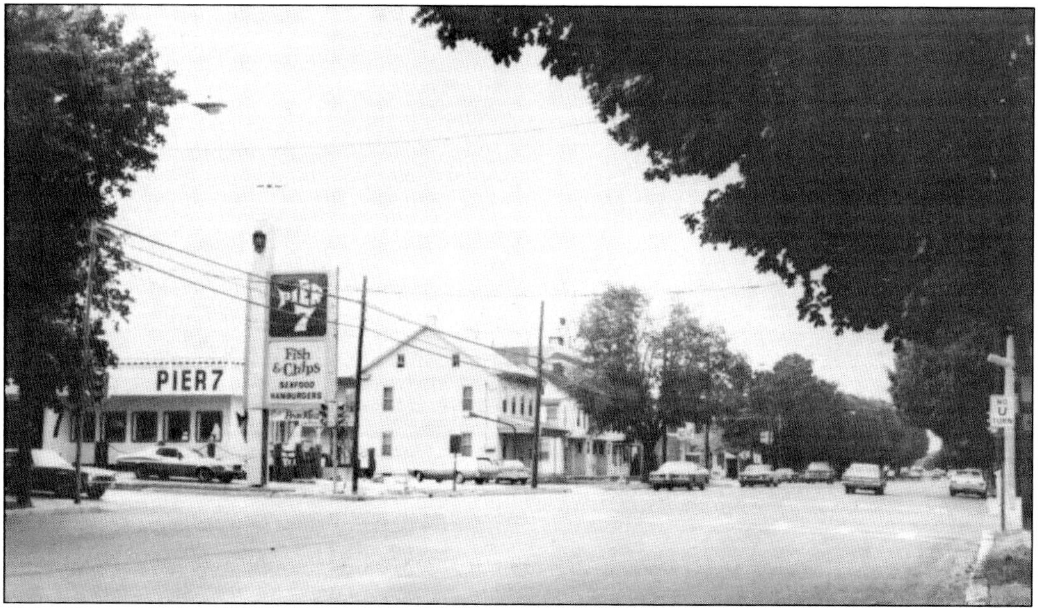

Pier 7 Fish & Chips at the corner of Penn Avenue and South Robeson Street is pictured around 1973. This lot was the former property of the Eagle Hotel. Though a popular spot, it only lasted until 1977, then was razed. (Courtesy of Carl Reidler.)

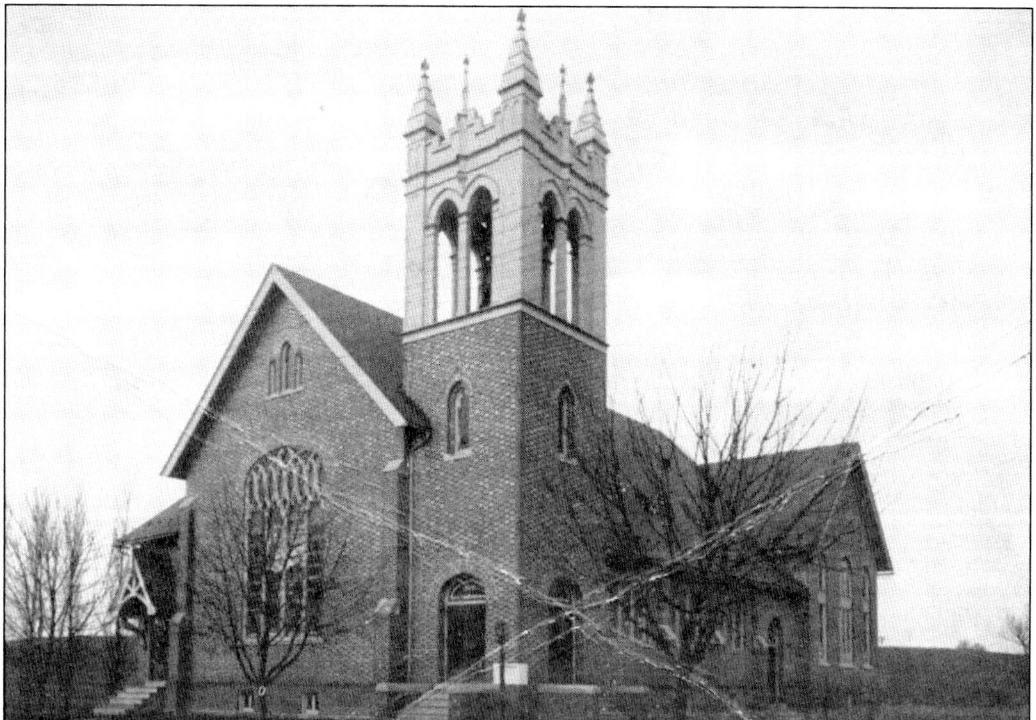

This view from the early 1900s shows St. Paul's Reformed Church on Penn Avenue. Notice there are no buildings around it yet. The church has been very active in its life; although membership has decreased, it is still a pillar of the community. (Courtesy of Carl Reidler.)

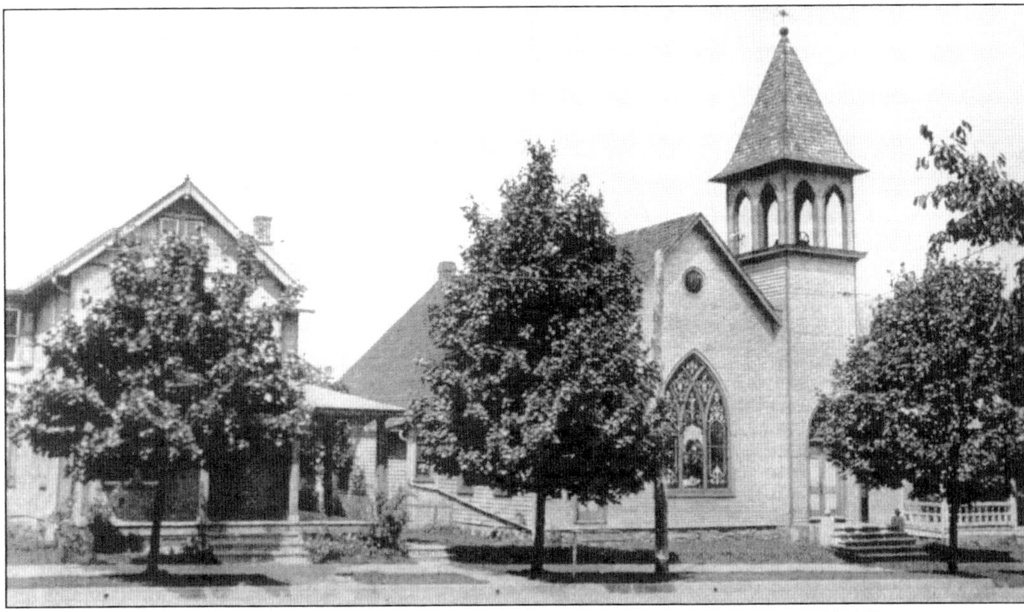

The former Bethany Evangelical Church was built on West Penn Avenue in 1902. The congregation disbanded in 1958 due to poor attendance. The building was later razed around 1960. (Courtesy of Carl Reidler.)

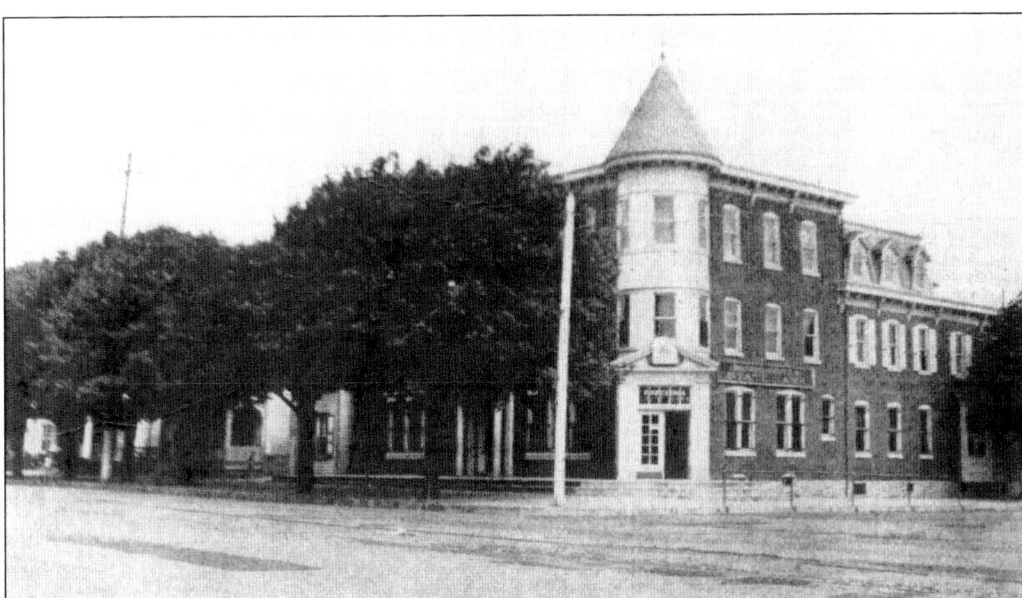

The Robesonia State Bank, with the attached post office, is seen here in 1945. Formerly the Mansion House, this building stood at the northwest corner of Penn Avenue and North Robeson Street. (Courtesy of Carl Reidler.)

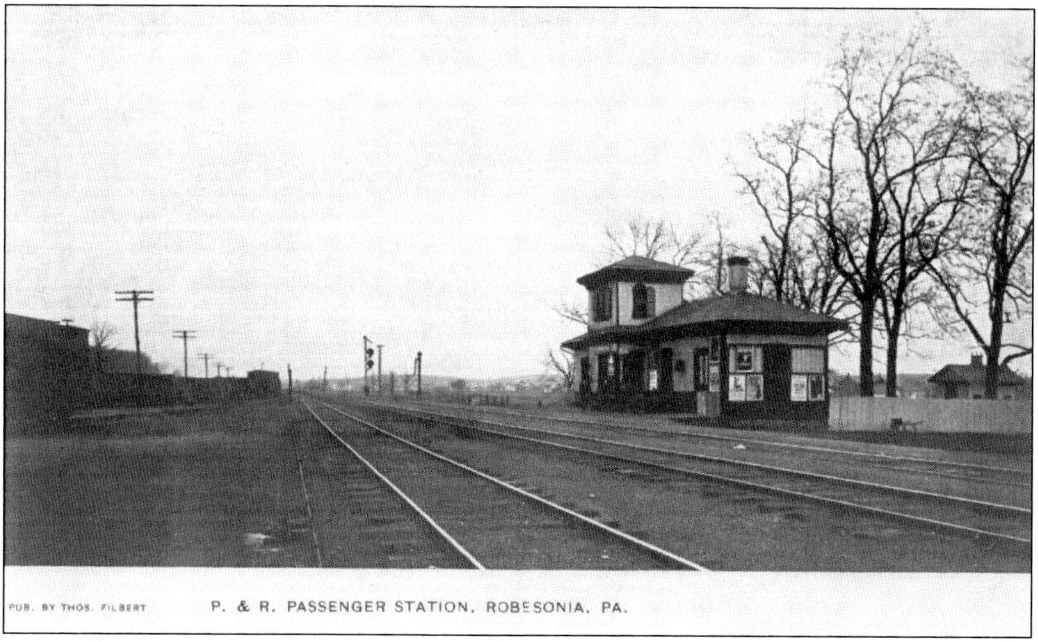

Pictured here in 1907 is another view of the Pennsylvania & Reading Railroad passenger station in Robesonia. To the right, out of view, were two large wooden water towers used to replenish the water tanks of the steam locomotives. (Courtesy of Carl Ganster.)

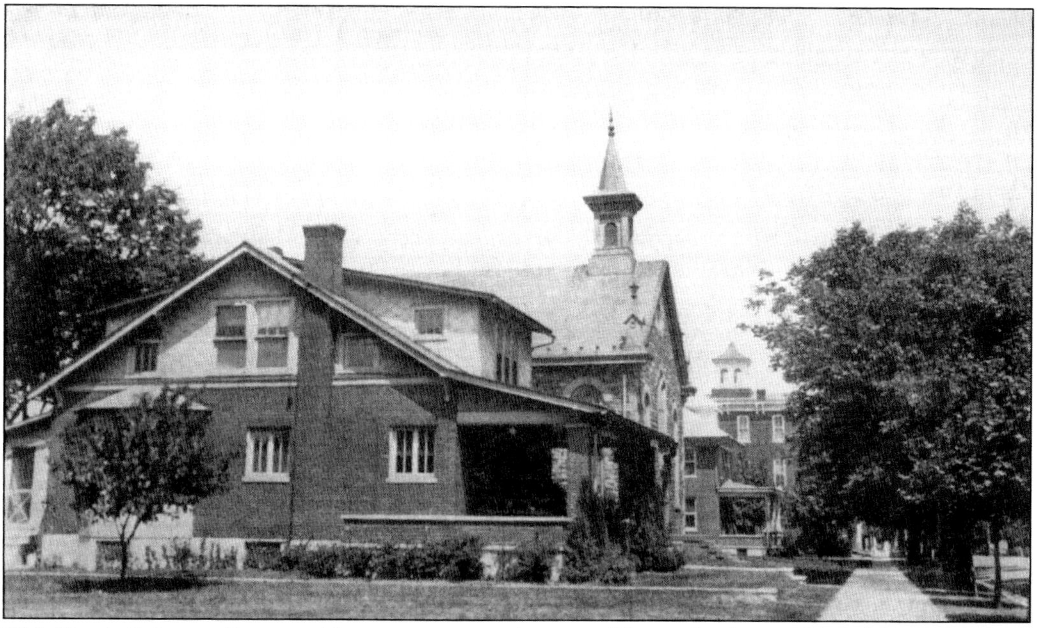

This South Robeson Street residence was situated next to Trinity Lutheran Church in Robesonia. Gerhart's Store, with its cupola on top, is visible down the street. This house was typical of those on Ruth Avenue, one of which was the home of author Carl Reidler for 25 years. (Courtesy of Carl Reidler.)

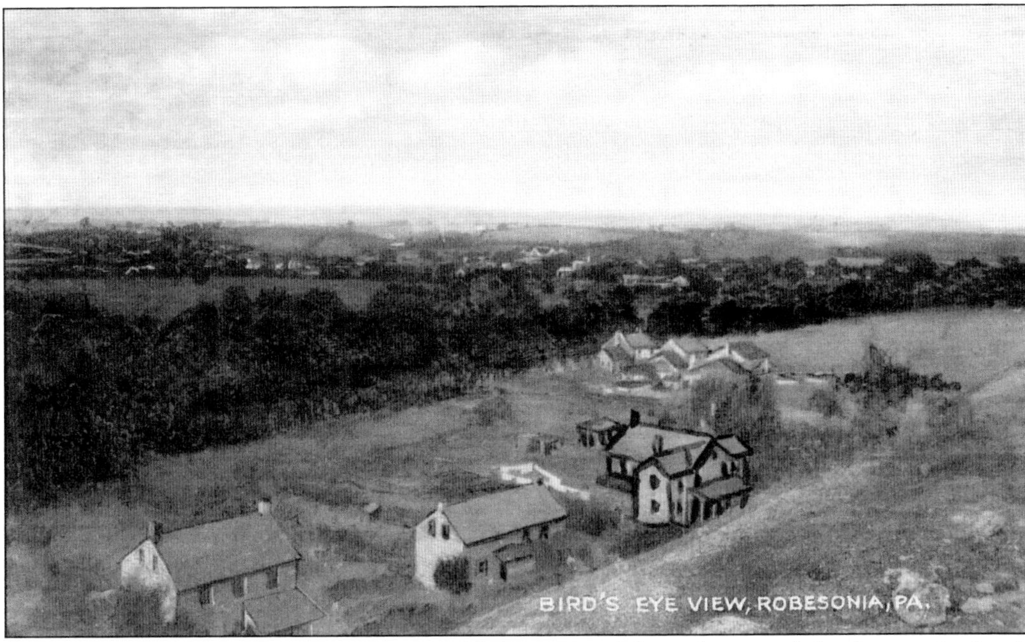

This view from the early 1900s was most likely captured from the top of the former slag bank, looking northwest. It shows some of the homes on Freeman Street and East Meadow Avenue, most of which are still standing. (Courtesy of Carl Reidler.)

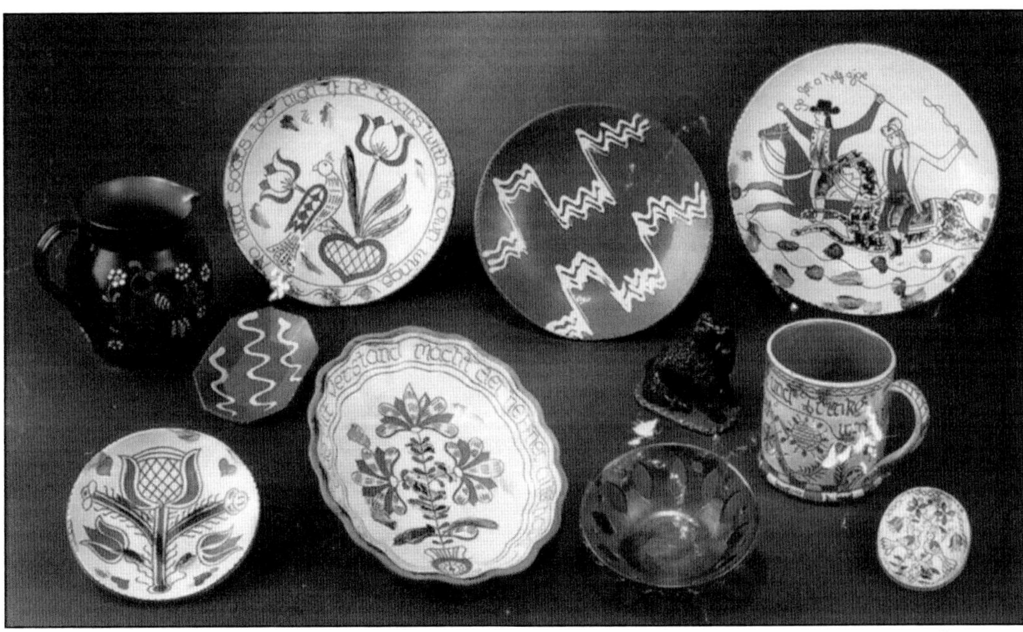

This postcard says it all for those from Robesonia or familiar with the area. Known as "the Porch Potter," Lester Breininger held an annual porch show in which he displayed and sold his award-winning Pennsylvania German redware pottery. Breininger's legacy and his many contributions to the area are pivotal to the history of Robesonia. (Courtesy of Carl Reidler.)

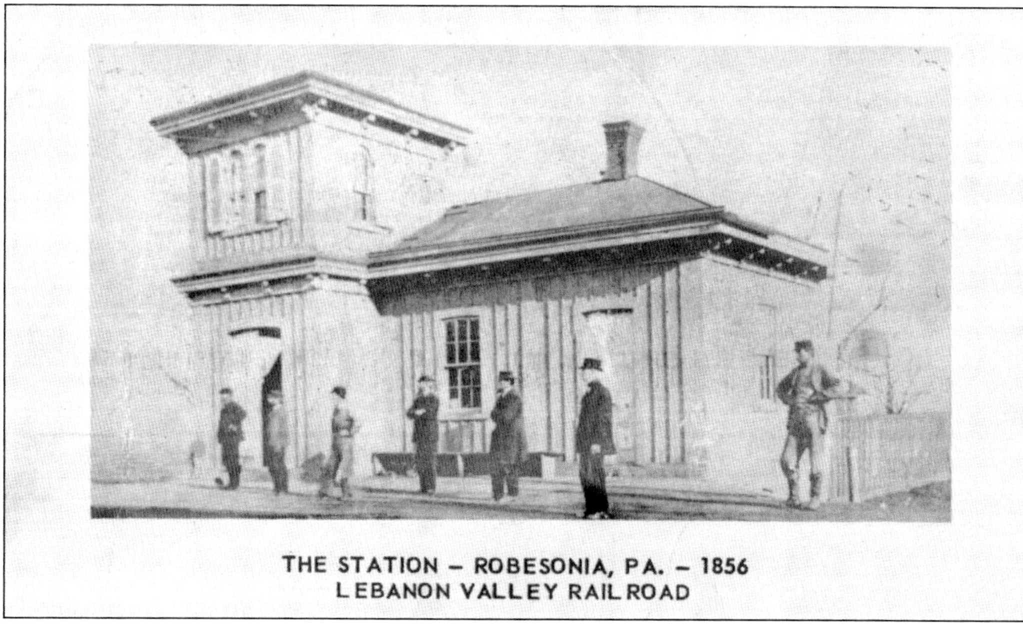

This is an 1856 postcard from an early version of the Lebanon Valley Railroad station in Robesonia. It is the same station featured on page 80, but that image displays additions and modifications made at a later date. (Courtesy of Carl Reidler.)

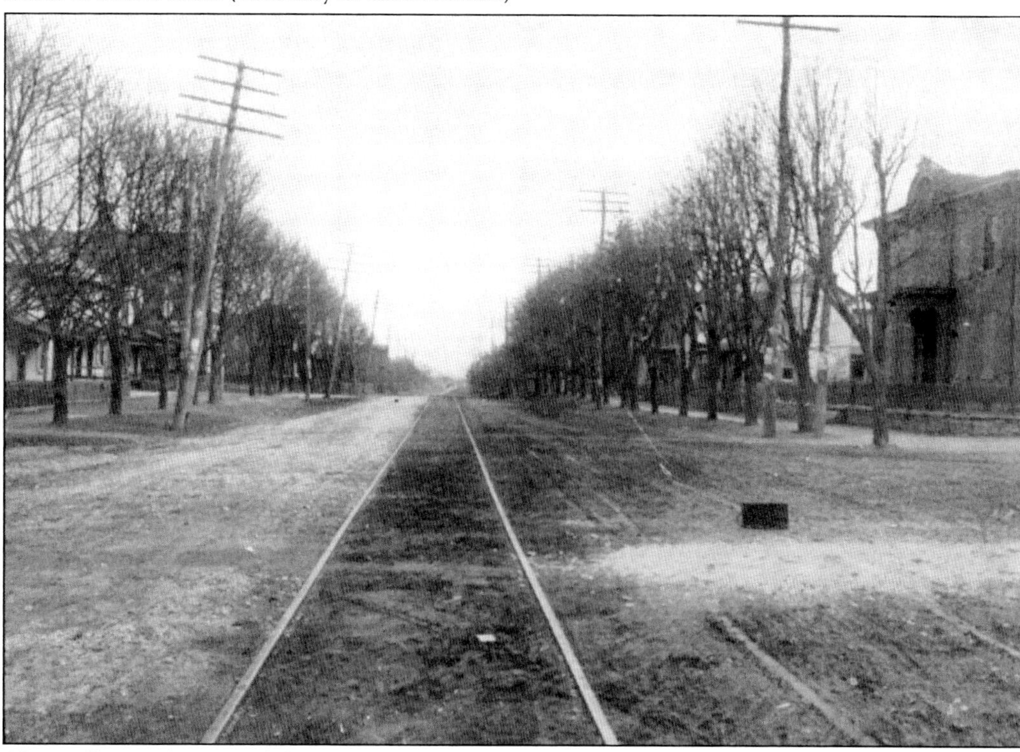

The trolley tracks extend through town in this photograph of Centre Street, looking east toward Wernersville. What was formerly Kalbach's apartment building on the right side, with the cupola on top, still stands today. (Courtesy of Ryan A. Zerbe.)

The former public school of Robesonia, built in 1916, still stands today as apartments. It served as the administration building of the Conrad Weiser School District for a few years and as the Robesonia Elementary School from 1955 to 1970. Before that it housed grades one through twelve. (Courtesy of Ryan A. Zerbe.)

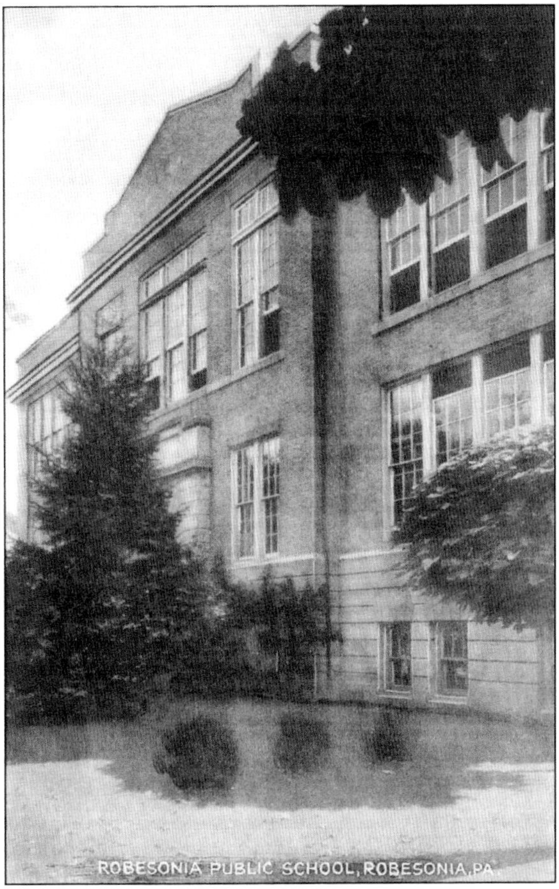

During this time period around 1910, many furnace buildings were massive in size, as evidenced by this rare view of the interior of the furnace cast house. (Courtesy of Ryan A. Zerbe)

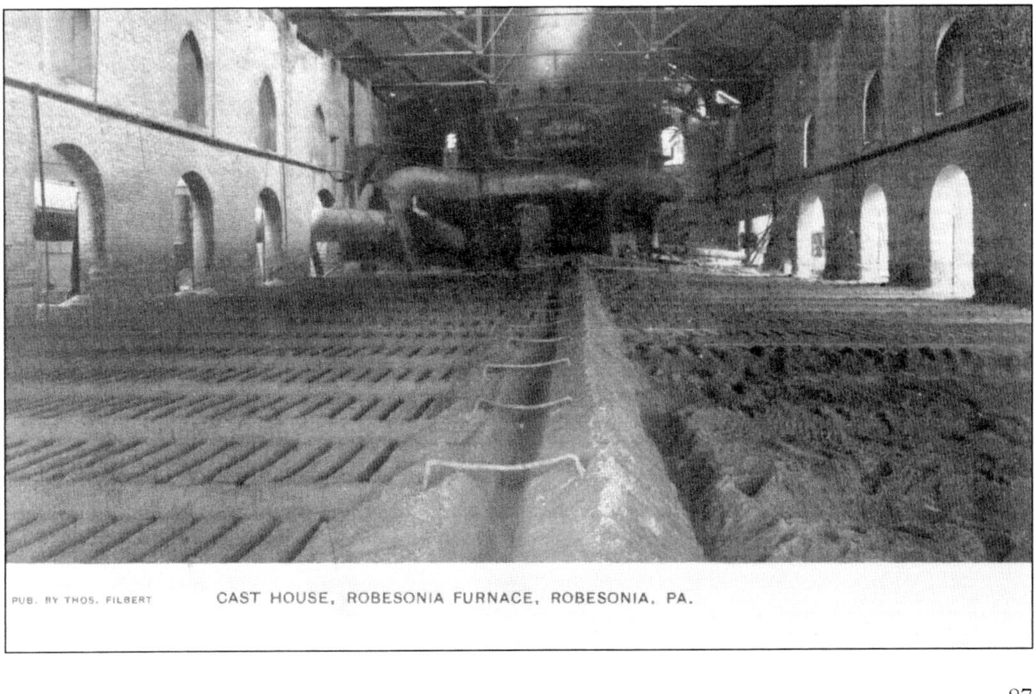

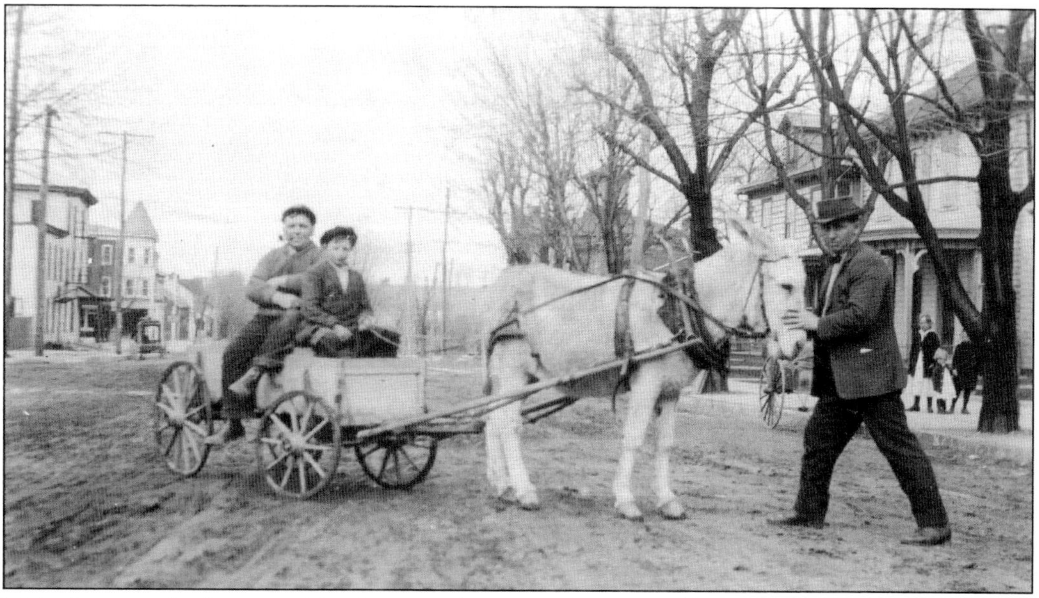

This photograph of a man with a horse and two people in a small wagon, likely a Gruber wagon, was taken in front of what is now the Pioneer Fire Company. The Mansion House is visible on the left, down the street. (Courtesy of Ryan A. Zerbe.)

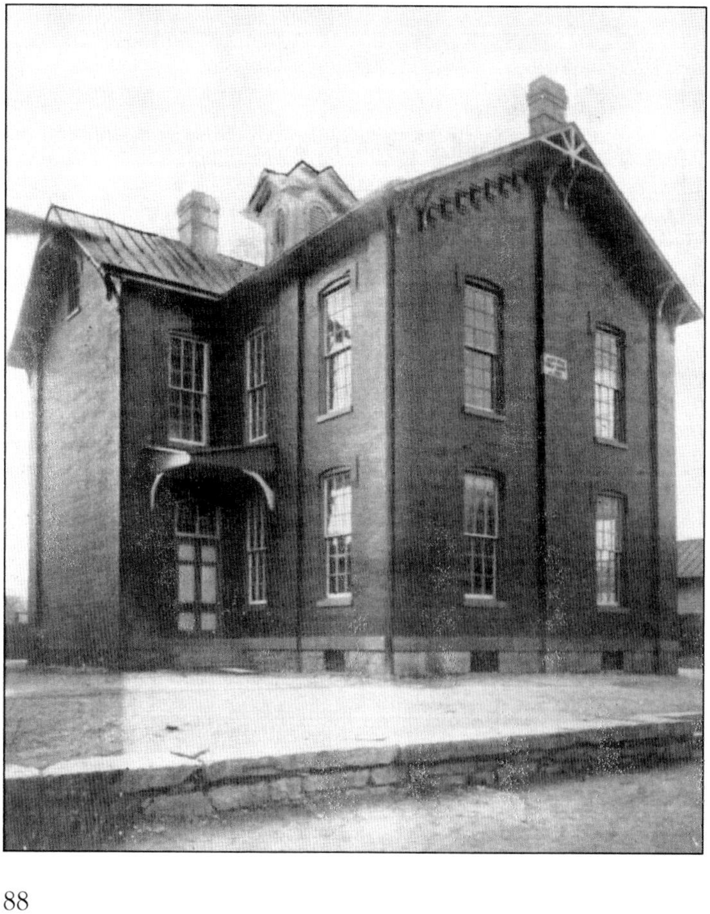

The second public school in Robesonia was located at 200 West Penn Avenue in the village. It is no longer there today. (Courtesy of Ryan A. Zerbe.)

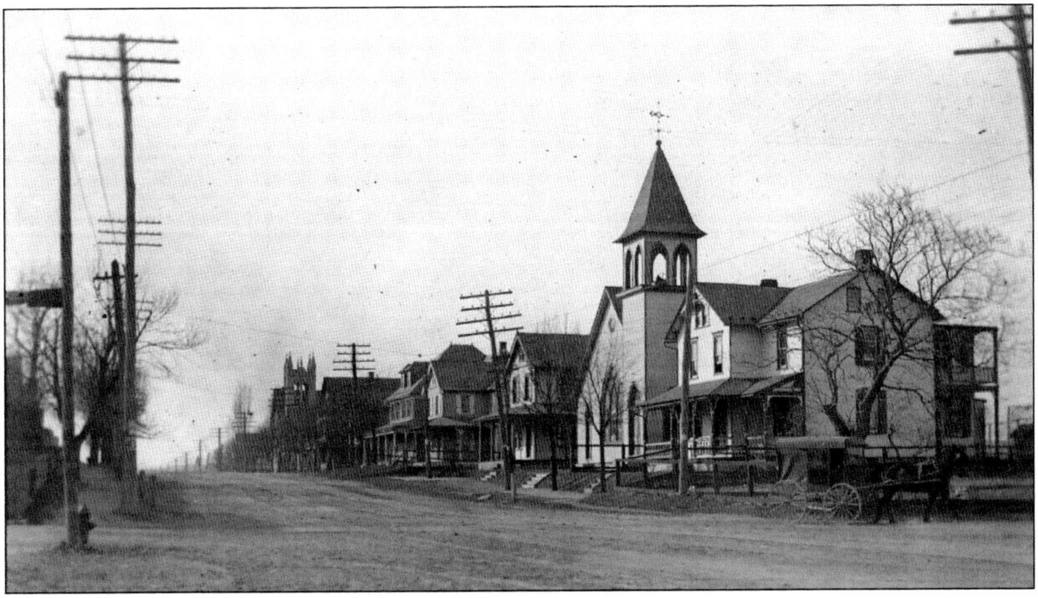

Bethany Evangelical Church, seen here at the intersection of Penn Avenue and Church Street, was razed in 1958. The church in the distance is St. Paul's United Church of Christ, which is still there today. (Courtesy of Ryan A. Zerbe.)

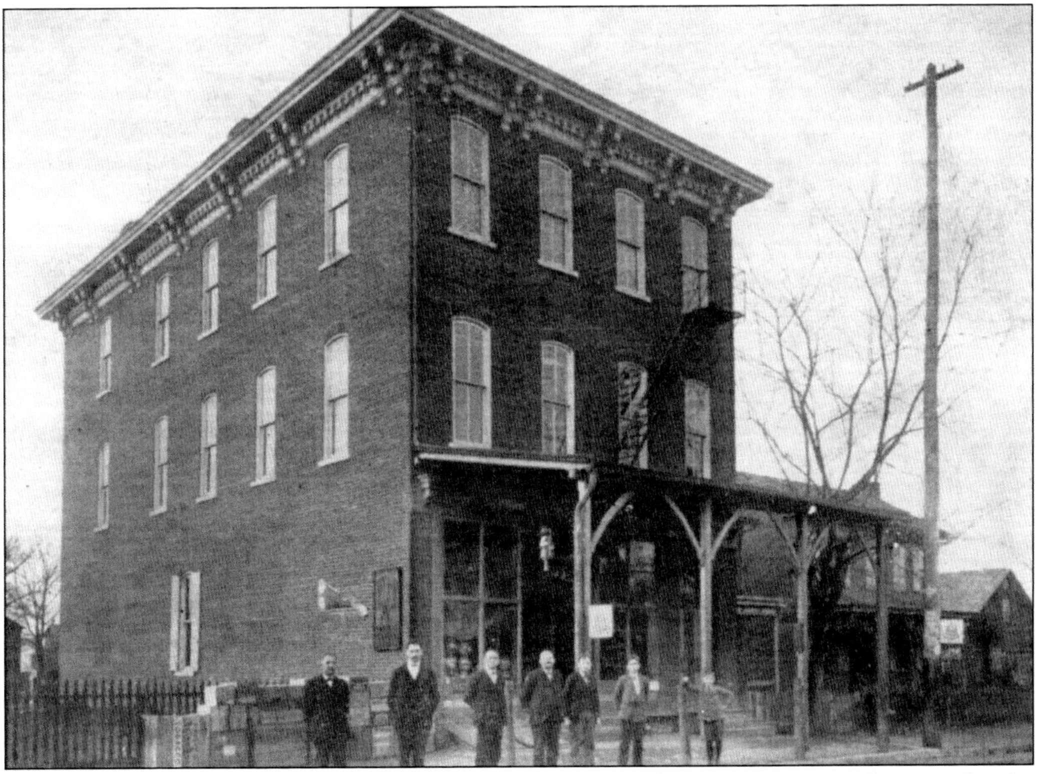

This view shows the general store of Gerhart and Moyer. In later years, it was taken over by the Henry family as a small grocery and meat store. Today, it still stands as the current home of Mike Henry. (Courtesy of Ryan A. Zerbe.)

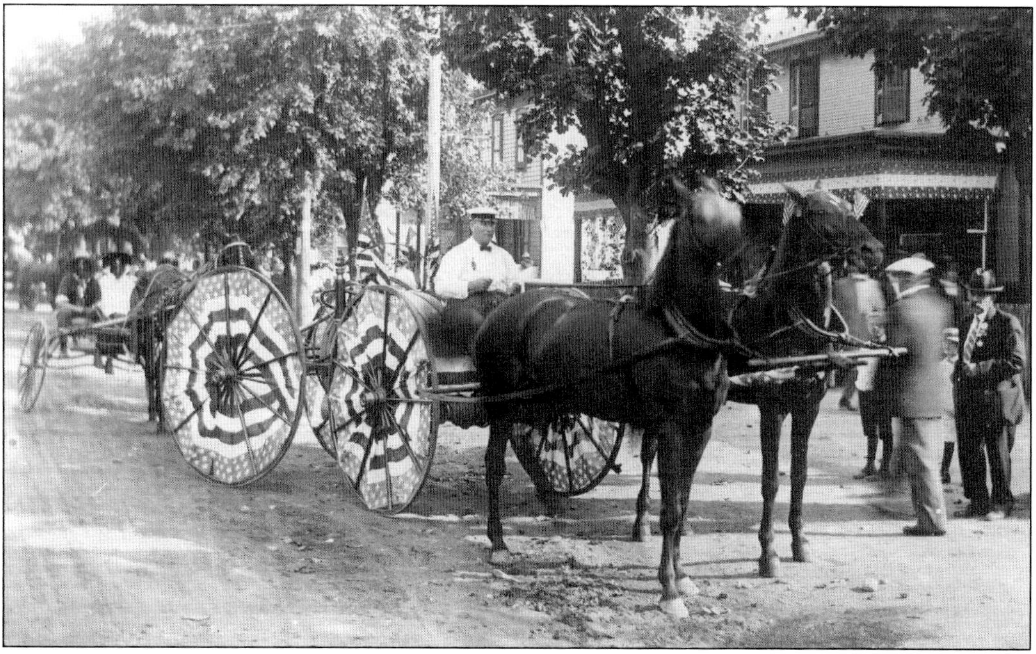

The Pioneer Hose Company has decorated their horse-drawn firefighting apparatus for what appears to be a holiday parade. The fire department is still in possession of this antique today. (Courtesy of Ryan A. Zerbe.)

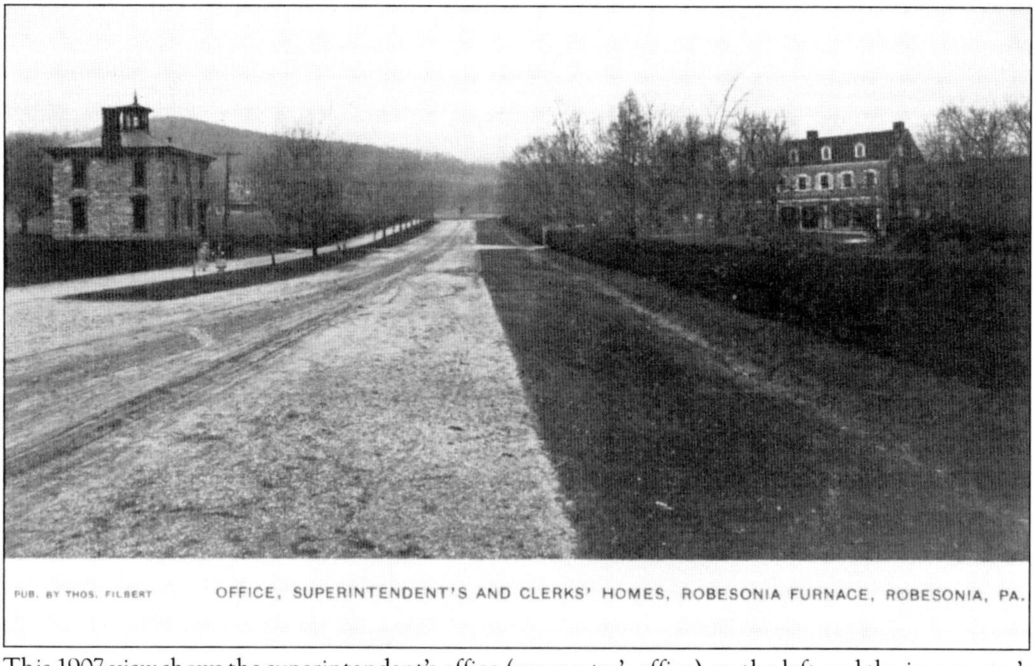

This 1907 view shows the superintendent's office (paymaster's office) on the left and the ironmaster's mansion on the right. Notice the dirt street and neatly manicured landscaping. The mansion is now a private residence, and the paymaster's office is owned by the estate of the late Lester Breininger Jr. It is the current home of Camp 113 of the POS of A. (Courtesy of Carl Reidler.)

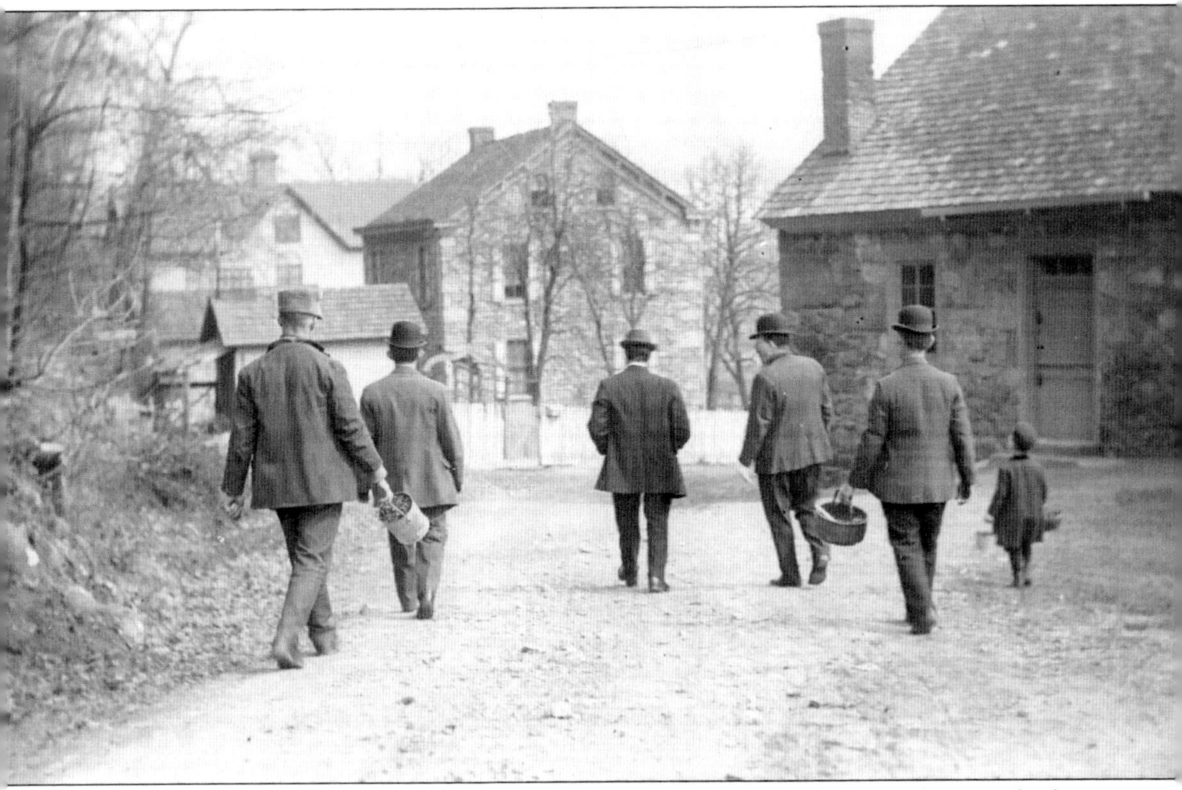

Here, furnace workers are probably headed to work with their lunch pails. It is unknown whether the little boy worked or was off to the Furnace Schoolhouse. (Courtesy of Ryan A. Zerbe.)

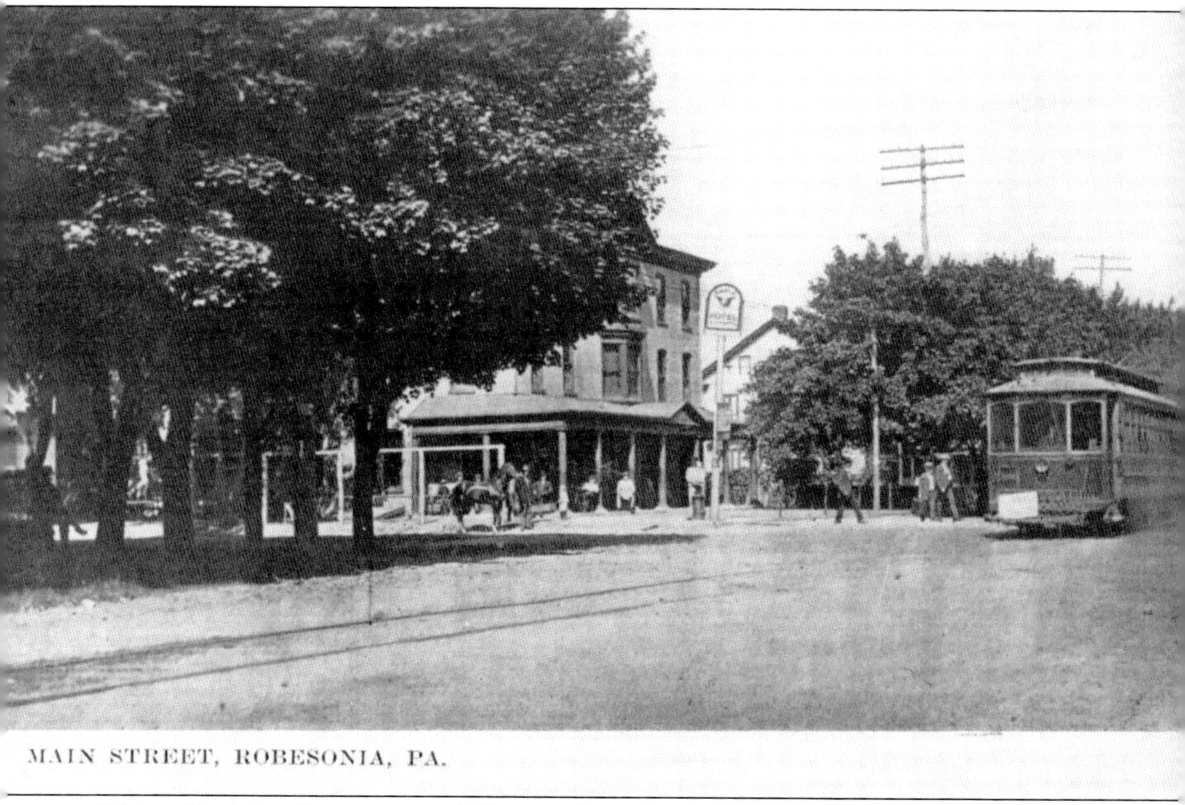

This trolley is heading east toward Wernersville at the intersection of Penn Avenue and Robeson Street. The Eagle Hotel sits to the left. (Courtesy of Ryan A. Zerbe.)

Six

Wernersville Borough

Wernersville, like South Heidelberg, was first inhabited by the Lenni-Lenape Indians. Artifacts found at Saddlebrook One, Elm View Court, and the old Reber farm on Lincoln Drive have proven they lived here long before the settlers, who came to the area in the late 1700s. Wernersville grew by leaps and bounds because of the mountain resorts and the train station that brought people to those resorts.

Also like South Heidelberg, Wernersville was carved out of Lower Heidelberg Township. On January 13, 1914, Wernersville was no longer a village, but a borough. The founder William Werner laid out the town with George Wertz, who was a very influential businessman. Wertz sold his original mill to help pave the way for the state psychiatric hospital. He built a new mill on Werner Street, formed both the Wernersville Electric and Wernersville Water Companies, and served on the board of the Wernersville National Bank and the borough's school board. This town easily could have been named Wertzville for all his accomplishments and improvements to the area.

Over the years, many small shops and businesses opened. Most notable were the car dealers in town, as they provided much revenue and employment. Local businesses kept the town strong despite the decline of the mountain resorts and the closure of the train station. Today, the car dealers are all but gone, as are Briner's Grocery Store, Wernersville Dry Cleaners, Charlie's Pastry Shop, Wernersville Hardware, both the M.E. Witman and Worley Lumber Companies, and many other small shops. The future for Wernersville could be in limbo, but only time will tell. The town has provided pleasant living for years, and it still has some good places left. The Penn Werner is still a fine place to dine, pizza places abound, and some new shops are trying to make a go of it. The borough's current population is 2,494.

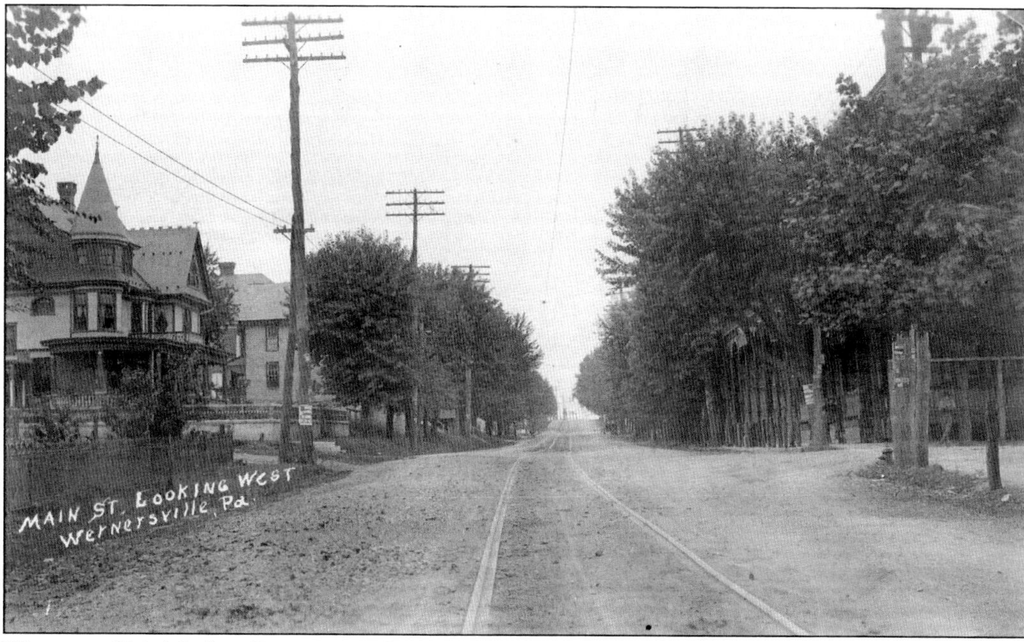

Wernersville's Market Street, now Penn Avenue, or Route 422, is pictured here around 1910. On the right, behind the trees, is the Lebanon Valley House. The building across the street is now a private residence, but it once served as the borough hall and library. (Courtesy of Carl Reidler.)

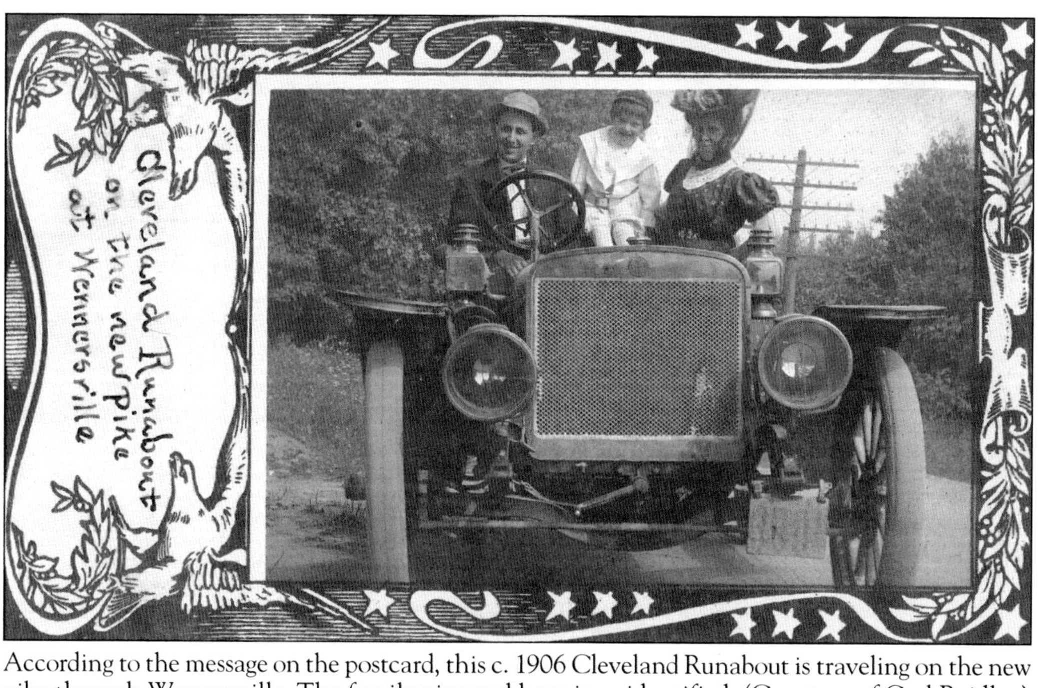

According to the message on the postcard, this c. 1906 Cleveland Runabout is traveling on the new pike through Wernersville. The family pictured here is unidentified. (Courtesy of Carl Reidler.)

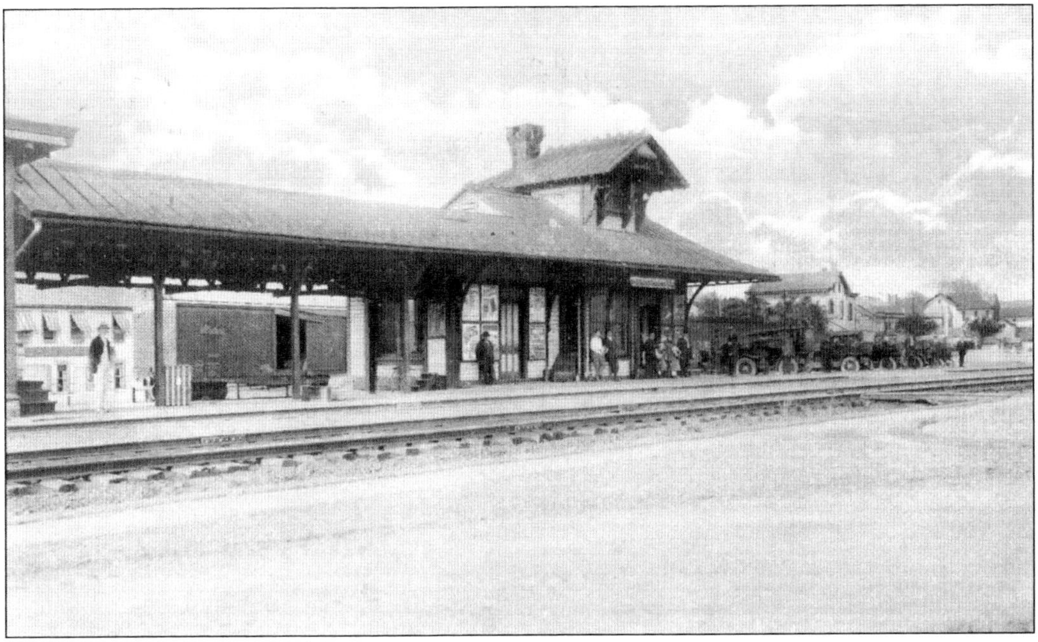

Pictured here in 1922 is Wernersville's wooden train station on the Pennsylvania & Reading Railroad line. Notice there is a rail siding on the north side of the station, where the cars for local deliveries were placed. The building with awnings seen at left is the Wernersville National Bank. (Courtesy of Carl Reidler.)

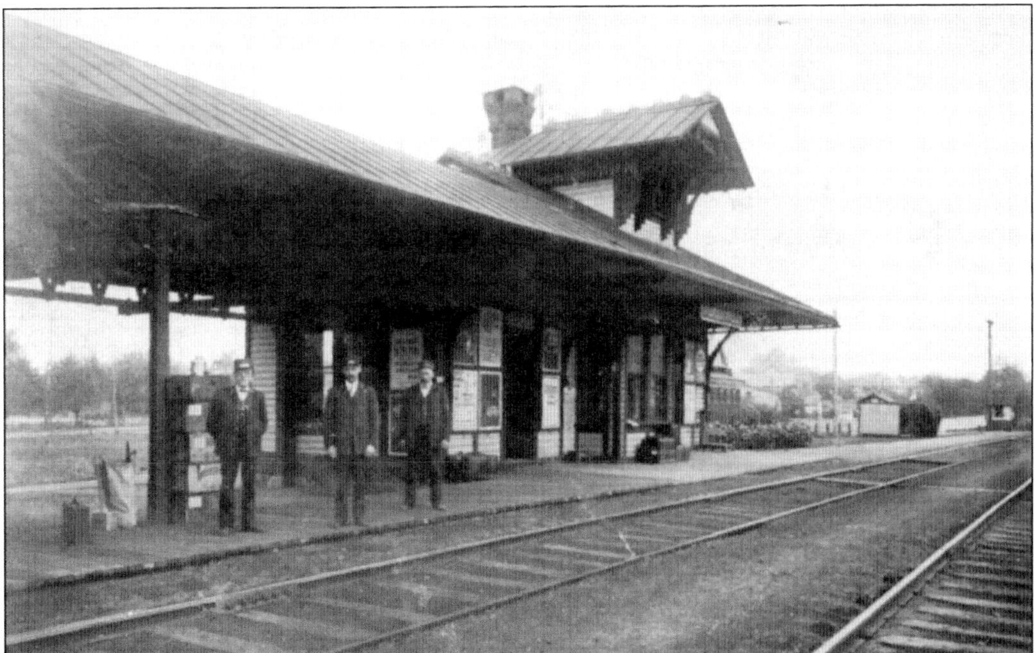

Here is another view of the wooden station in Wernersville, along with the ticket agent and baggage clerks. In 1907, the date of this image, the rail was just steps from the platform. (Courtesy of Carl Reidler.)

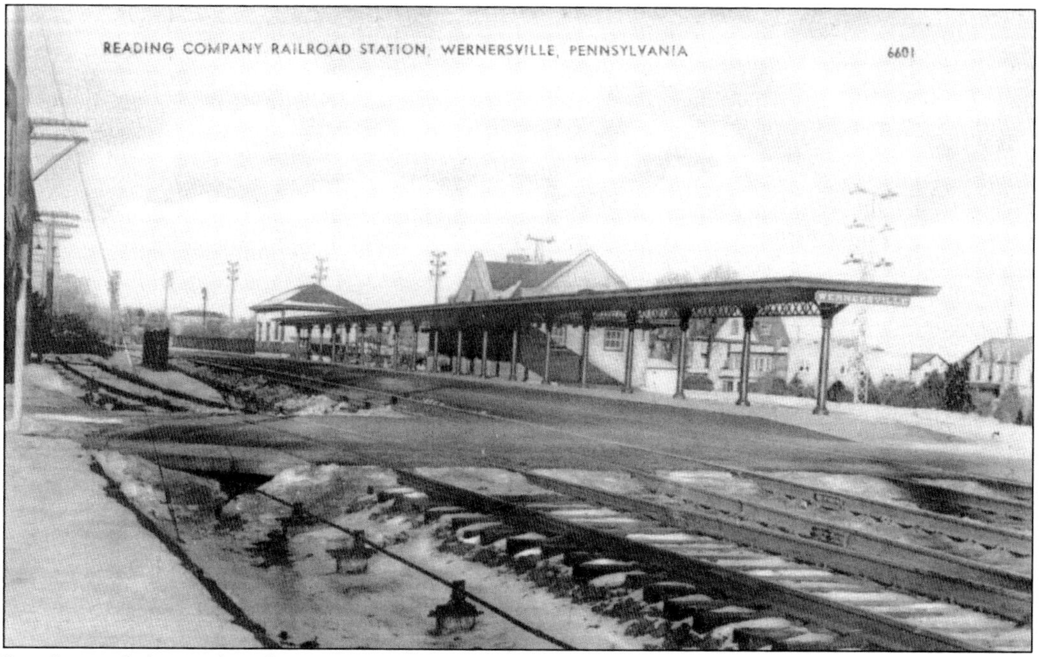

Just beyond this railroad crossing at Werner Street is the newly constructed stone station in Wernersville, pictured here in 1928. (Courtesy of Carl Reidler.)

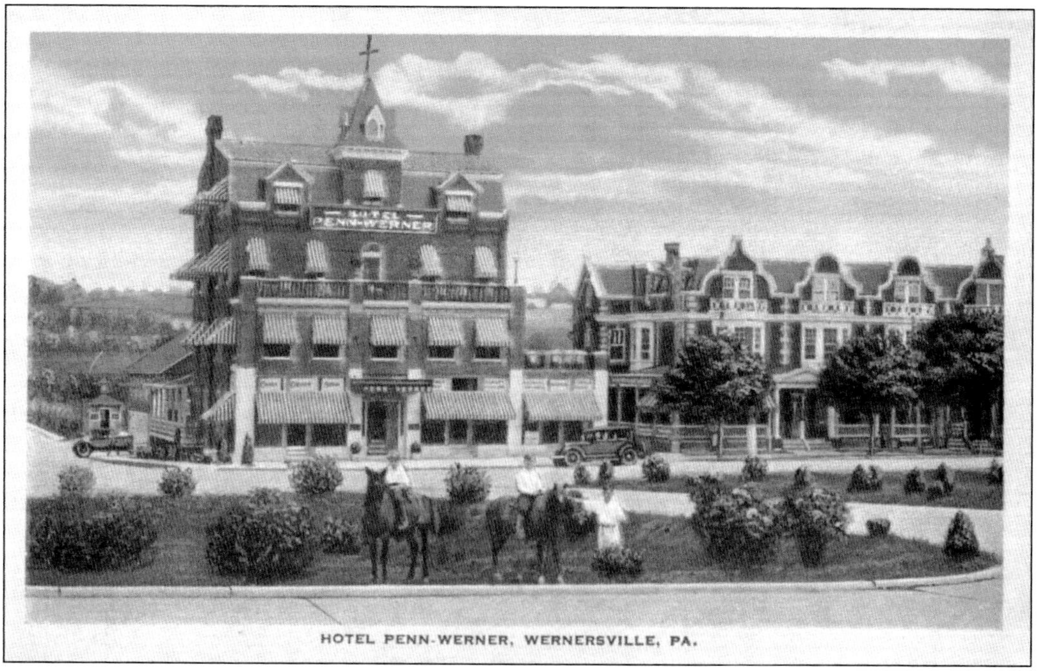

The Penn Werner Hotel on Market Street, pictured on this postcard from the late 1920s to early 1930s, was located across the park from the railroad station. Note the classic striped awnings on the hotel. The back of the postcard advertises a full-course meal for $1 to $1.50 and sandwiches for 50¢. (Courtesy of Carl Reidler.)

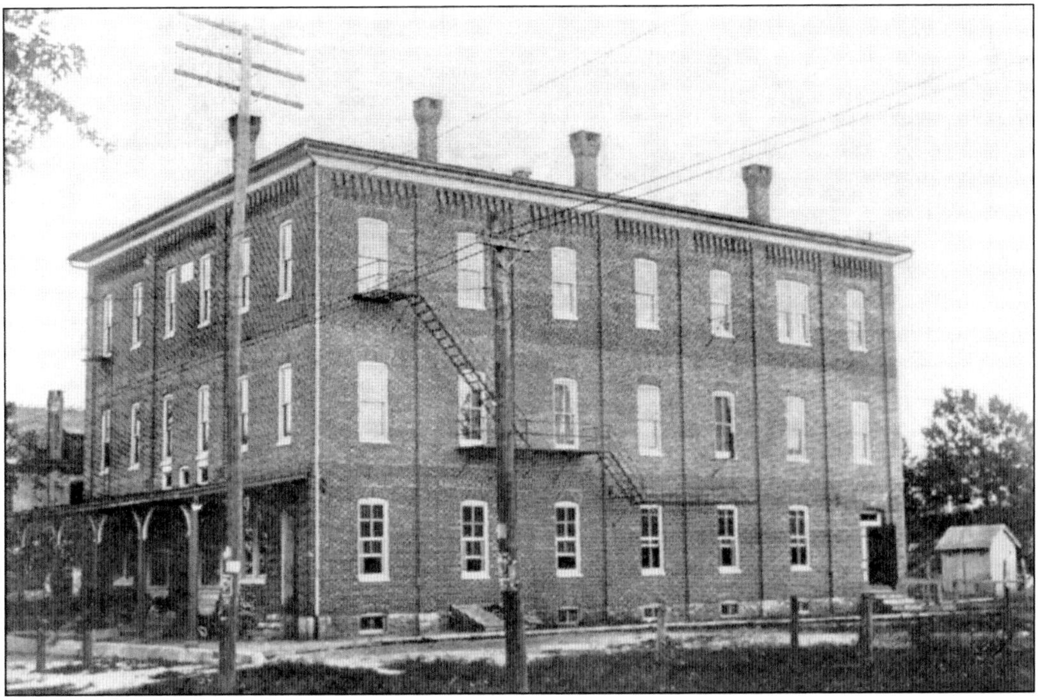

The lodge hall and auditorium was also located on Market Street. Over the years, this building has served as a town hall and meeting place for groups like the POS of A and Knights of Pythias, among others. It also housed a bar and restaurant called the Brass Rail. Later, the VFW took over the first floor, the second floor became a venue for wedding receptions and parties, and the third floor remained a lodge hall. The VFW closed around 1996, and it was sold. Today, the building is divided into apartments. (Courtesy of Carl Reidler.)

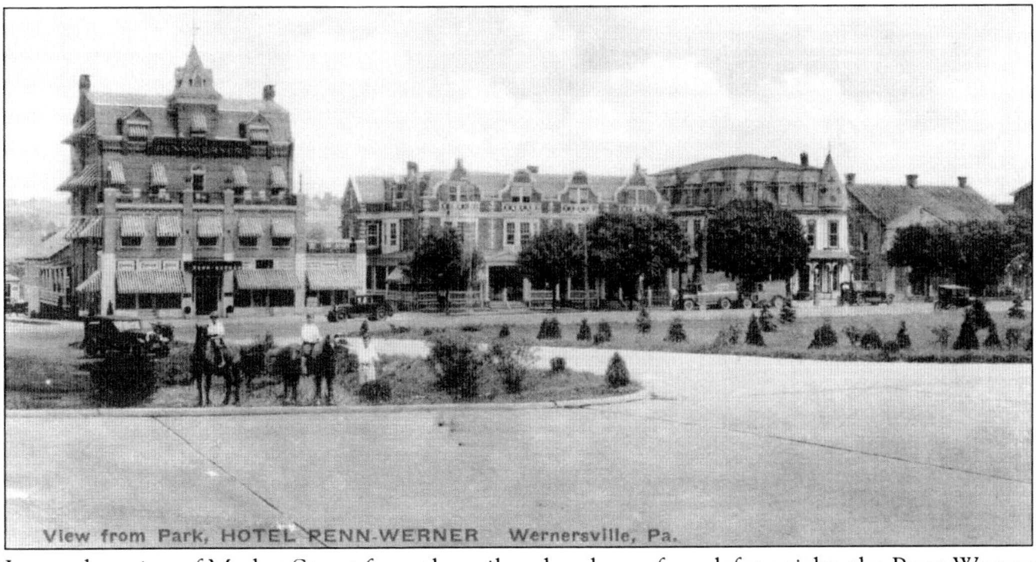

In another view of Market Street from the railroad park are, from left to right, the Penn Werner Hotel, a row of homes, an unidentified building, and the Wernersville National Bank. It appears the men on the donkeys posed for several photographs taken from this location. The Penn Werner boasted a billiard parlor, barbershop, tailor, drugstore, and bar. (Courtesy of Carl Reidler.)

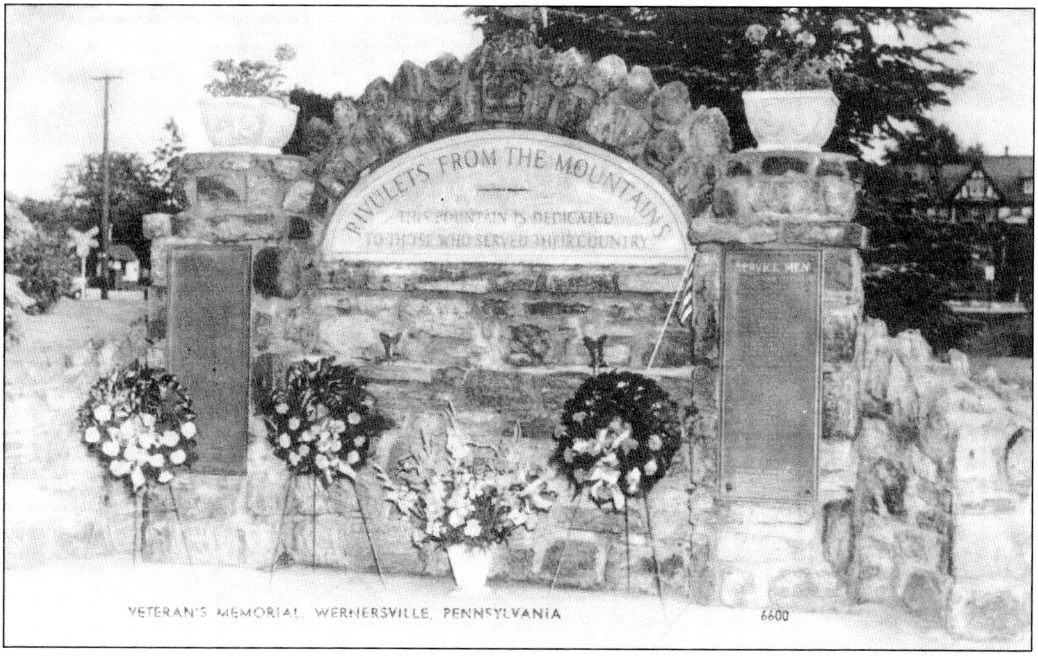

The Veterans Memorial was originally part of railroad park. This site was its home until the early 2000s, when Hoover Motors requested that it be moved and helped pay for its relocation. It is now located on Stitzer Avenue, in front of the former Citizens Hose Fire Company. (Courtesy of Carl Reidler.)

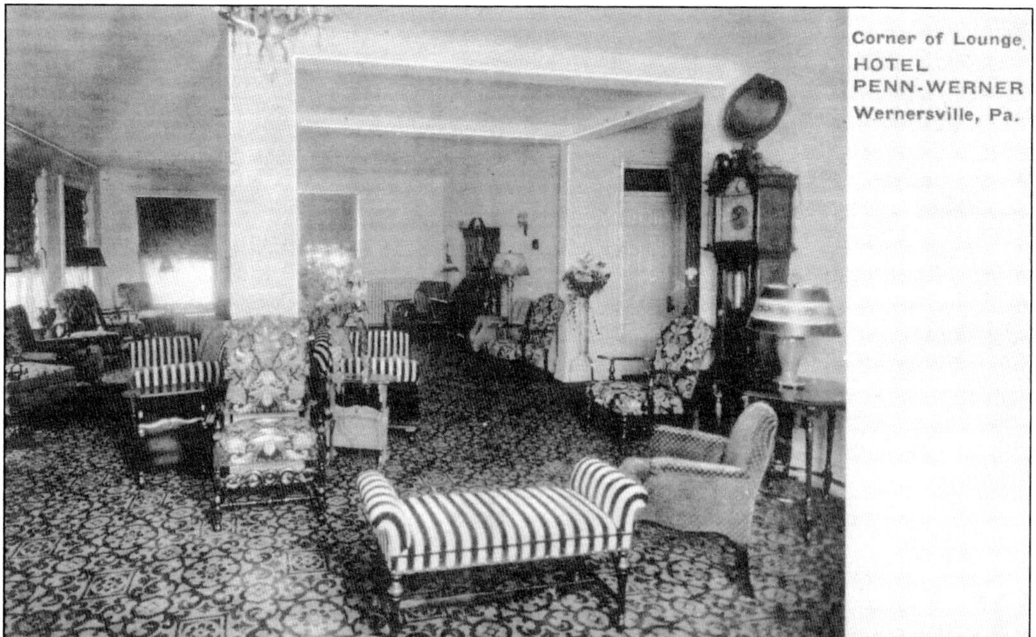

This is a postcard of the lounge, or day room, on the third floor of the Penn Werner Hotel. It was a pleasant setting for that time period. (Courtesy of Carl Reidler.)

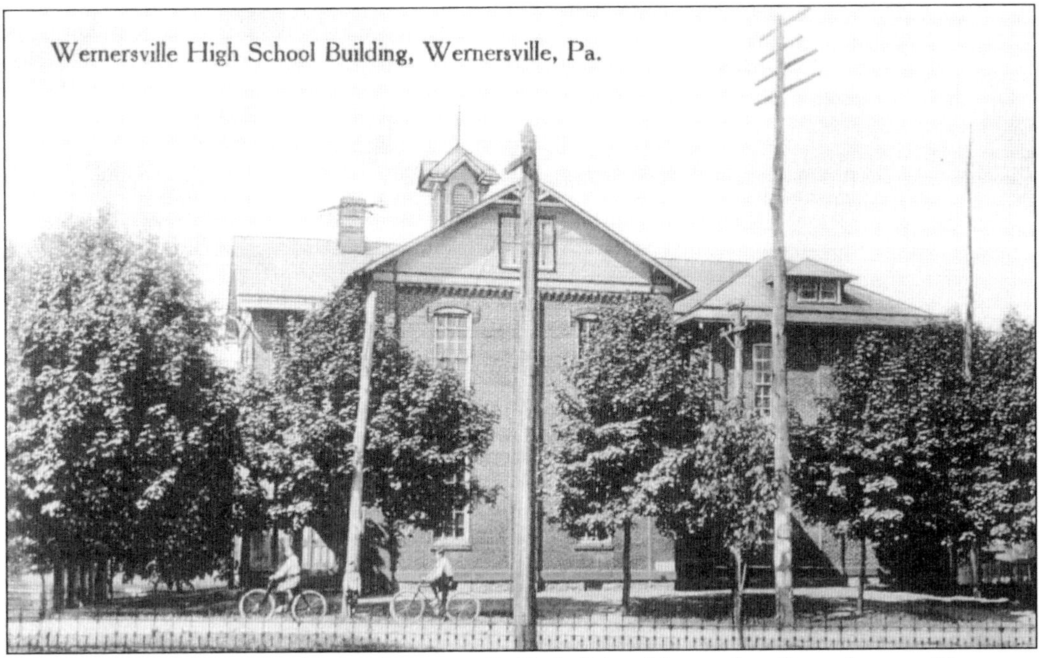

Pictured here in 1912 is the former Wernersville High School, located on Penn Avenue. Two years later, Wernersville became a borough. It served as a school until 1931, when a new school was built behind it. Over the years, the school was rented for storage, and the former Foy Laboratories occupied it for years. Today, it is an apartment building. (Courtesy of Carl Reidler.)

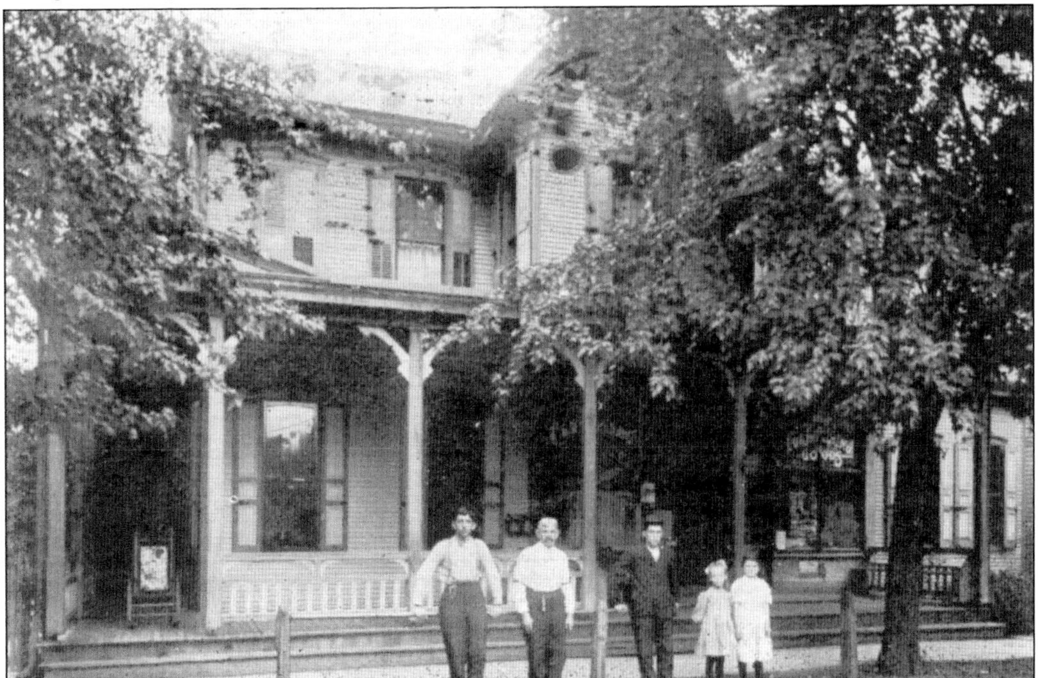

This 1920 postcard depicts the store and residence of E.S. Hassler on Market Street in the village of Wernersville. (Courtesy of Carl Reidler.)

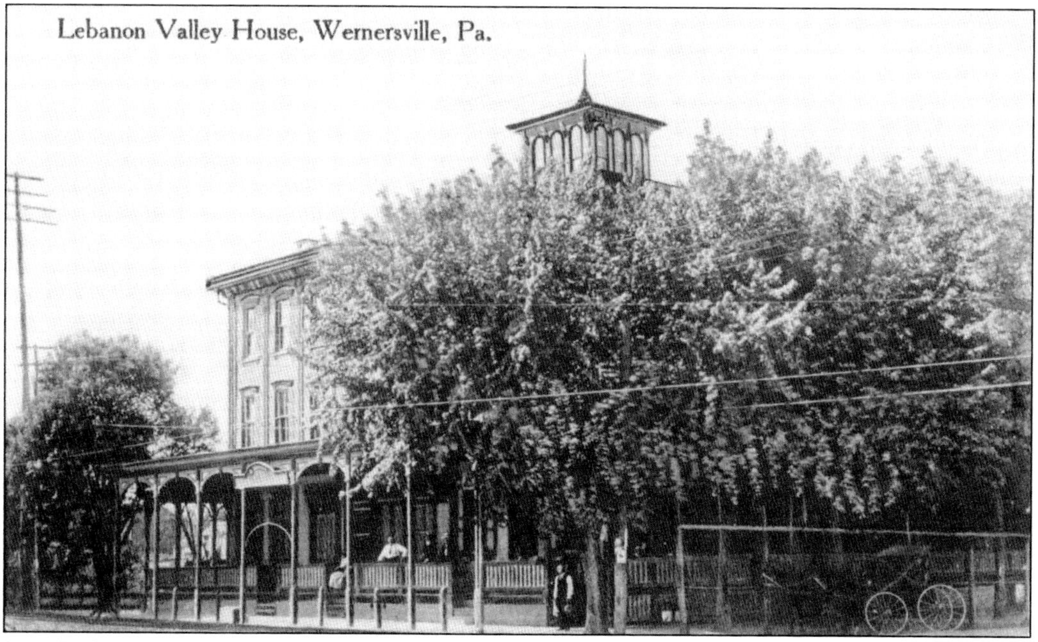

In 1871, Dr. James W. Deppen built the Lebanon Valley House at the corner of Market and Elm Streets for his medical practice and to accommodate stage coach travelers. The building has seen many business over the years, including the Lebanon Valley House Bar and Warner's Cut Rate Store, a pharmacy. Today, it is a bicycle shop called the Crank, with apartments above it. The building has changed since the time of this photograph taken in 1911, losing its porch and several windows from the Penn Avenue side. (Courtesy of Carl Reidler.)

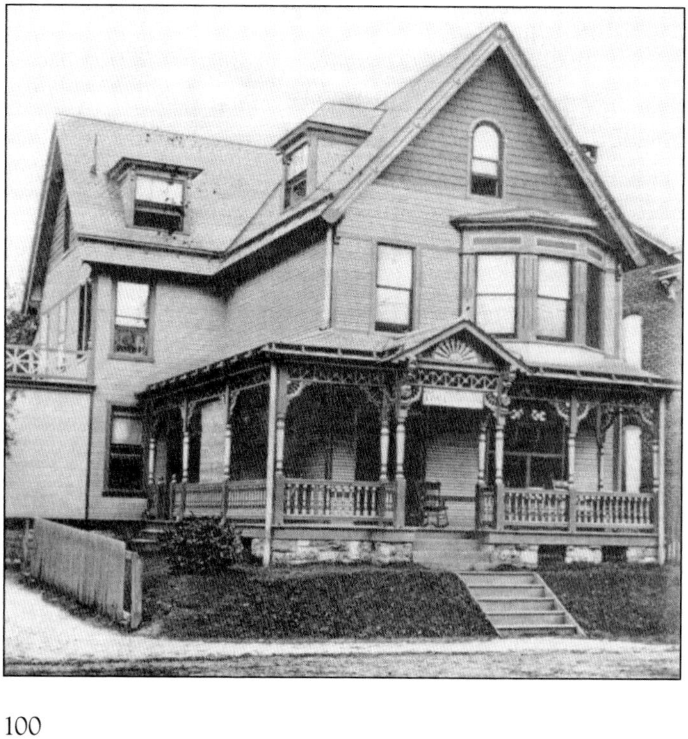

Pictured here is the Ellenora on Market Street, near the corner of Stitzer Avenue. This establishment generally took in people when the Penn Werner was full or if a train arrived late. Back then, buggies did not transport visitors to a resort after dark. The building still stands today, and it is in fine shape. (Courtesy of Carl Reidler.)

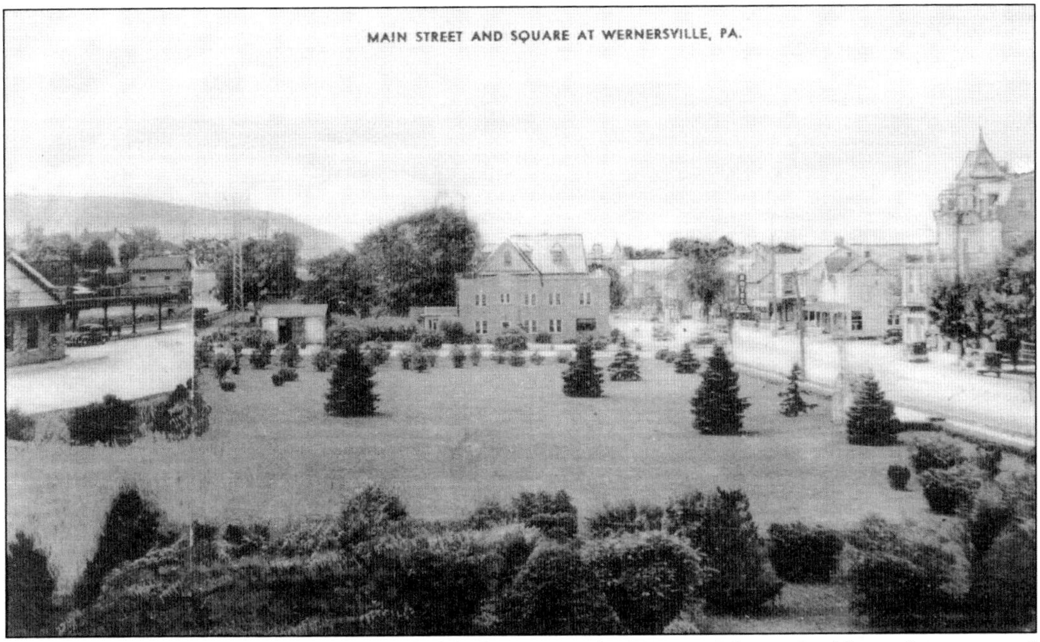

Looking west from Werner Street, probably from atop the Hoover Motors building, this postcard shows the overall size of railroad park. Other visible landmarks are, from left to right, the train station, Wartluft's Restaurant, and the Penn Werner, along with the old business district down West Market Street. (Courtesy of Carl Reidler.)

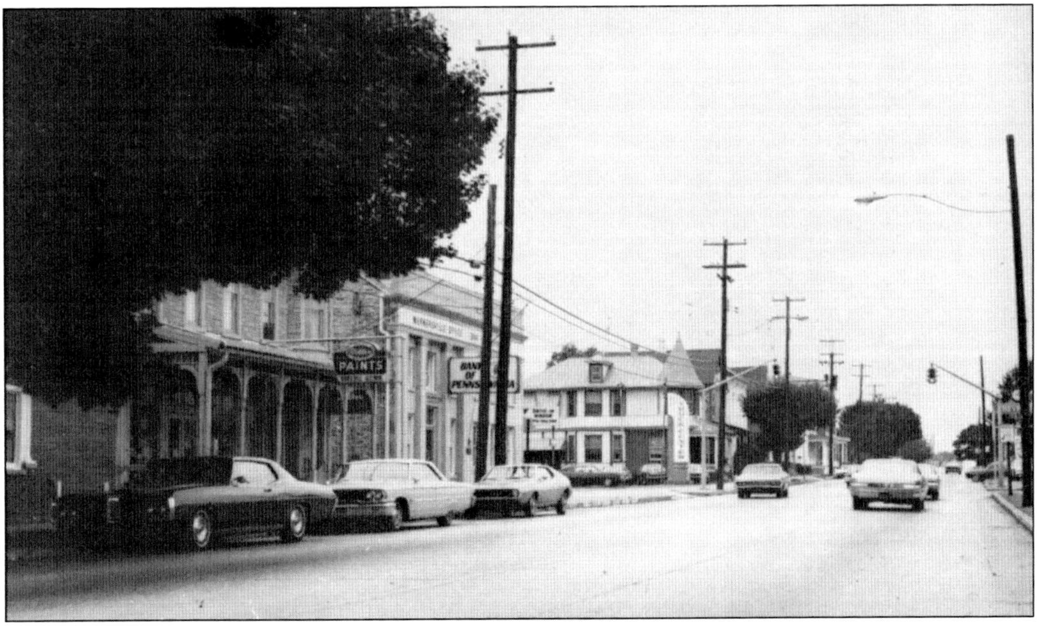

Penn Avenue is pictured here about 1975. The old Wernersville Hardware and the Bank of Pennsylvania are visible in this eastern view. (Courtesy of Carl Reidler.)

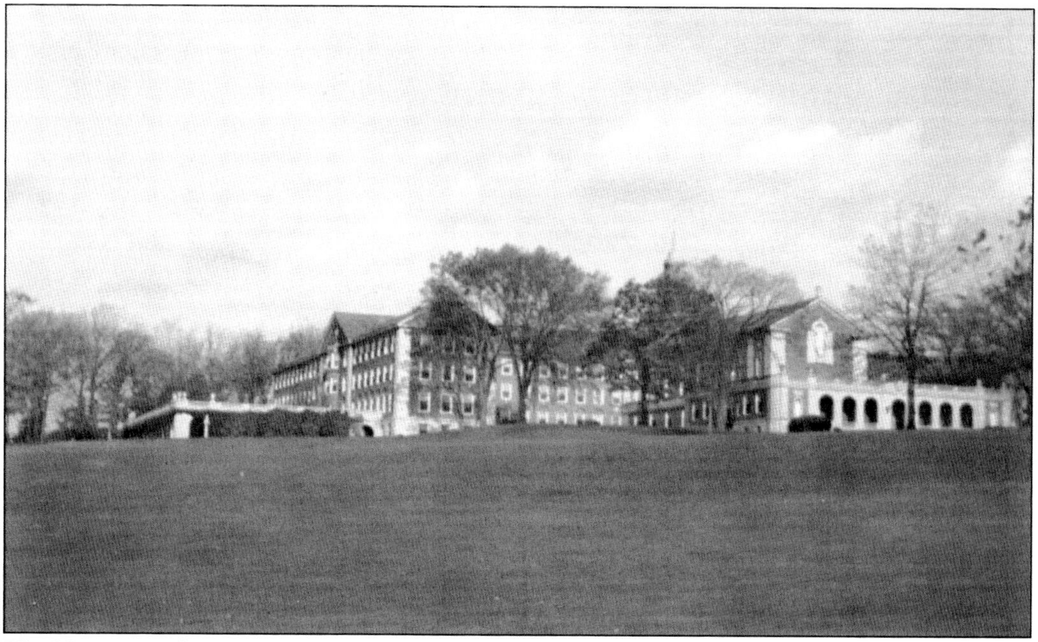

The Novitiate of St. Ignatius Loyola and Jesuit Center is pictured here. It now serves as a retreat house, mainly for Catholics. The center is a beautiful place, and the cemetery is a must-see. Today, it is known as the Jesuit Center for Spiritual Growth. (Courtesy of Carl Reidler.)

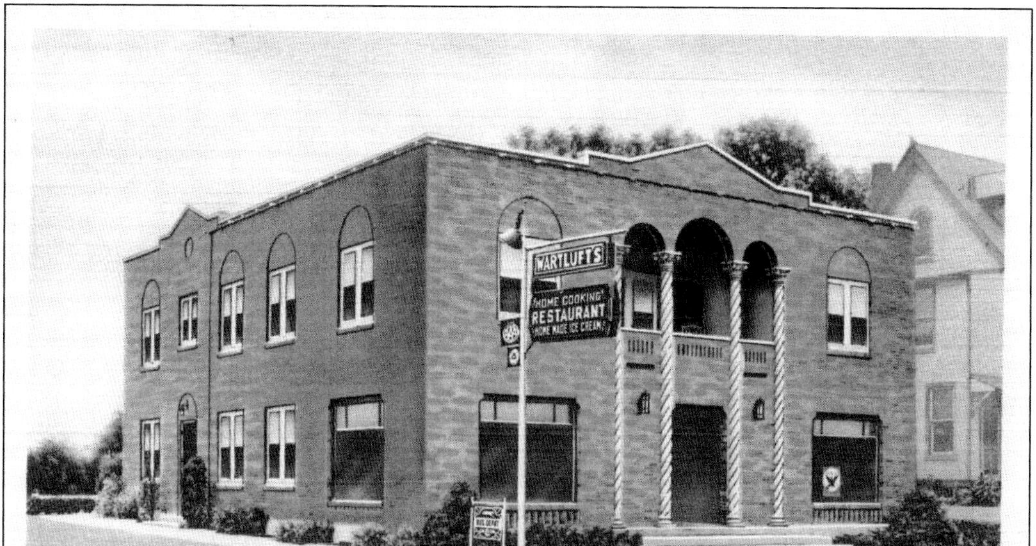

This is a view of Wartluft's Restaurant on the corner of Penn and Stitzer Avenues. The Ellenora sits to the right. Dr. Raylene Devine had her office here for years, and the second home of Woody's Sporting Goods was located in the basement for a few years. The top floor has contained apartments for some time. (Courtesy of Carl Reidler.)

Pictured here is the First Reformed Church in Wernersville on West Penn Avenue. It remains a very active church, and the building is in wonderful condition. (Courtesy of Carl Reidler.)

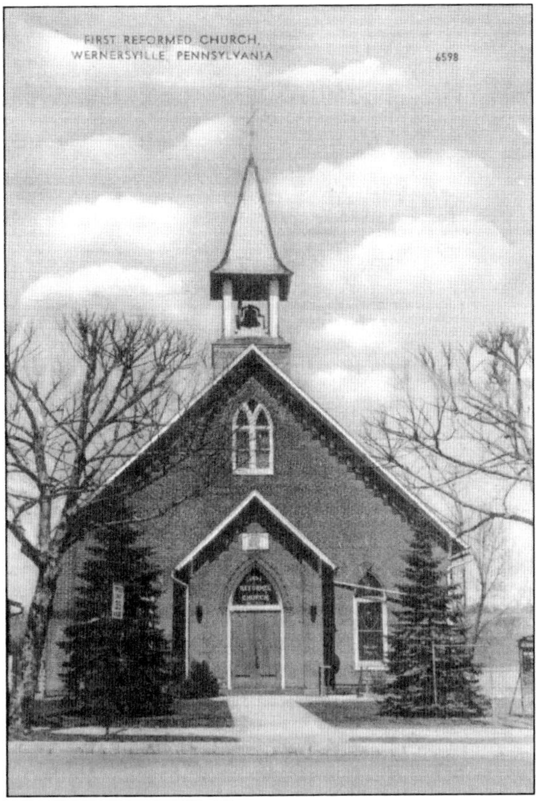

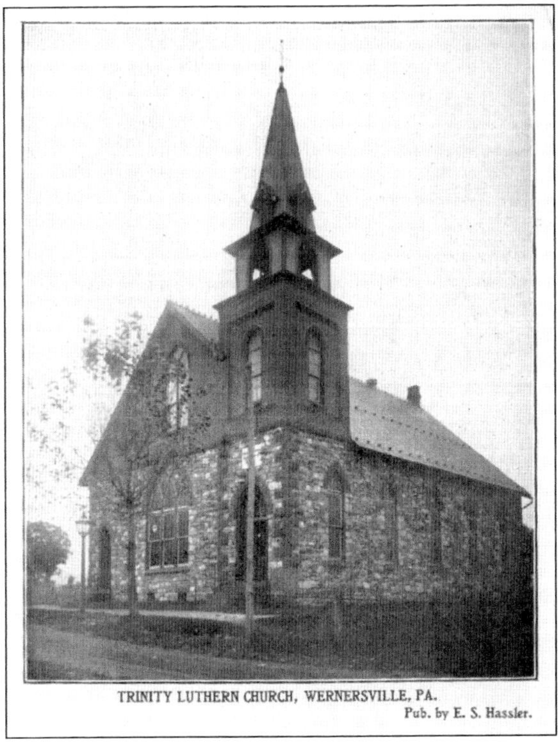

This is an early postcard of Trinity Lutheran Church on Beckley Street in Wernersville. Since this photograph, the church has undergone several additions and upgrades. (Courtesy of Carl Reidler.)

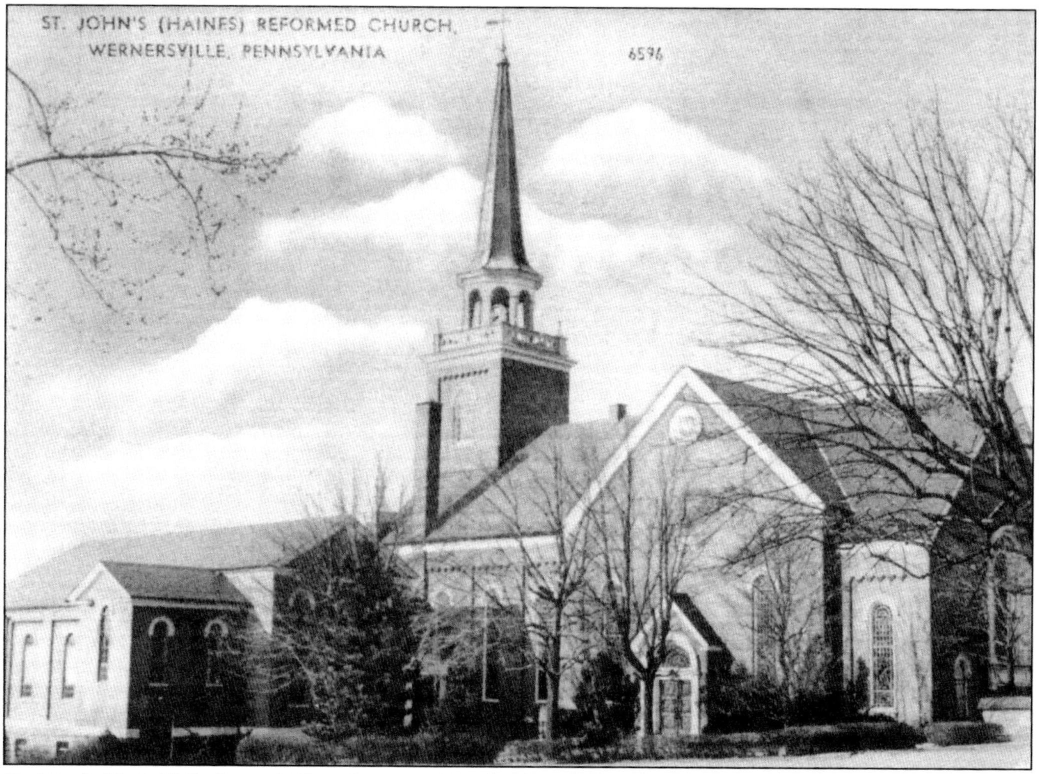

St. John's (Hain's) Reformed Church sits on North Church Road. The Hain family donated land for the church, so it is also known as Hain's Church. It is a very large church, and like the other local churches, it is well kept. Many important locals are buried in its huge cemetery. (Courtesy of Carl Reidler.)

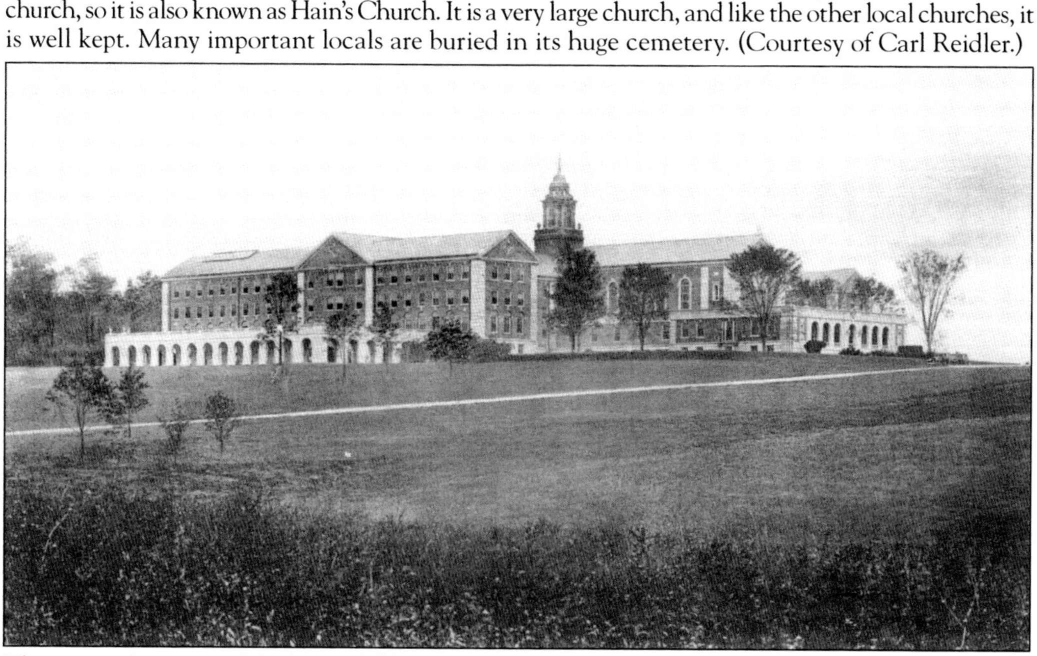

This is another view of the beautiful Jesuit complex in Wernersville. More information about the novitiate turned retreat center can be found in Kathy Scogna's book *A House of Bread*. (Courtesy of Carl Reidler.)

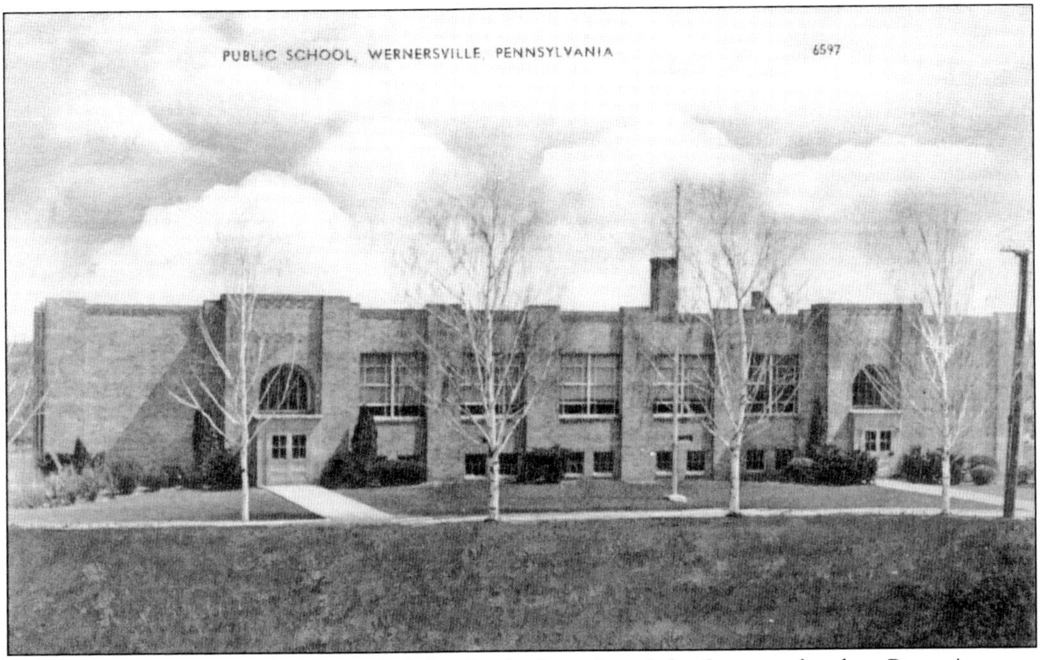

Built in 1931, the Wernersville High School, which replaced the former school on Penn Avenue, is located on Pine Street in the borough. After the Wernersville School District merged into the Conrad Weiser School District, this institution became the Wernersville Elementary School. In 1989, the district built a new elementary school on Lincoln Drive, and this building was sold, becoming apartments. (Courtesy of Carl Reidler.)

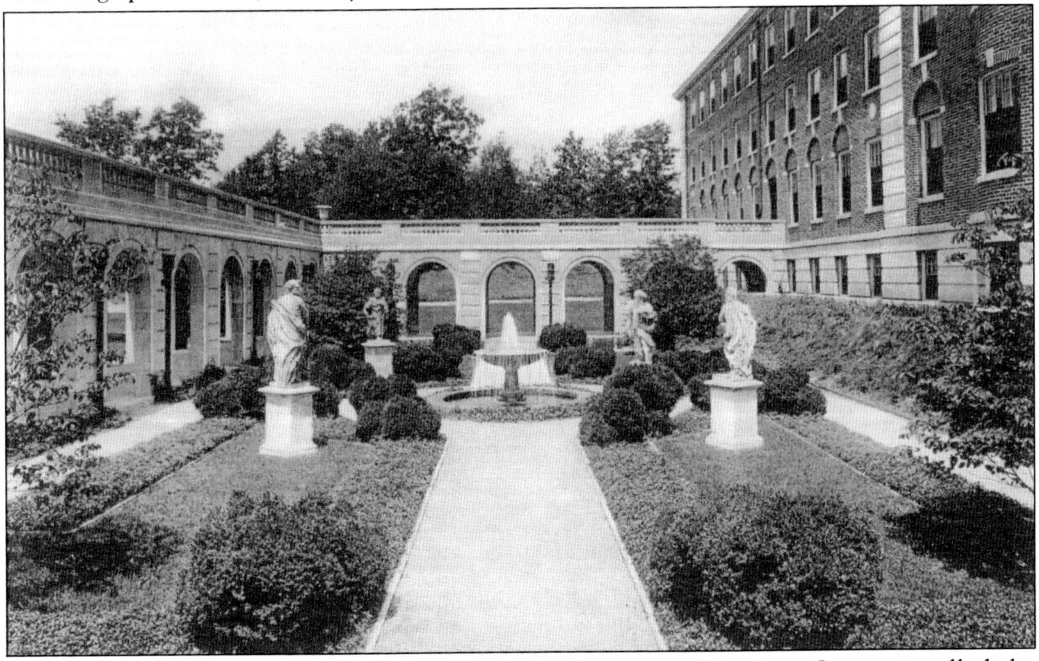

The well-maintained, open-air courtyard at the Novitiate of St. Isaac Jogues is called the Cloister Garden. The garden, pictured here, is still a beautiful retreat to this day. (Courtesy of Carl Reidler.)

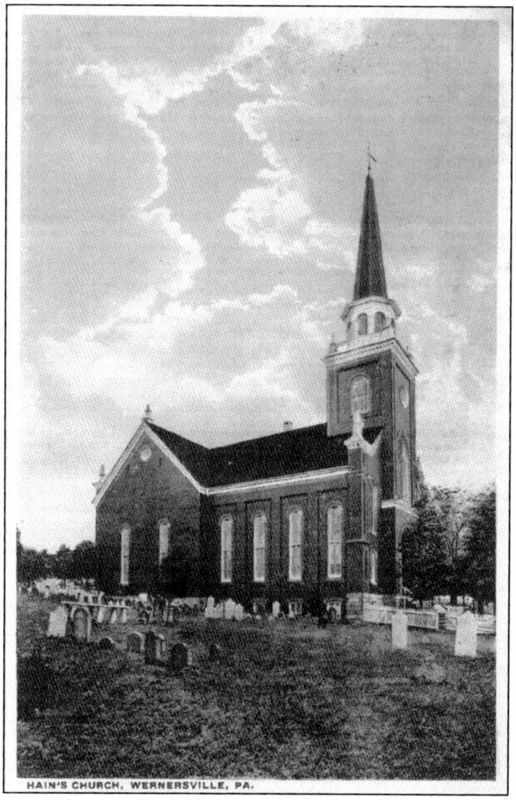

This 1914 postcard shows another view of St. John's (Hain's) Church, along with some of the cemetery. (Courtesy of Carl Reidler.)

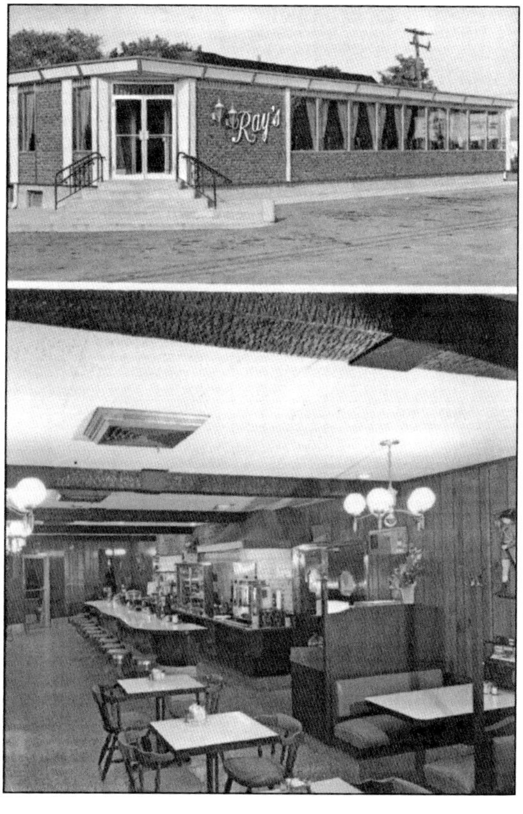

Locals and those from the surrounding area know Ray's Diner very well. After Ray's, the eatery became the Village Pantry Restaurant. Both places have been enjoyed by groups of all ages. (Courtesy of Carl Reidler.)

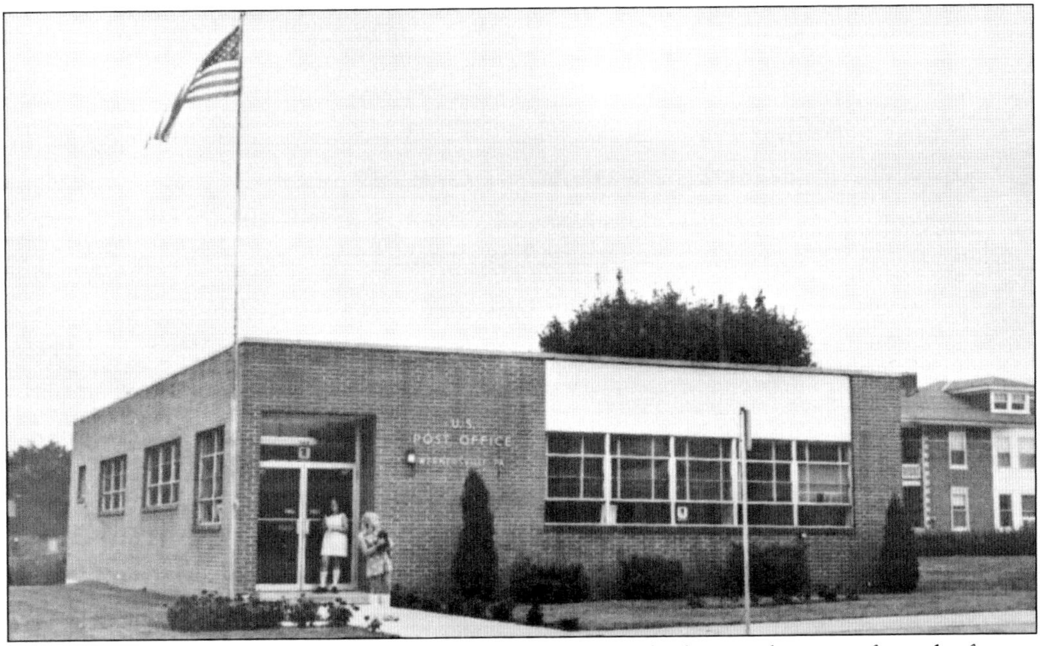

Pictured here in 1975 is the post office on Stitzer Avenue, which sat right across from the former Citizens Hose Fire Company. This post office was closed about 2005, and a new one was built on South Church Street. The building is currently a day care center. (Courtesy of Carl Reidler.)

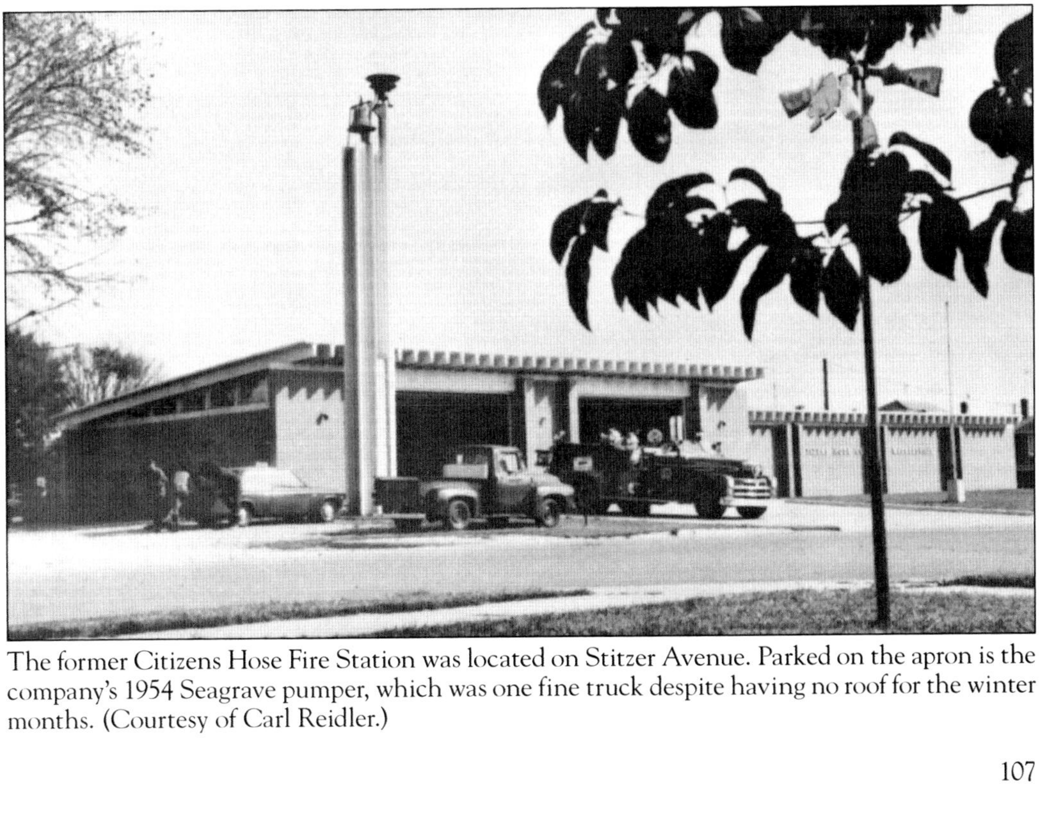

The former Citizens Hose Fire Station was located on Stitzer Avenue. Parked on the apron is the company's 1954 Seagrave pumper, which was one fine truck despite having no roof for the winter months. (Courtesy of Carl Reidler.)

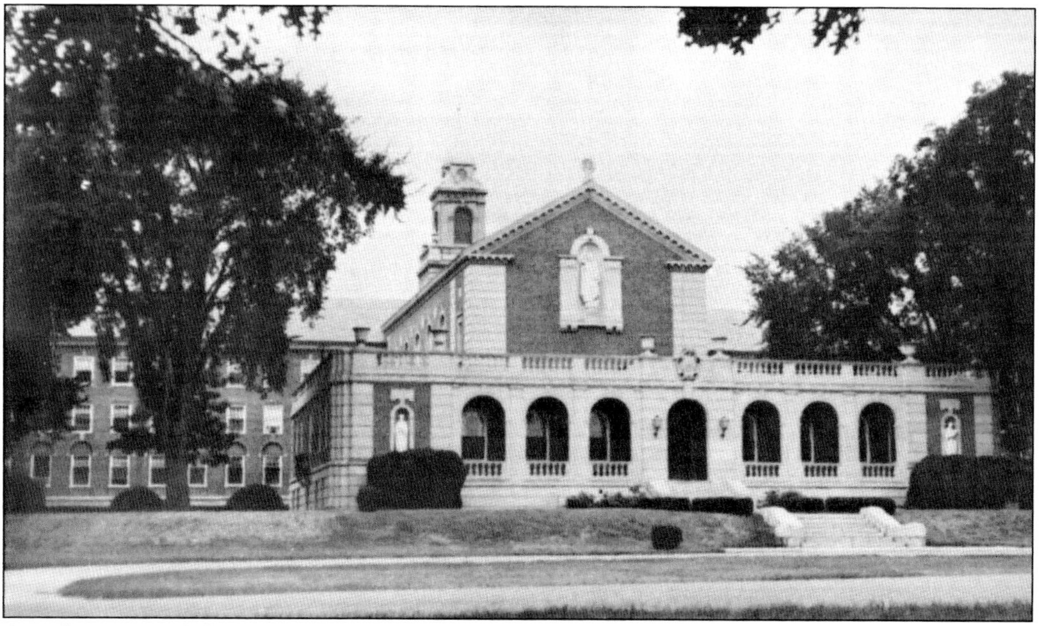

Another view of the Novitiate of St. Isaac Jogues in Wernersville provides a glimpse of the complex's beautiful architecture. (Courtesy of Carl Reidler.)

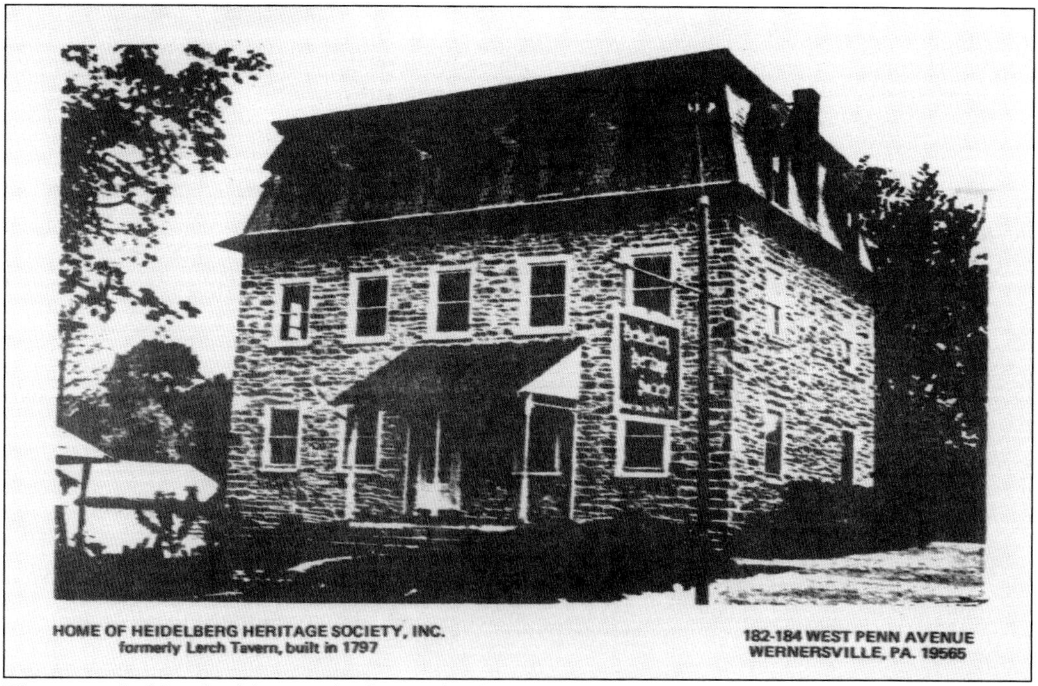

The second-oldest building in the borough, the former Lerch Tavern, was built in 1797. Today, it serves as the home of the Heidelberg Heritage Society, an organization that collects and preserves historic materials, structures, and landmarks. (Courtesy of Carl Reidler.)

Seven

South Heidelberg Township

South Heidelberg became a township in 1914. It was almost named Cacoosing Township, which means "place of owls" in the language of the Delaware Indians. South Heidelberg was cut out of Lower Heidelberg Township, and Lower Heidelberg was cut away from its parent, Heidelberg Township, in 1842. The Lenni-Lenape Indians roamed this area. Even today, farmers who still till the land can find artifacts in their fields.

This area was established primarily by German settlers, the same ones who came from the Palatinate region. It also played an important role in the country's independence. In the Furnace and Preston Roads area was the Berkshire Furnace, which produced cannonballs and shot to keep Washington's army well equipped. Farther west, behind the current Wernersville State Hospital Dam, was the old Bore Mill Gun Barrel Factory, where octagon gun barrels were forged to further supply Washington's troops. This factory lasted until after the Civil War, producing gun barrels for the War Between the States and the War of 1812.

In the mid-1800s, the area had many resorts, such as Grand View, Walter's Park, Bynden Wood, Preston's Sunnyside, and Mountain Sunset. Most of these did well until the Great Depression; after that, only Galen Hall and South Mountain Manor survived. Due to poor business for one and a devastating fire for the other, that era of history is gone.

Today, South Heidelberg is mostly residential, with a commercial area along Route 422. Considering all the changes that have happened over time, the township seems to still be doing well. Today, the township's population is 7,271.

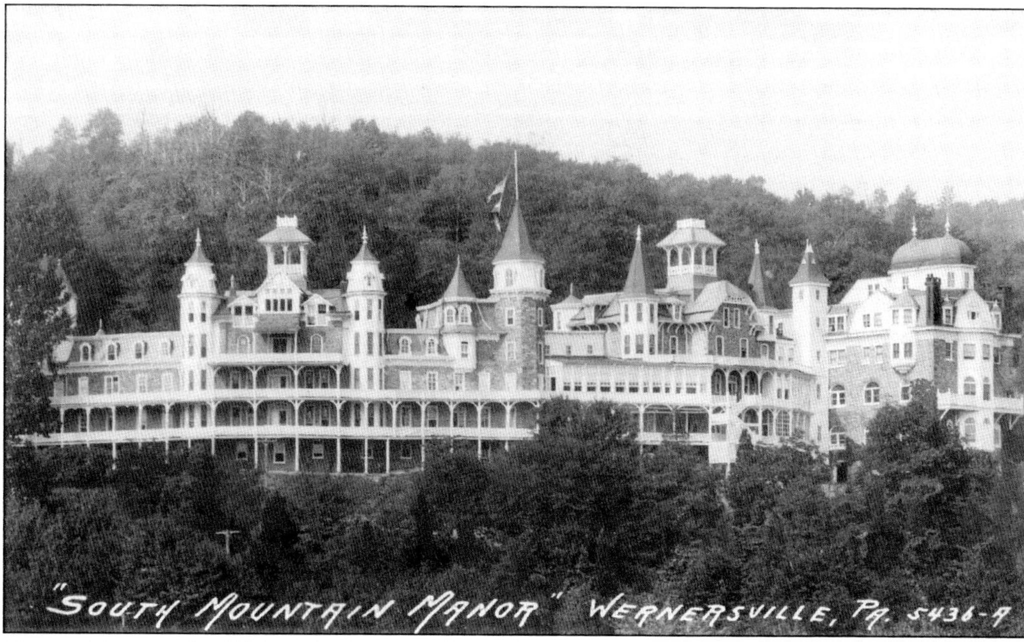

Pictured here is the Walter Sanitarium. South Mountain Manor, as the postcard states, is the name it received after changing hands. The new owners made this notation on the card, most likely using up old postcard stock. As one can see, this was a gorgeous place. The manor is no longer there, and the property is now the source for Wernersville's water supply. (Courtesy of Carl Reidler.)

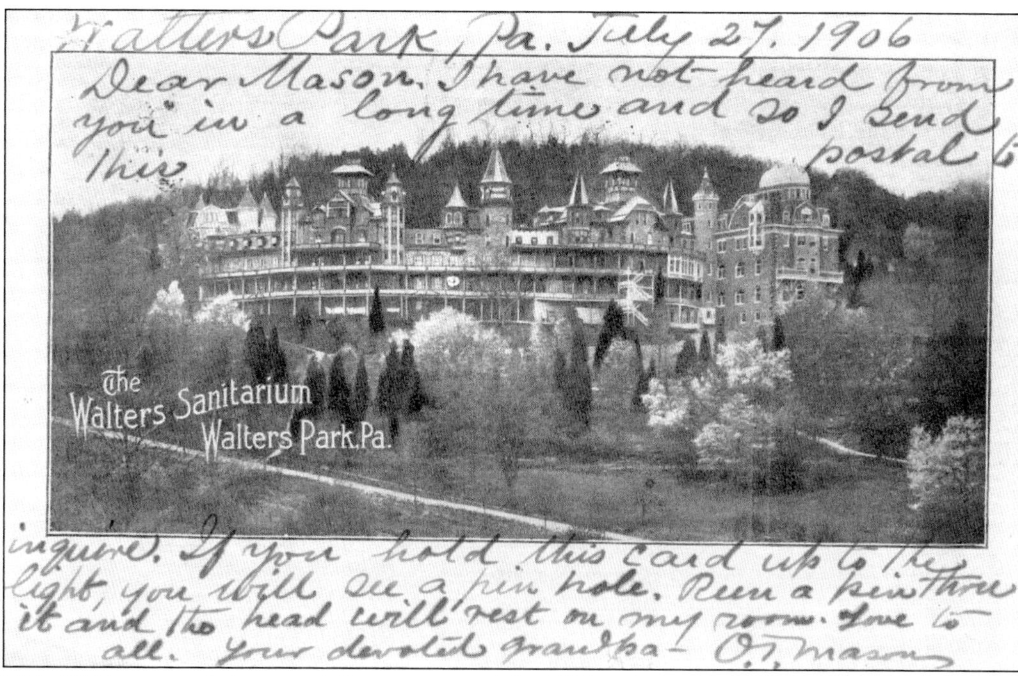

This 1906 postcard shows a different view of the Walter Sanitarium, located on 500 acres of mountain land known as Walter's Park. The architecture is exquisite; by today's standards, this retreat would still attract visitors. (Courtesy of Carl Reidler.)

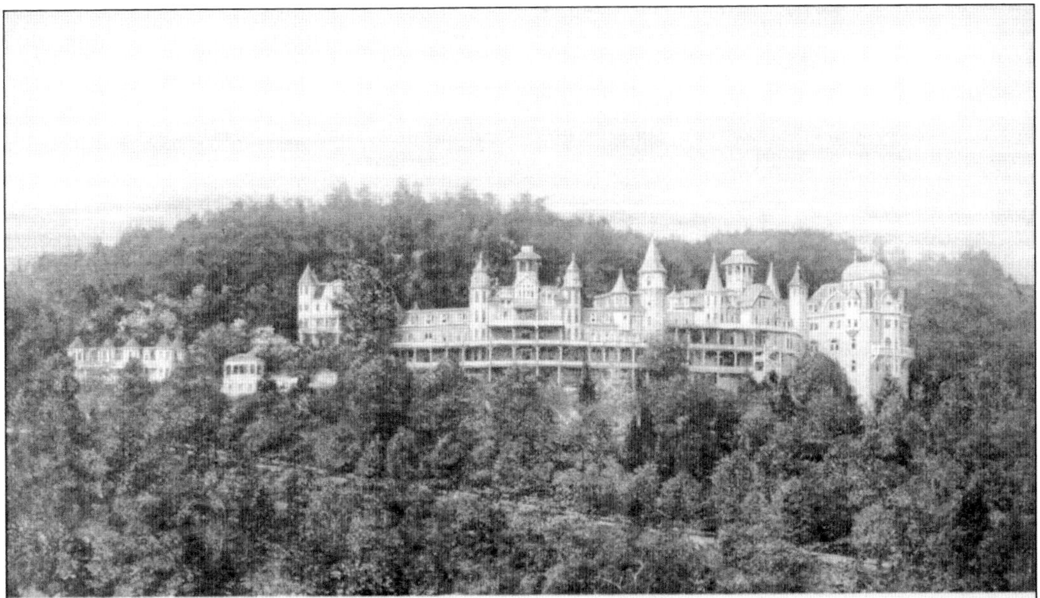

THE WALTER SANITARIUM, WALTER'S PARK, PA.

A panoramic view of the Walter Sanitarium illustrates the expanse of the resort, which was large enough to merit its own post office. The cancellation on the back of this postcard is dated July 27, 1906, Walter's Park, Pennsylvania. (Courtesy of Carl Reidler.)

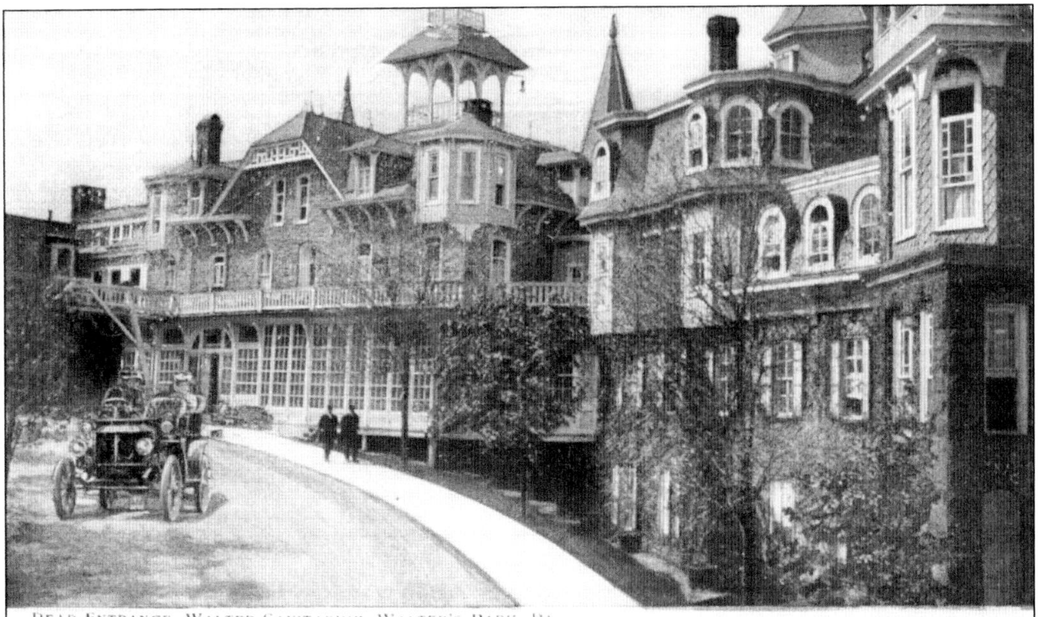

REAR ENTRANCE, WALTER SANITARIUM, WALTER'S PARK, PA.

This 1910 postcard shows the rear entrance of the Walter Sanitarium. Again, note the architecture of this fine structure. (Courtesy of Carl Reidler.)

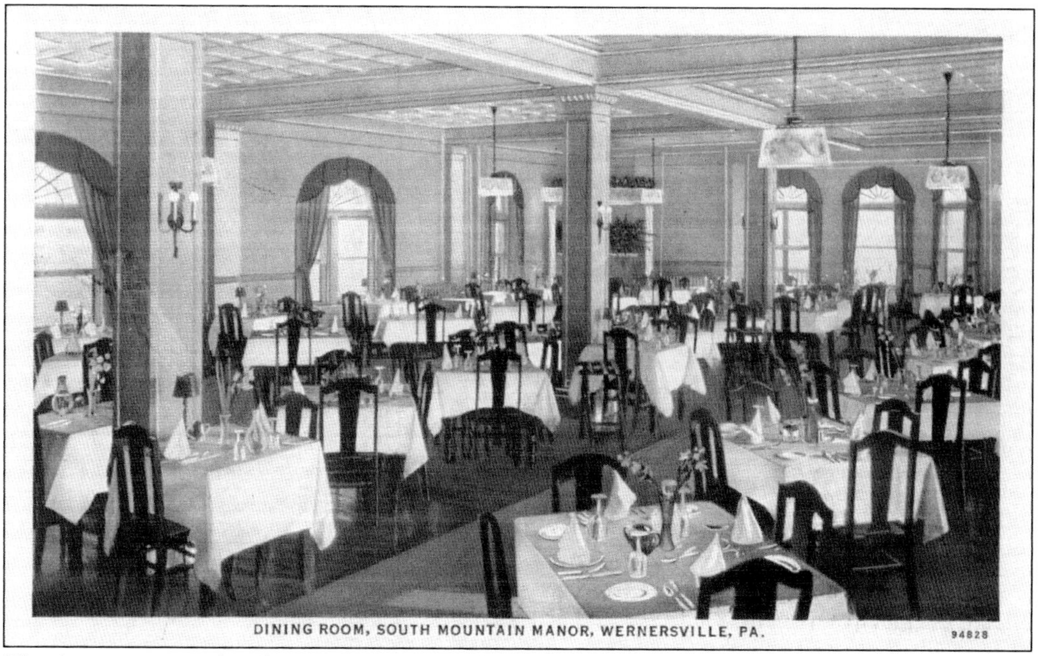

The dining room at South Mountain Manor featured tin ceilings and hardwood floors. This hotel could accommodate 250 guests. Among its offerings were golf (at Galen Hall), swimming, tennis, saddle horses, music, dancing, and more. (Courtesy of Carl Reidler.)

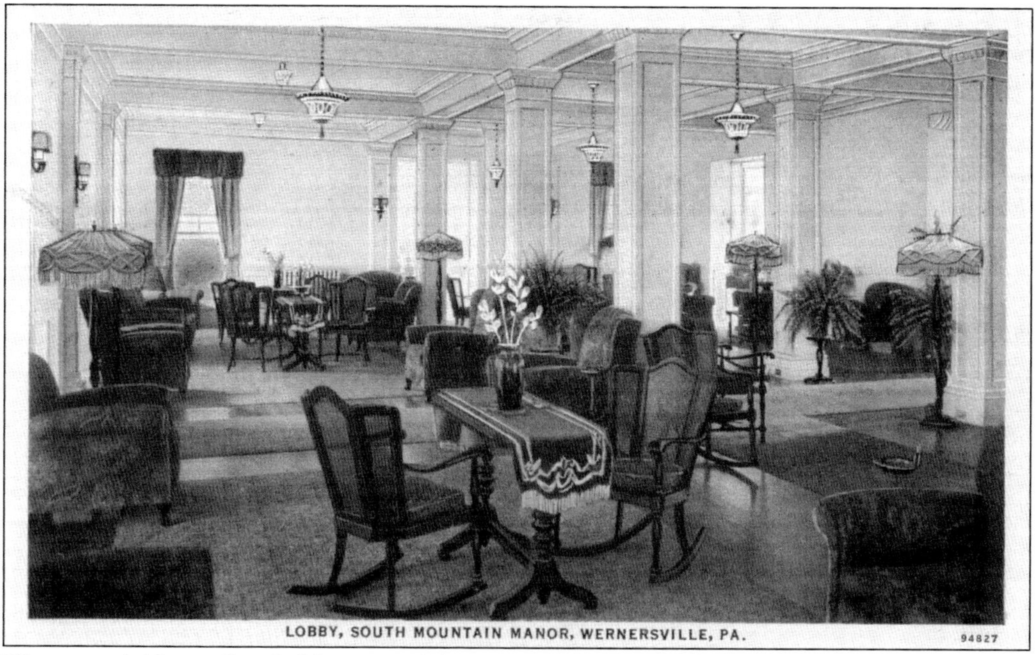

The main lobby at South Mountain Manor was spacious and well furnished. (Courtesy of Carl Reidler.)

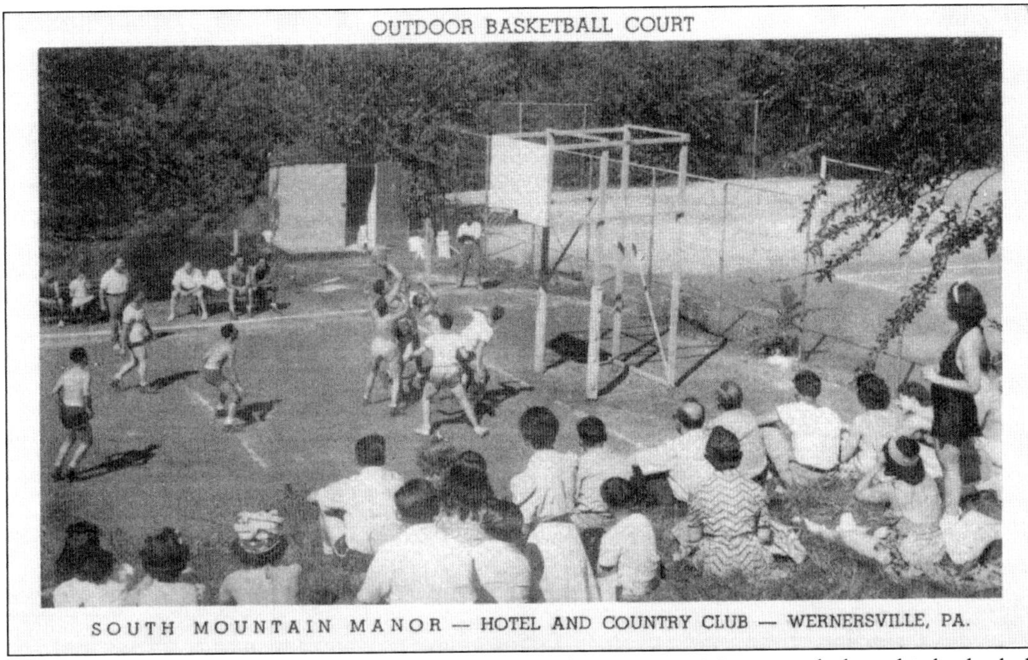

This postcard shows some of the activity areas at South Mountain Manor, including this basketball court and the tennis courts in the background. Other recreational activities included badminton, volleyball, baseball, and handball, just to name a few. (Courtesy of Carl Reidler.)

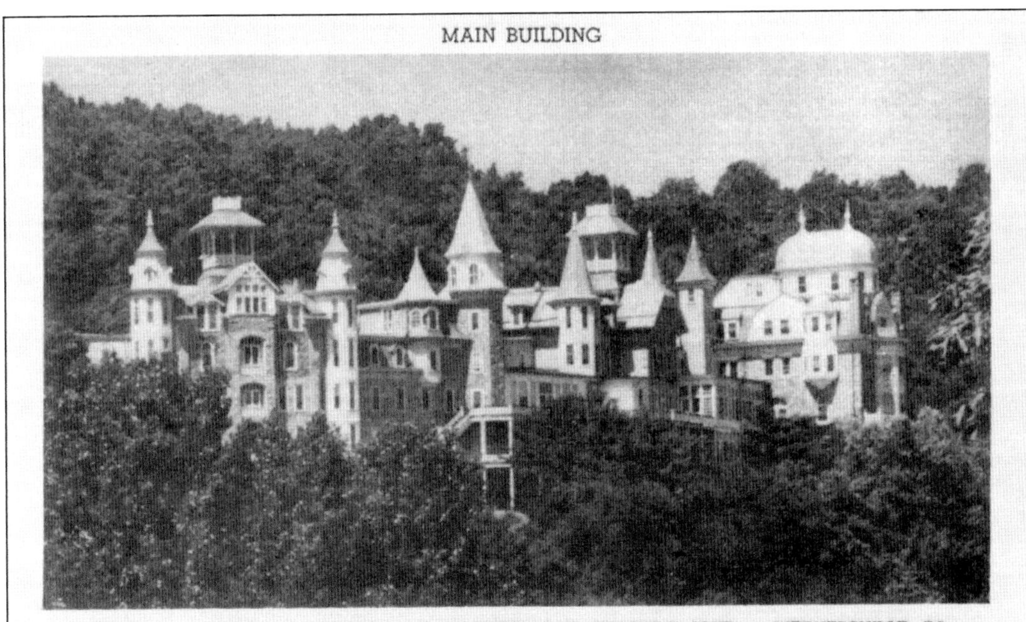

Pictured here is another slightly different view of South Mountain Manor, Wernersville. Again, the splendor of this building is just magnificent. (Courtesy of Carl Reidler.)

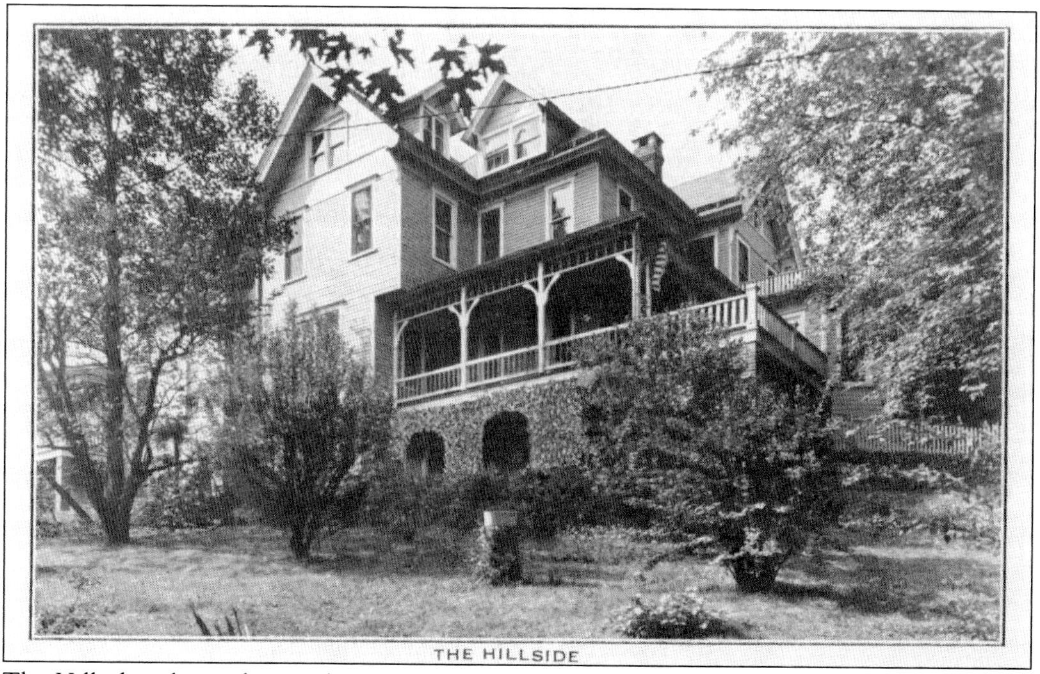

The Hillside is located on Galen Hall Road, on the steep hill above the old South Heidelberg School. This resort accommodated those waiting to get a room at Grand View. The interior has been restored and converted into apartments. (Courtesy of Carl Reidler.)

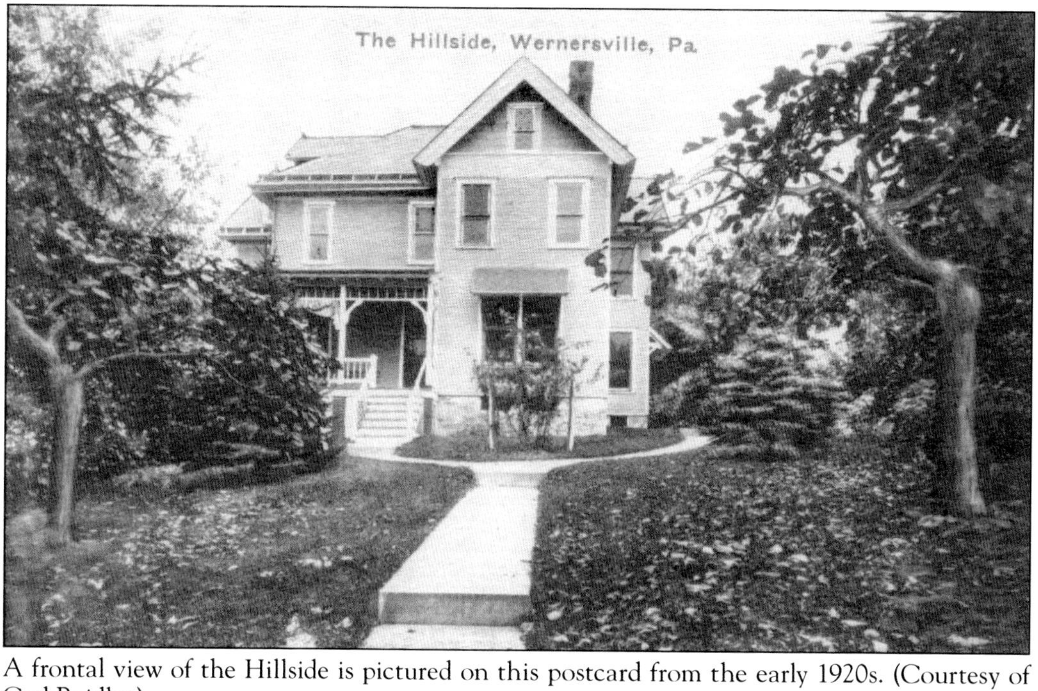

A frontal view of the Hillside is pictured on this postcard from the early 1920s. (Courtesy of Carl Reidler.)

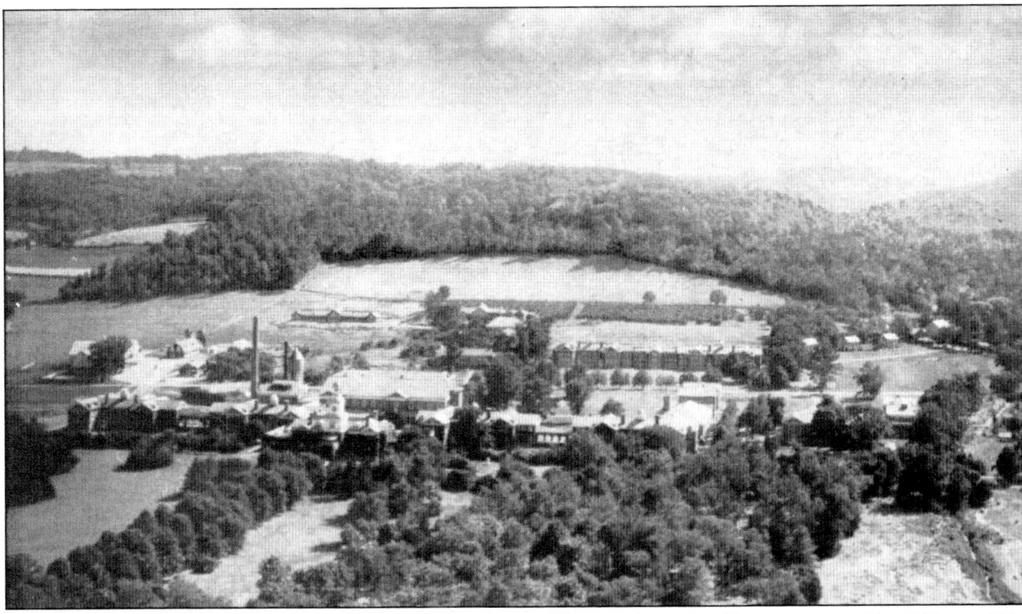

This is an aerial view of the Wernersville State Hospital with all its original buildings. The approximate date of this image is 1940. (Courtesy of Carl Reidler.)

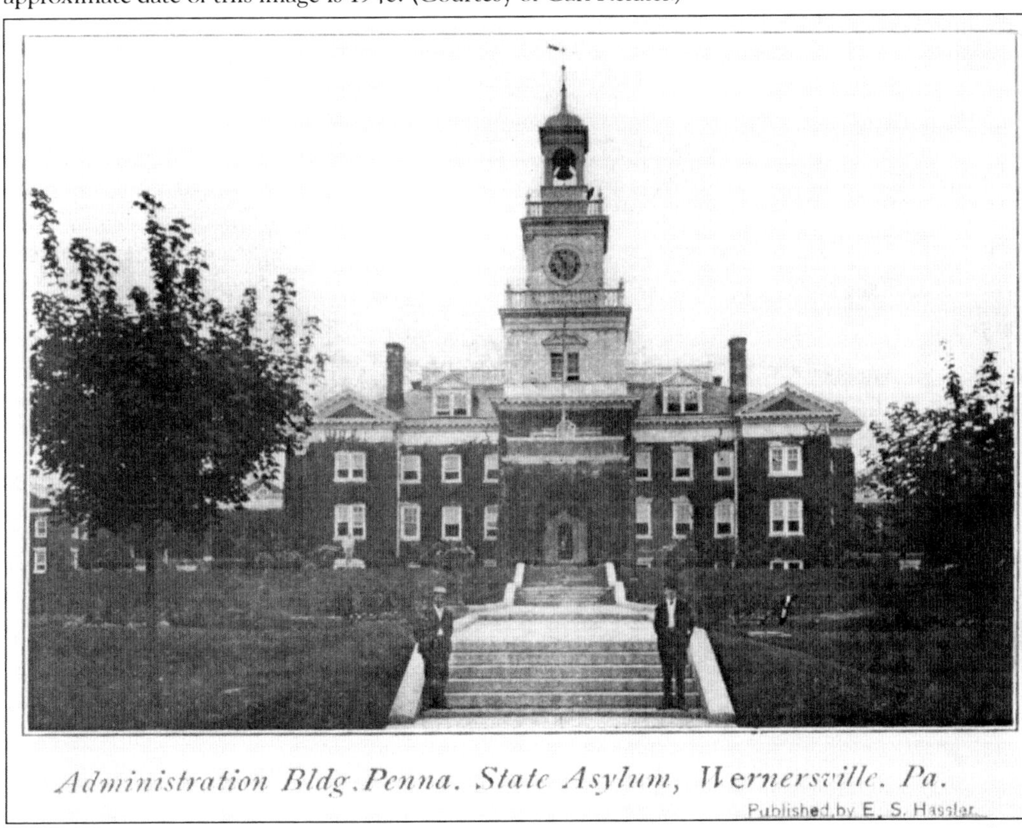

This is a 1908 postcard showing the administration building at the Wernersville State Asylum, as it was originally known. (Courtesy of Carl Reidler.)

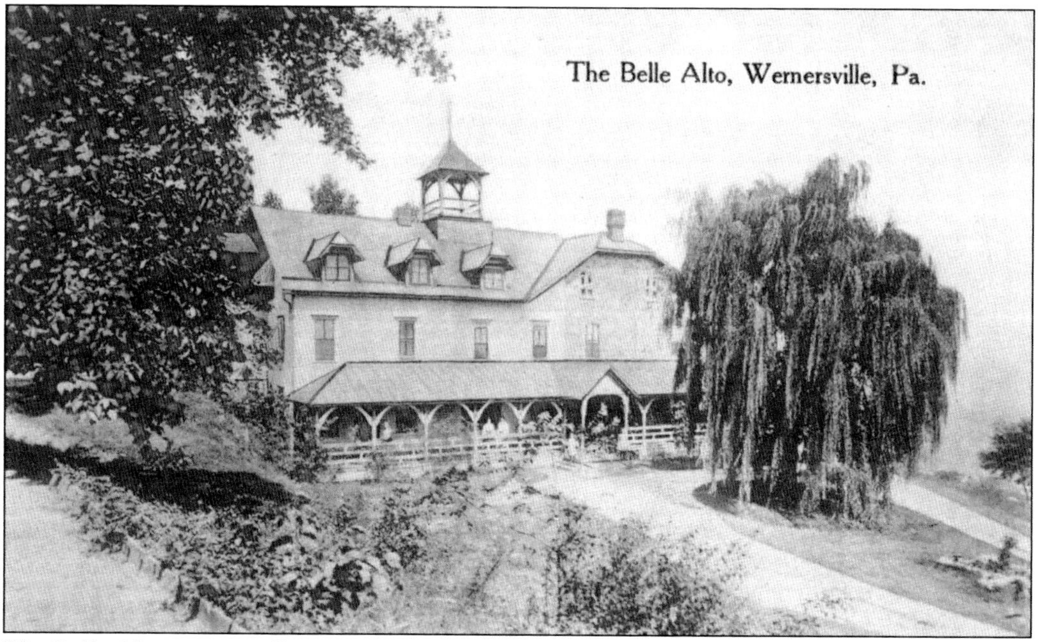

The Belle Alto was a smaller resort-type building located on the mountain. It is pictured here in the early 1920s. (Courtesy of Carl Reidler.)

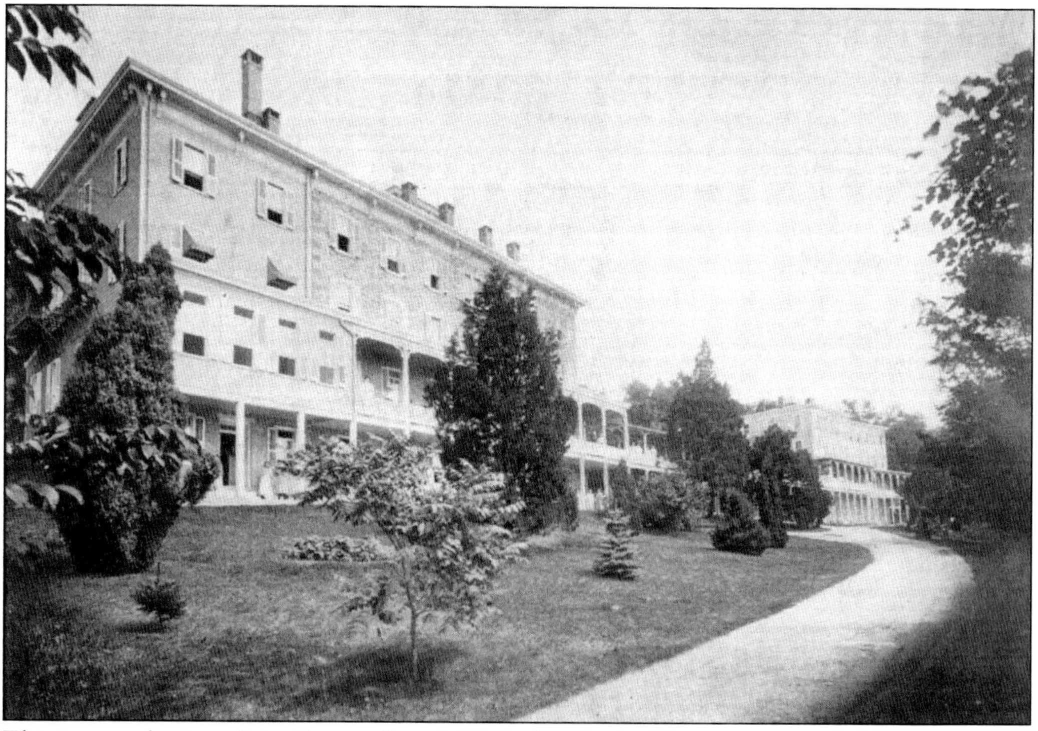

This is an early view of the Preston from 1910, before the building was expanded into what later became Galen Hall. Originally known as Preston's Sunny Side, its name was changed because the owners felt people would not stay here if the hotel was in the sun all the time, although it primarily was. (Courtesy of Carl Reidler.)

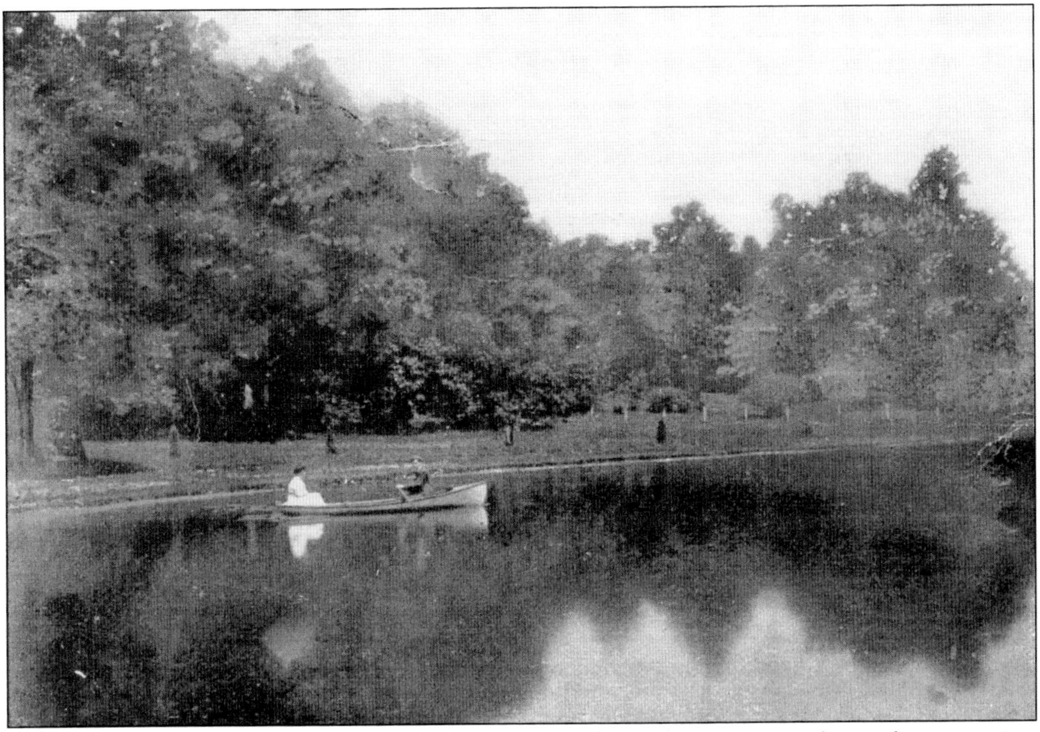

The lake at the Preston, pictured in this 1904 postcard, was later converted into the swimming pool at Galen Hall, which still stands today in a restored condition thanks to the Masano family. (Courtesy of Carl Reidler.)

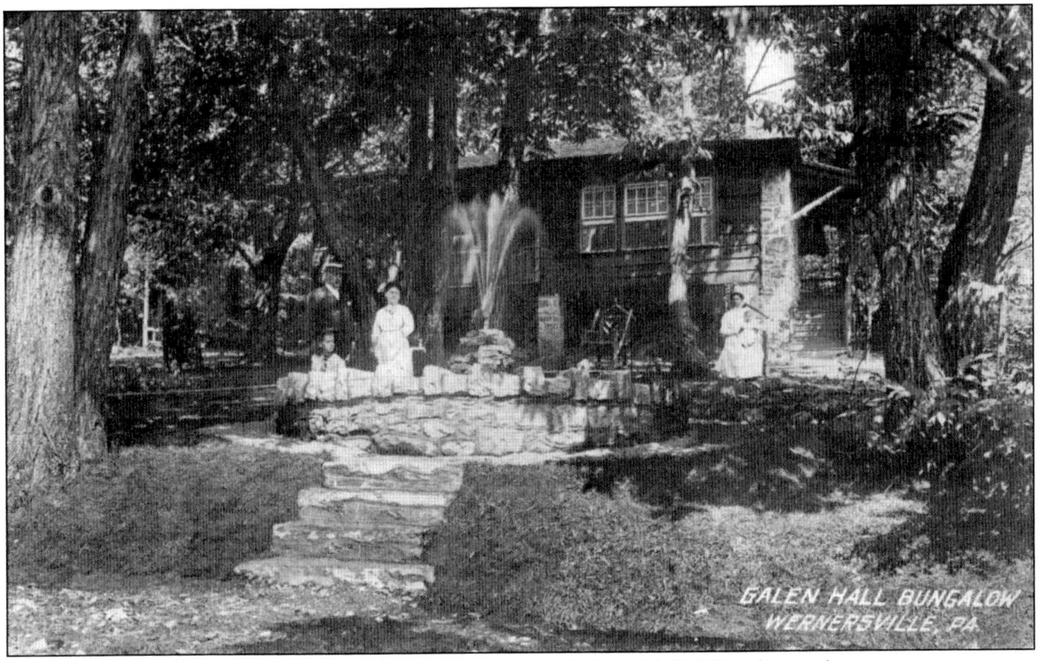

This view from 1912 shows one of the cottages at Galen Hall. This bungalow now serves as a private residence. Its fountain remains intact as well. (Courtesy of Carl Reidler.)

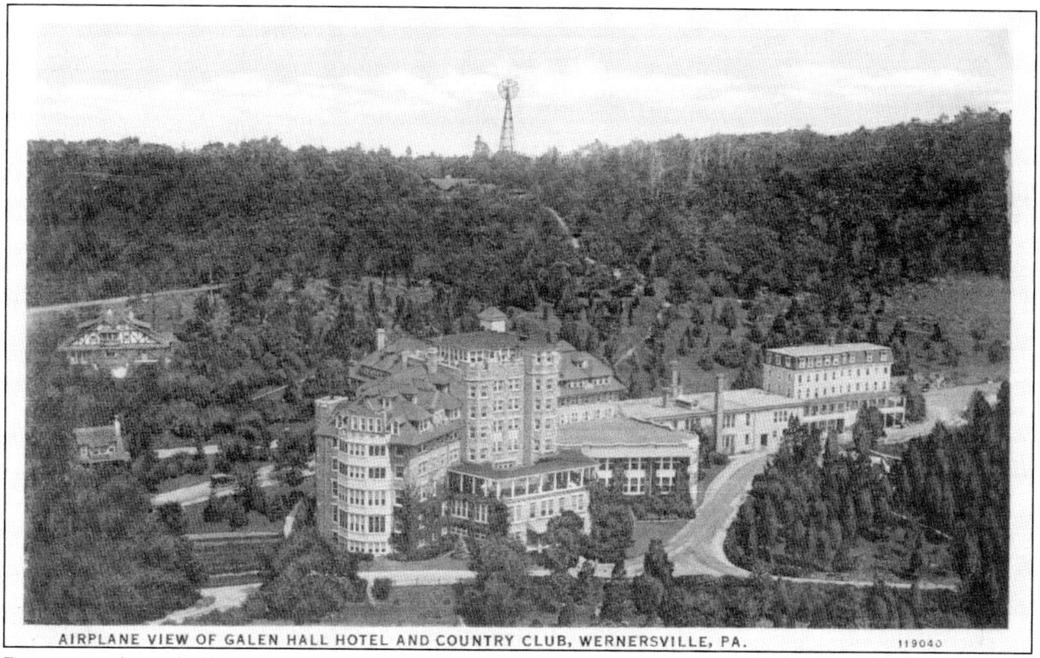

Boasting a large ballroom and championship golf course, the Galen Hall Hotel, seen in this aerial view from the 1940s, could accommodate 300–310 guests. (Courtesy of Carl Reidler.)

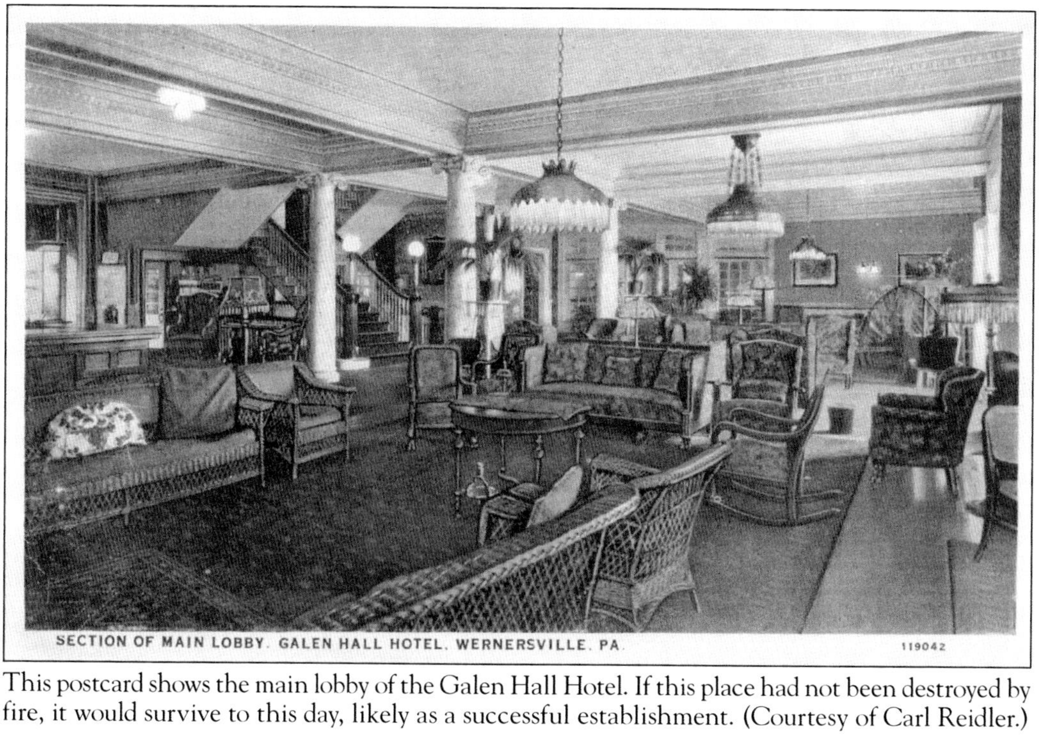

This postcard shows the main lobby of the Galen Hall Hotel. If this place had not been destroyed by fire, it would survive to this day, likely as a successful establishment. (Courtesy of Carl Reidler.)

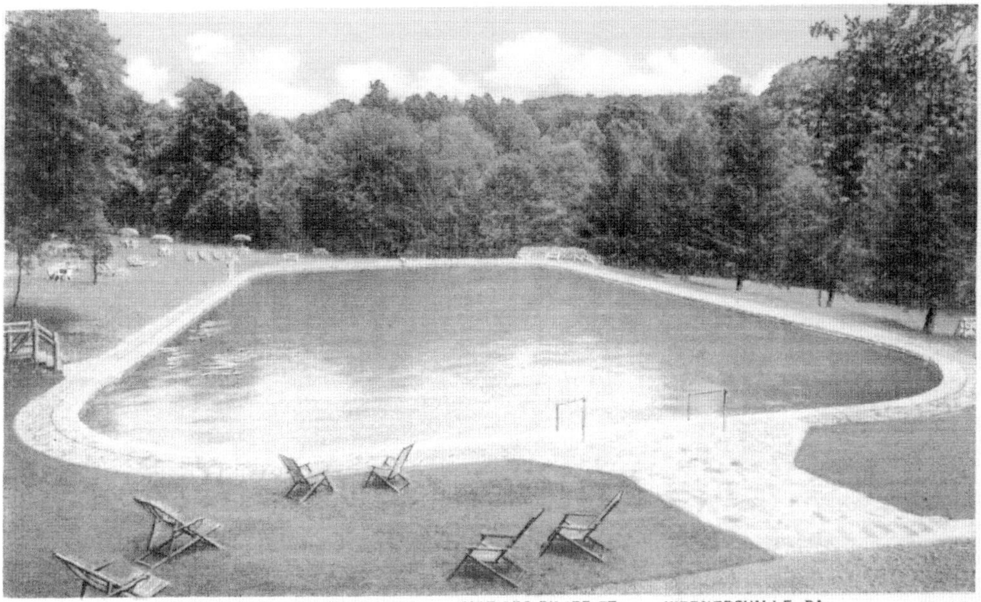

After some modifications, the Preston lake became a beautiful swimming pool. It is still there today, but the only swimmers are about 500 fish. It is fed by a natural spring. (Courtesy of Carl Reidler.)

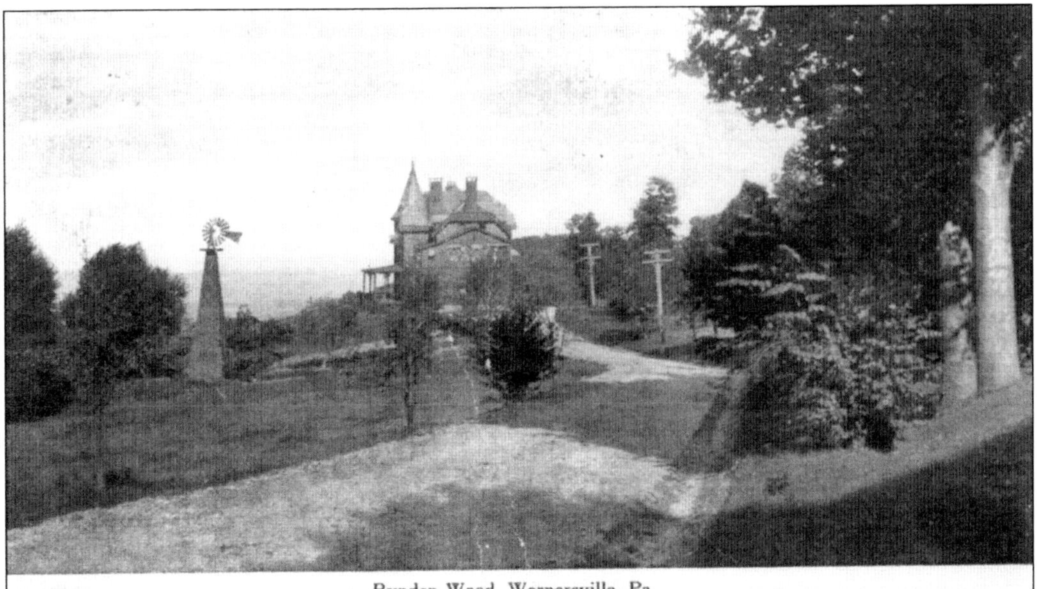

The Bynden Wood Hotel on Cushion Peak Road sat high on the hill, with a tremendous view of the city of Reading and Berks County, as well as Lancaster County. The hotel, pictured here in 1920, could accommodate 45–50 guests. It was razed in the 1960s by the YMCA of Reading, which owns the complex today. (Courtesy of Carl Reidler.)

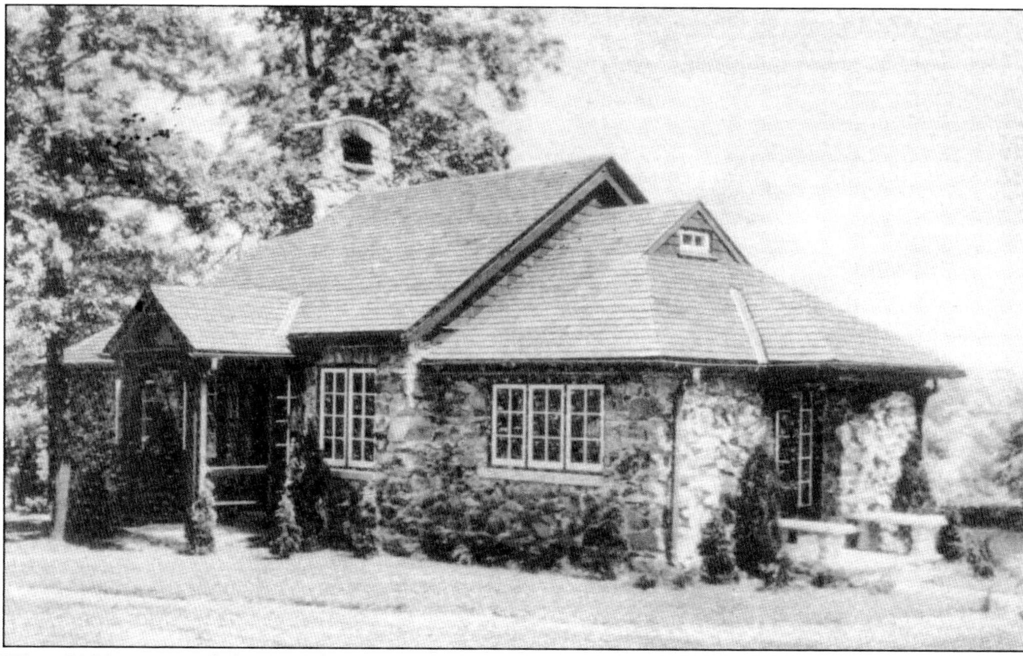

This 1928 postcard depicts the Bynden Wood teahouse and gift shop at the Bynden Wood Hotel. This building stands today, along with an addition made by its current owners, the South Mountain YMCA. (Courtesy of Carl Reidler.)

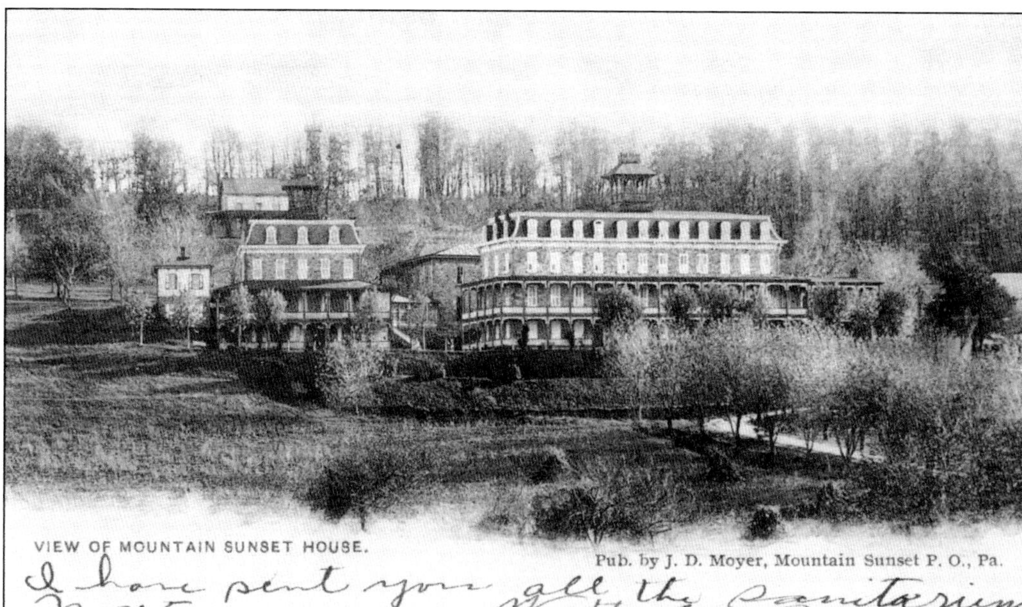

Pictured here in 1906 is the Mountain Sunset House on Galen Hall Road, which could host 200 guests. Like Walter's Park, it had its own post office. The hotel later became Sunset Hall, then the Villa Maria, which is now owned by the Caron Foundation. (Courtesy of Carl Reidler.)

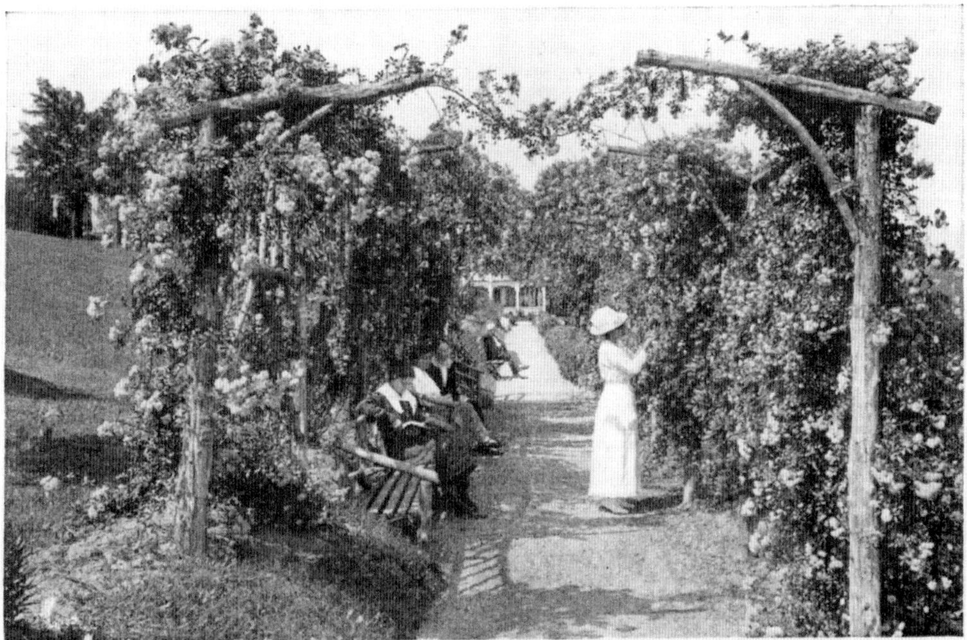

Rose-Arbor and Flower-Bordered Walk to Hall

A rose arbor lines the walkway to Sunset Hall (formerly Mountain Sunset). As detailed on this postcard from 1921, this site was 1,000 feet above sea level, and visitors could arrive via Wernersville Station direct from Boston, New York, and Washington. (Courtesy of Carl Reidler.)

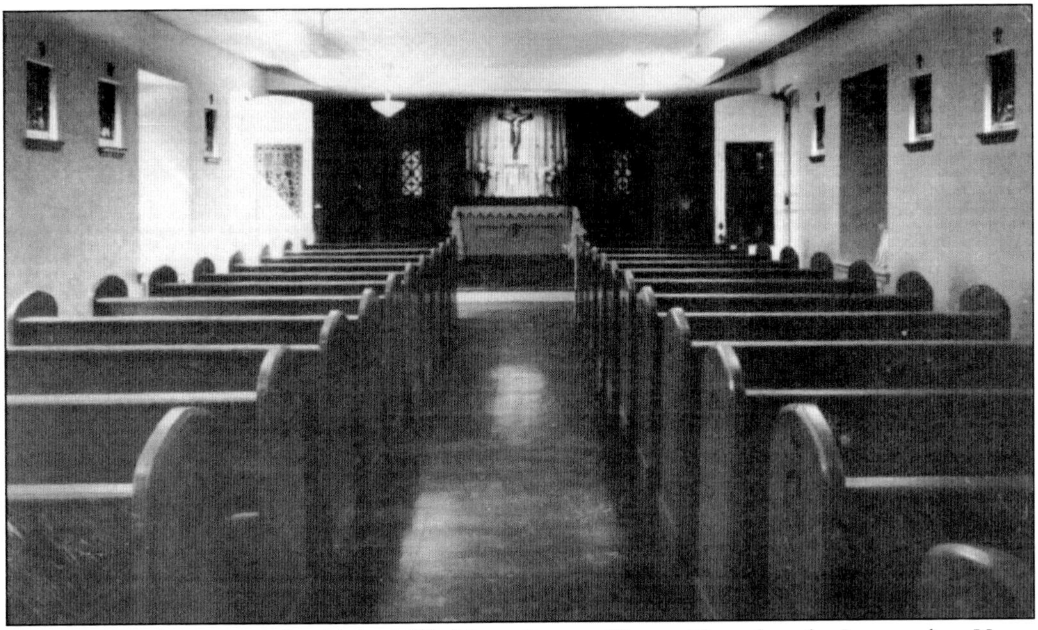

The owners of Sunset Hall sold the Villa Maria Retreat House Chapel to the Immaculate Heart of Mary. The chapel remained in this state until 1987, when the Caron Foundation bought it as part of its drug and alcohol treatment facility. (Courtesy of Carl Reidler.)

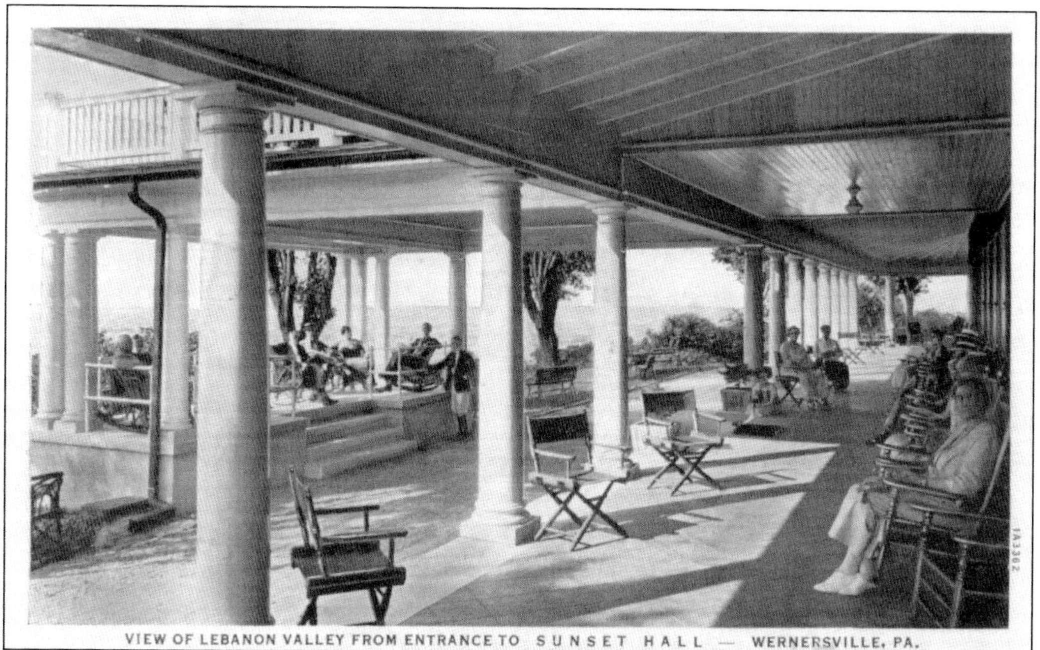

This is a front porch view from Sunset Hall. The postcard reads, "A Most Superior Spot, spend a day, a week, and a month. The Simple Life and Friendly Cheer May all those find who gather here." (Courtesy of Carl Reidler.)

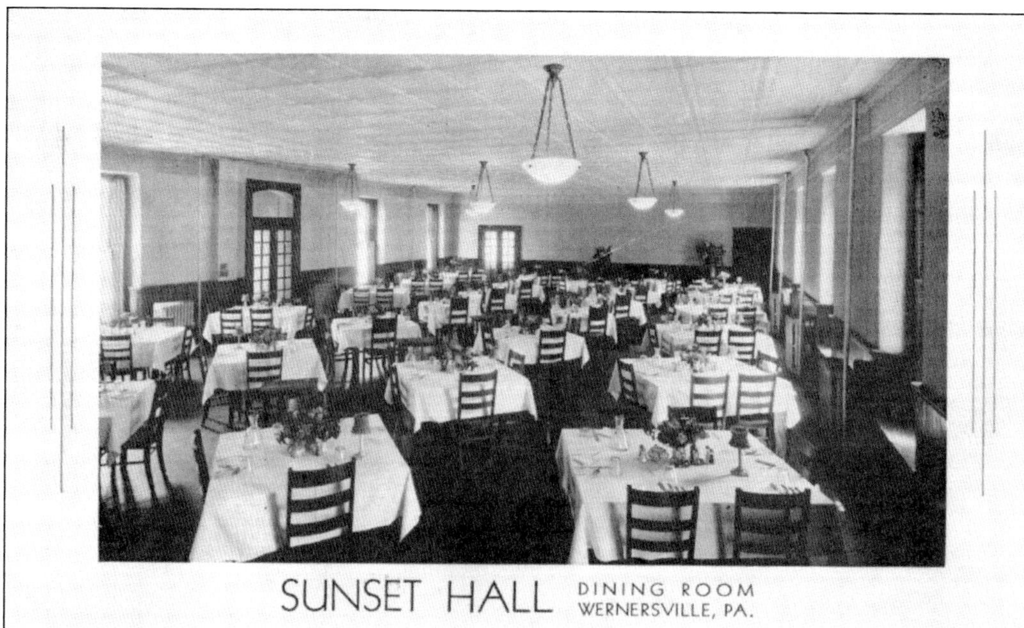

This is the dining room at Sunset Hall, complete with beautiful, and rare, tin ceilings. (Courtesy of Carl Reidler.)

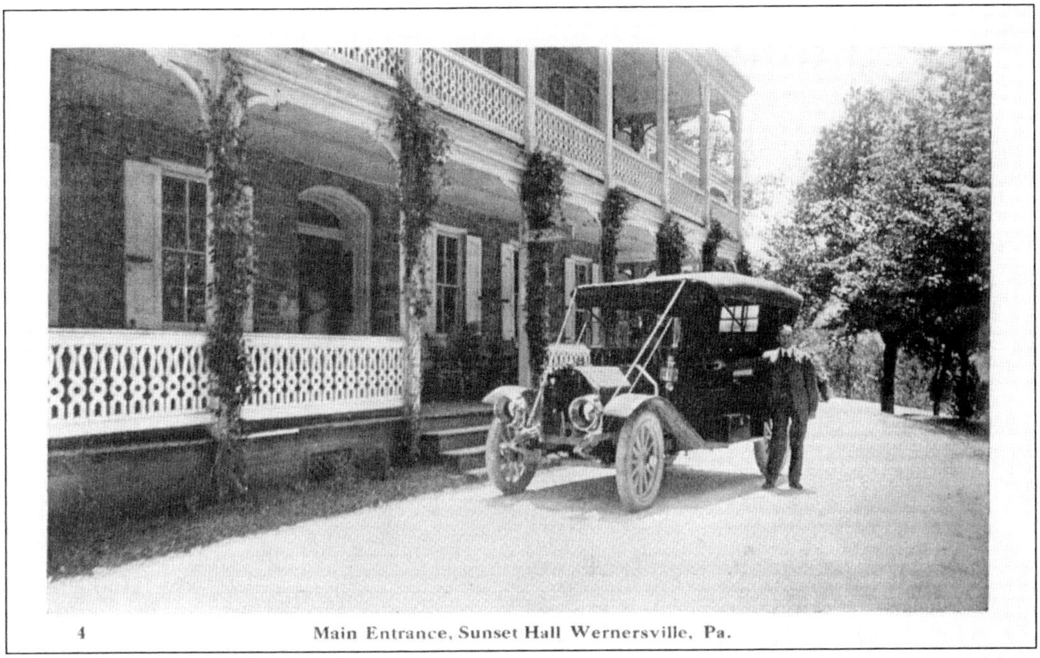

This view from the early to mid-1910s shows the main entrance at Sunset Hall. This building stands today as part of the Caron Foundation. (Courtesy of Carl Reidler.)

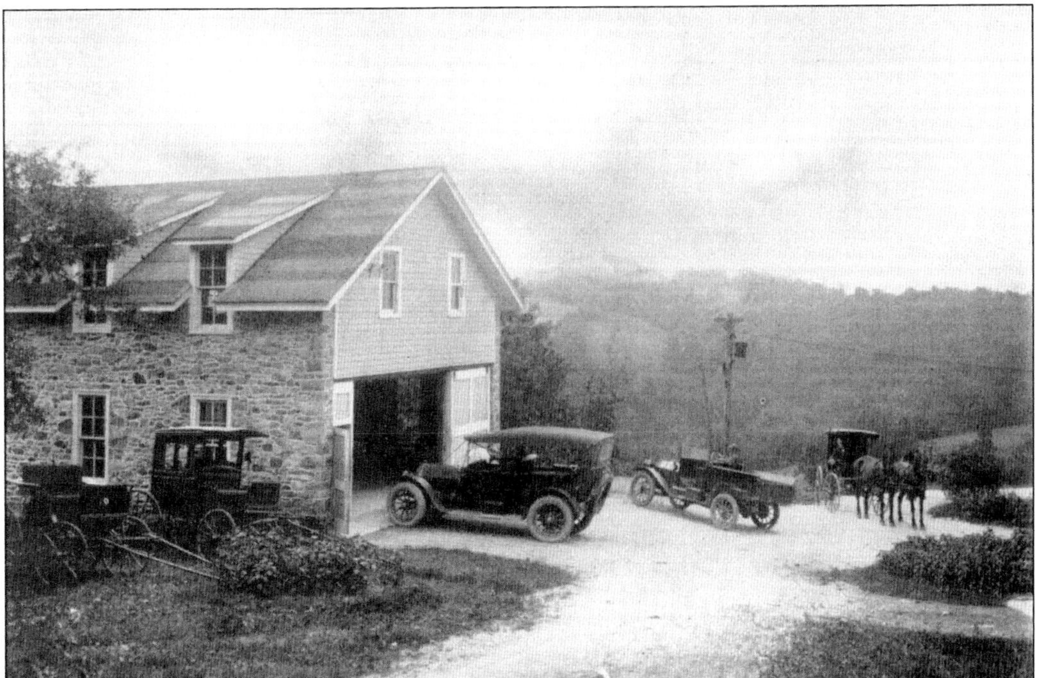

This view from the early 1910s shows the garage at Sunset Hall. Notice horses and cars were still sharing the road at this time. (Courtesy of Carl Reidler.)

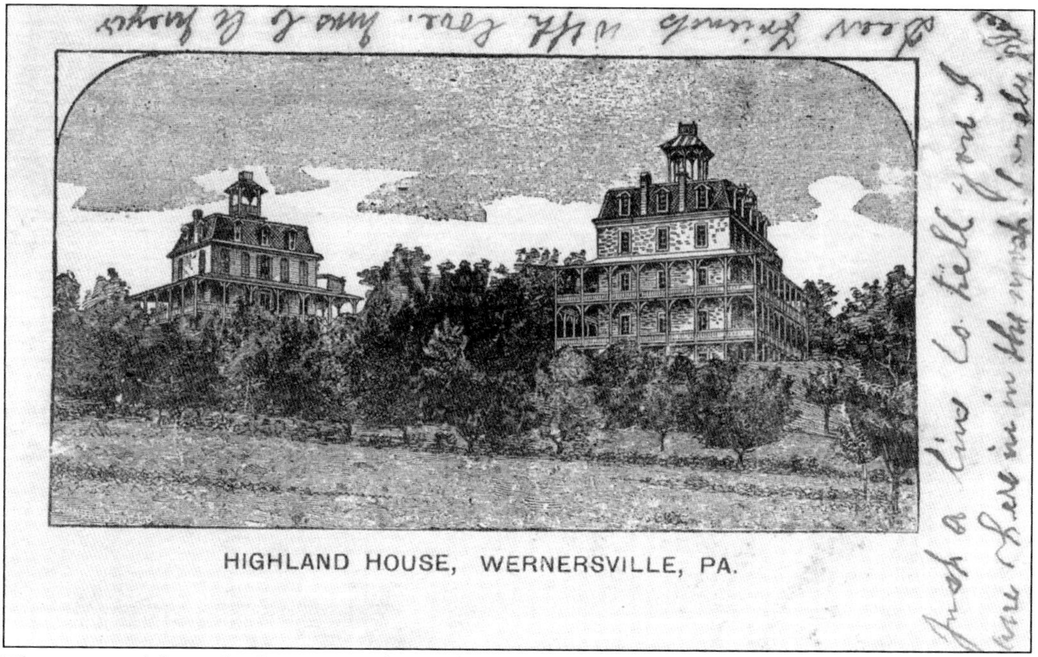

This postcard from the late 1800s shows the Highland House, which sits across the street from Sunset Hall. It still stands today as part of the Caron Foundation. During World War II, spotters would sit in the cupola atop the building and search for German planes that might have entered American airspace. (Courtesy of Carl Reidler.)

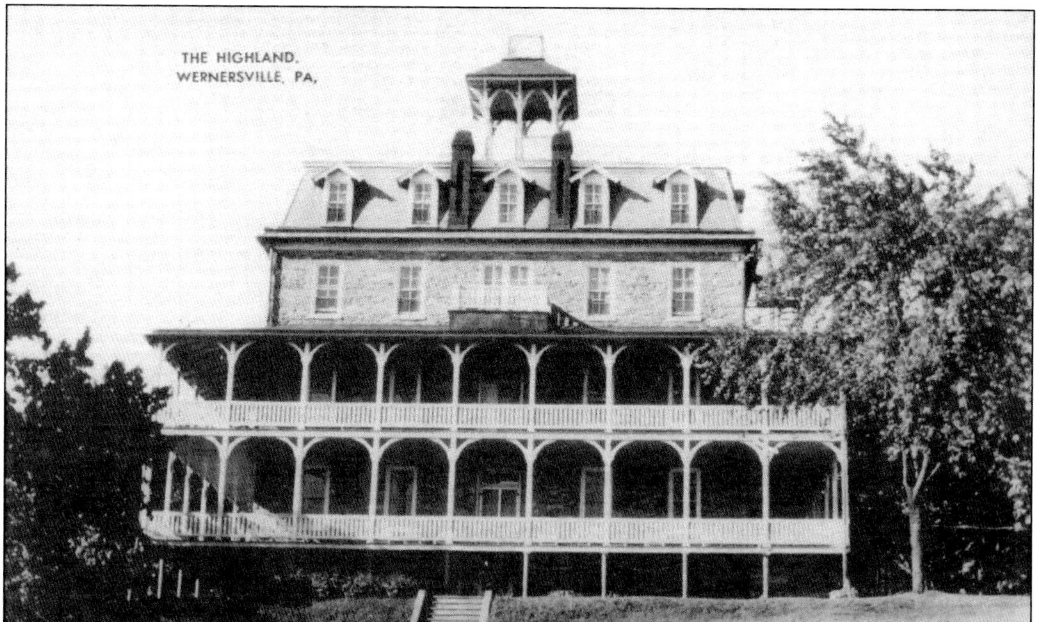

This is a close-up view of the Highland House. Although a large building in appearance, it could accommodate only 35 guests at a time. (Courtesy of Carl Reidler.)

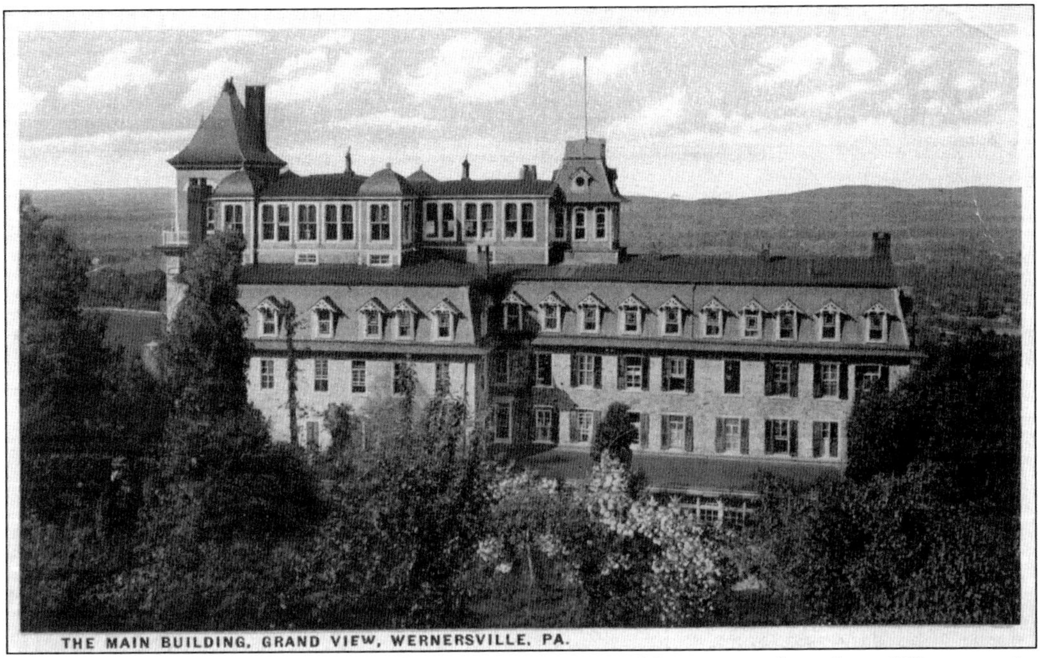

Overlooking Wernersville, the Grand View Sanitarium could accommodate about 150 guests. As the only self-sufficient resort on the mountain, the sanitarium had its own farm for beef, chicken, eggs, fruits, and vegetables, along with ice dams in the winter to cool the underground locker. (Courtesy of Carl Reidler.)

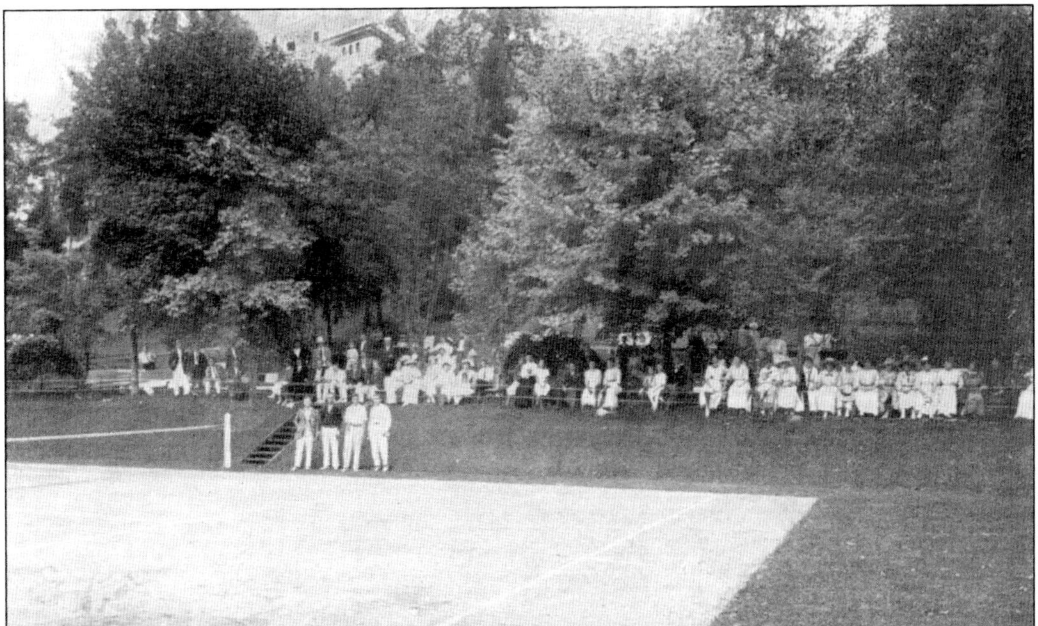

Tennis was one of the many activities at Grand View. Golf was also available at Galen Hall. (Courtesy of Carl Reidler.)

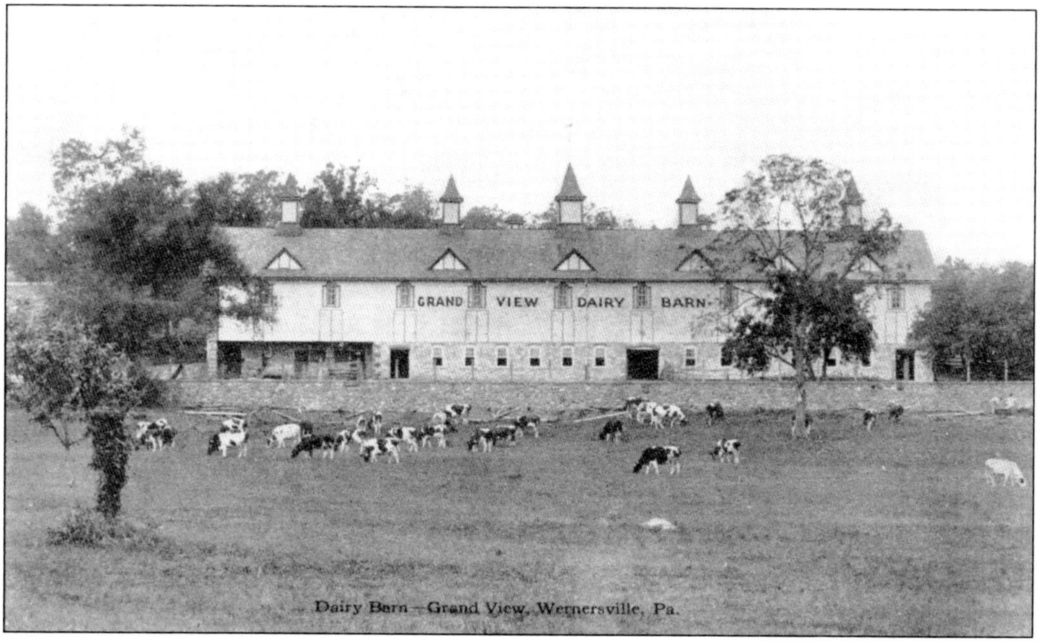

The Grand View Diary Barn, pictured here in 1917, serviced the Grand View Resort. Built around 1890, the structure still stands, and the Schaeffer family has used it for many years. (Courtesy of Carl Reidler.)

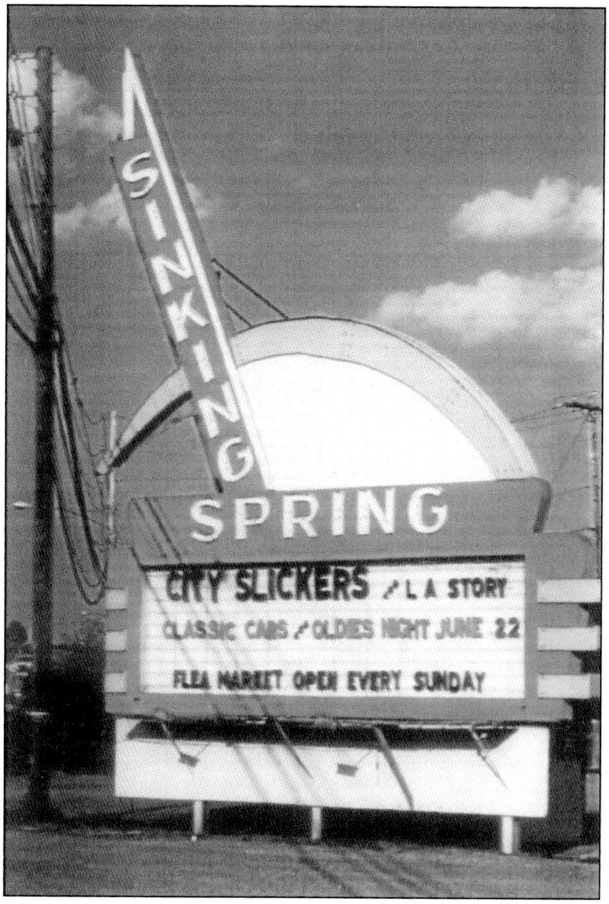

From its opening in the 1950s to the early 1980s, the Sinking Spring Drive-In on Route 422 West was the only one of its kind in western Berks County. In later years, it was home to a Sunday flea market. Today, it is the site of a small commercial shopping center. (Courtesy of Carl Reidler.)

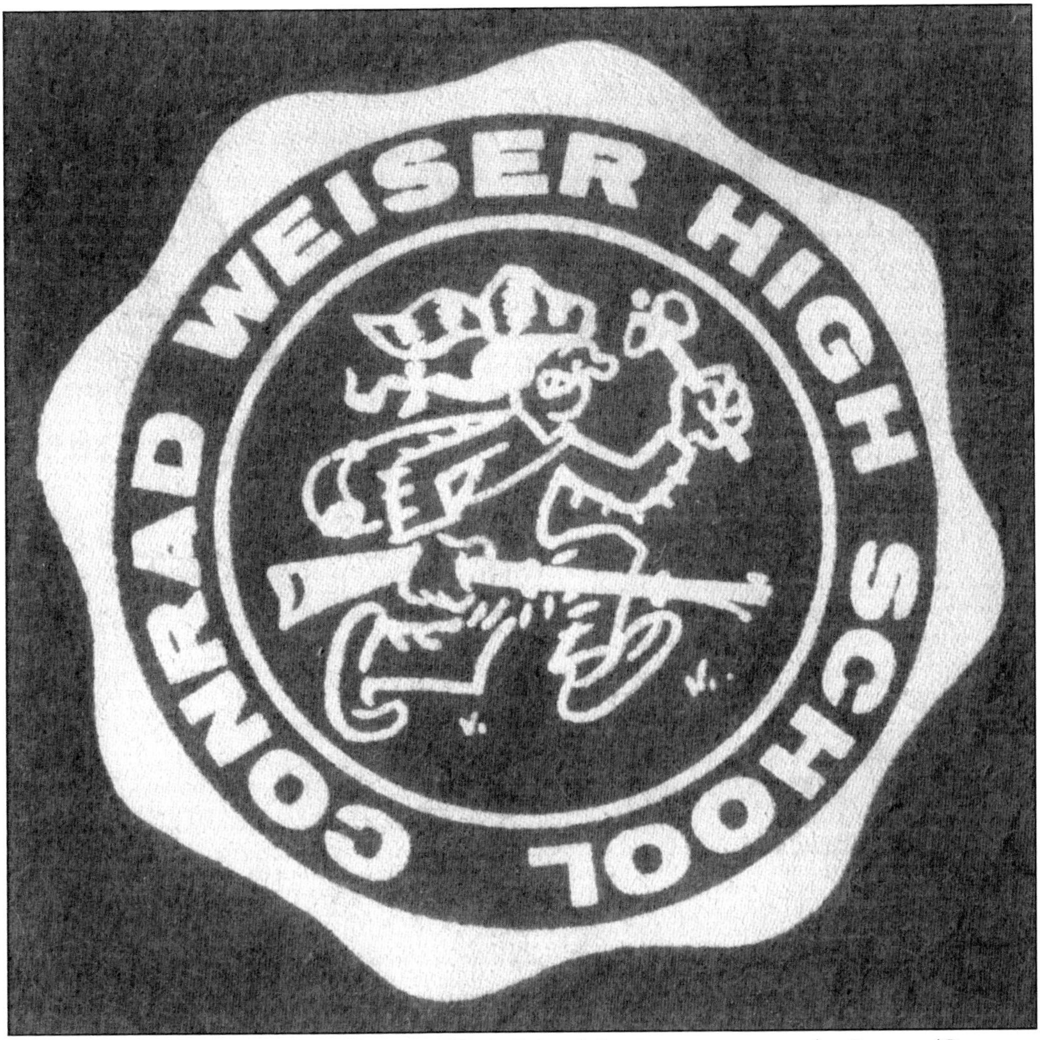

An early emblem for the Conrad Weiser High School displays its mascot, the Scouts. (Courtesy of Carl Ganster.)

Consistent with our mission to preserve history on a local level, this book was printed in South Carolina on American-made paper and manufactured entirely in the United States. Products carrying the accredited Forest Stewardship Council (FSC) label are printed on 100 percent FSC-certified paper.